Vis...
...
BLA...

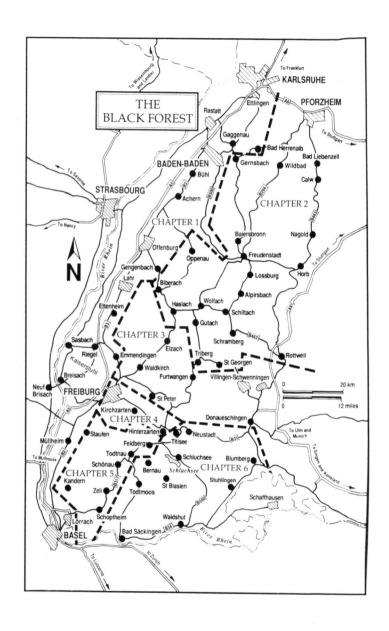

THE
BLACK FOREST

To Frankfurt

KARLSRUHE

PFORZHEIM

Ettlingen [A8]

Rastatt

Gaggenau

Bad Herrenalb

Gernsbach   Bad Liebenzell

Wildbad

To Stuttgart

BADEN-BADEN

Bühl

CHAPTER 2

Calw

Achern

STRASBOURG

CHAPTER 1

Baiersbronn

Nagold

Offenburg

Oppenau

Freudenstadt

To Stuttgart

Gengenbach

Biberach

Lossburg

Horb

Lahr

Haslach   Wolfach

Alpirsbach

Ettenheim

Schiltach

CHAPTER 3   Gutach

Sasbach

Elzach   Triberg

Schramberg

Riegel

Emmendingen

Rottweil

Breisach

Waldkirch   St Georgen

Neuf
Brisach

Furtwangen   Villingen-Schwenningen

FREIBURG

St Peter

20 km

Kirchzarten

Donaueschingen

12 miles

CHAPTER 4

To Ulm and
Munich

Hinterzarten   Neustadt

Müllheim   Staufen

Feldberg   Titisee

Todtnau

Schluchsee   Blumberg

Schönau   Bernau   CHAPTER 6

Kandern   Schluchsee

Stuhlingen

CHAPTER 5   St Blasien

Zell   Todtmoos

Schaffhausen

Schopfheim

Lörrach   Waldshut

BASEL   Bad Säckingen

River Rhein

To Lucerne   To Zurich

VISITOR'S GUIDE
Germany:
BLACK FOREST

GEORGE WOOD

MPC

HUNTER
PUBLISHING INC

Published by: Moorland Publishing Co Ltd,
Moor Farm Road West, Ashbourne, Derbyshire DE6 1HD, England

ISBN 0 86190 507 5

Published in the USA by: Hunter Publishing Inc,
300 Raritan Center Parkway, CN94, Edison NJ 08818

© George Wood 1994

1st edition 1984
2nd edition 1990, fully revised and redesigned
3rd edition, revised 1994

British Library Cataloguing in Publication Data:
A catalogue record for this book is available from the British Library.

Colour and black & white origination by: Scantrans, Singapore
Printed in Hong Kong by: Wing King Tong Co Ltd

Cover photograph: *Gengenbach* (MPC Picture Collection)

Illustrations have been supplied as follows: H. Alcock: pp 30, 79, 87, 98,
102, 103 (top), 118 (top), 126, 143, 182 (both), 186 (top), 191, 214 (centre &
bottom), 215; Stadt Blumberg: p 210 (bottom); MPC Picture Collection: pp
46, 47, 103 (bottom), 110 (both), 111 (both), 114, 115 (both), 118 (bottom),
179 (both), 207 (bottom), 214 (top). All other illustrations are by the author.

Acknowledgments
I would like to acknowledge the assistance given by many people in Britain and
Germany in the preparation of this book. My wife and other members of my
family have cheerfully followed me in my explorations and have made many
helpful suggestions along the way. Wolfgang Winter in Heidelberg kindly
checked the details of Allemanic history and customs for me. The *Fremdenverkehrsverband* in Freiburg was most helpful in providing background material
and in placing a number of photographs at my disposal.

G.W.

CONTENTS

	Preface	7
	Introduction	8
1	The Baden Wine Road	20
2	Valleys of the North	69
3	The Central Area	123
4	Freiburg and the Hell Valley	160
5	Mountains of the South-West	176
6	The South-Eastern Corner	195
	Useful Information for Visitors	229
	Index	251

Key to Symbols Used in Text Margin and on Maps

 Recommended walk

 Parkland

 Archaeological site

 Nature reserve/Animal interest

 Birdlife

 Garden

 Skiing facilities

 Caves

 Church/Ecclesiastical site

 Building of interest

 Castle/Fortification

 Museum/Art gallery

 Beautiful view/Scenery, Natural phenomenon

 Other place of interest

 Sports facilities

 Interesting railway

Key to Maps

 Main road

 Motorway

 Railway

 River

 Town/City

 Town/Village

 Lake/Reservoir

Canals

-----.----- Country Boundary

PREFACE

Before and between the world wars and prior to the days of mass tourism, the Black Forest was highly regarded by the discerning traveller; indeed, the British were in the forefront in encouraging the promotion of modest tourist developments. Since 1955, this part of Germany has been an officially recognised holiday and recreation area and most of the amenities found today have been introduced during this time. Unchanged, however, are the scenery, the good food, drink and accommodation, as well as the friendly hospitality of the inhabitants. A noticeable development in recent years has been the increase in the number of English-speaking visitors enjoying the undoubted delights of the Black Forest.

It is hoped that this updated and enlarged edition of the Visitor's Guide will prove useful to those who have already made plans to visit the area and that it will encourage others to do so. The Black Forest is very much a place in which to follow one's own inclinations and this guide aims to show just how easy it is to do that. Above all, it is a place in which to unwind from the trials and tribulations of the daily round, whether by relaxing beside a swimming pool, discovering the secrets of nature in the valleys and on the mountains, or by examining the treasures in the many museums.

INTRODUCTION

The 'Black Forest' (Schwarzwald) is usually regarded as the area measuring over 160km (100 miles) from north to south and some 65km (40 miles) from east to west which nestles neatly into the angle formed by the Rhine (Rhein) where the river also marks, broadly speaking, the borders with Switzerland and France in the south and west respectively. These boundaries are fairly obvious, but those on the east and north sides are much less precisely defined. However, for the purposes of this book, they may be taken as the Stuttgart-Lake Constance *Autobahn* 81 and the Stuttgart-Karlsruhe *Autobahn* 8.

The forest's name may be derived from the dense growths of pine trees which clothe many of the mountain slopes but the newcomer to the area should not expect from this that he will find mile upon mile of forest interrupted only by the occasional habitation. Of course, forestry is of great importance to the economy but there are large stretches of arable land, especially in the north and east, while dairy-farming is the main livelihood of many rural families. The huge traditional farmhouses provide shelter, not only for the family but also for the livestock, as well as accommodation for farm implements, vehicles and winter feed.

Today, space will often have been found to construct one or two very comfortable holiday flats as well. Most of the farmhouses have been modernised internally and the family enjoys the amenities of central heating, luxurious bedrooms and well-appointed bathrooms and kitchens. Such creature comforts will extend to, or may even have started in, the accommodation provided for paying guests. The life of the Black Forest farmer can be hard and members of the family often find employment in a nearby town to ease the financial burden.

The modest income from tourism is obviously an important factor too. Those family members with a paid job are not excused their share of farm work and find their evenings and weekends taken up with such tasks as milking, hay-making and repairing fences.

Another significant contribution to the rural economy comes from the wine industry. The great vineyards of Baden (this part of Germany is in the state of Baden-Württemberg) are mainly to be found along the sunny western slopes facing the Rhine. The wines of Baden are highly esteemed and the interested tourist can explore the wine country by following the Baden Wine Road (*Badische Wein-strasse*) which runs almost the entire length of the Forest, from Baden-Baden in the north to Basel on the Swiss border. Opportunities for sampling the product (*Weinproben*) abound.

The mountains of the Black Forest are fairly modest, rarely exceeding 1,000m (3,300ft) in the north. The main peaks are in the south but even the highest of these, the Feldberg, does not quite reach 1,500m (5,000ft). In clear weather, some of them offer superb views of the snow-covered Swiss Alps to the south. However, one should not expect too much of such distant views because a heat-haze frequently intervenes, particularly in summer. Nevertheless, the mountain tops are nearly all delightful in their own right and some of them will be mentioned in more detail later.

Apart from the Rhine on the southern and western boundaries, there are no big rivers in the Black Forest but there are many small ones which contribute greatly to the scenic interest. Indeed, one might say that the bubbling streams and numerous waterfalls are as typical of the Black Forest as the woodlands themselves. The famous Neckar rises near Schwenningen and then meanders northward out of the Forest, through Stuttgart and Heilbronn, before turning west towards Heidelberg and the Rhine. As it grows it becomes, like the Rhine itself, an important traffic artery for water-borne goods. An even better known waterway, the Danube (Donau), originates near Donaueschingen and leaves the Black Forest as a modest little river to continue its lengthy journey eastwards to the Black Sea. Similarly, although there are no very large lakes, a number of small ones provide boating facilities. The largest and best-known of these are the Schluchsee and the Titisee, both in the south-east.

There are no wholly industrial towns in the Black Forest. The busy cities of Stuttgart and Karlsruhe lie just outside its borders, as do Strasbourg, on the French side of the Rhine, and Basel which is mostly in Switzerland. Freiburg (im Breisgau, to distinguish it from any of several other towns of the same or similar name) is regarded as the capital of the Forest, with a population of some 180,000. Apart from Pforzheim (population 97,000), few other towns reach 50,000 and the vast majority are much smaller.

While discerning tourists have patronised the Black Forest for many years, it is only in about the last thirty years that it has developed into a proper holiday area. It has all the facilities modern visitors expect but there is also an emphasis on the features for which the area is renowned. There are well-marked and cared-for footpaths, long-distance paths, nature parks, health resorts and varied winter sports possibilities. This defined holiday area, embracing the 5,000 square miles of the 'forest', is now the most visited of Germany's many holiday regions.

It is the Black Forest's geographical nature which makes it unique. Some 50 million years ago, there occurred the literally earth-shattering developments which produced the remarkable contours of this part of Europe. The Alps were folded up and with them a mountainous chain stretching from the Massif Central of France, through the Vosges (Vogesen) and Black Forest, to the Erzgebirge in far-off Saxony. There was, at that time, no real division between the Vosges and the Black Forest, and it was not until about 42 million years later that another natural upheaval occurred. The middle section of the range broke free and plunged some 1,000m (3,300ft) into the earth's crust, creating what eventually became the Rhine plain — the mighty river flowing northwards through it from its source in the snows of the Swiss Alps to the North Sea. Further modifications of the landscape were caused by volcanic eruptions and the arrival of the Ice Age. The ice-cap was responsible for planing some 1,000m (3,300ft) from the tops of the mountains on both sides of the plain before it withdrew about half a million years ago to leave the generally rounded summits which distinguish these mountains from the craggy outlines of the Alps.

The original rocks consist of granite and gneiss, as can clearly be seen in a number of places in the southern Black Forest, in the rock wall of the Feldberg above the Feldsee for example . Gneiss can also be seen in the central and northern parts of the Forest, as well as in the stone terraces of the waterfall at Triberg or the rock walls of the Murg valley. In other places the rock is hidden by a thick layer of red sandstone or by yellow-white chalk. The area is rich in minerals, and in earlier days iron, felspar and silver were all mined. Until the beginning of this century, coal was obtained near Offenburg and Baden-Baden. Significant deposits of uranium exist at the foot of the Feldberg but conservationists have so far hindered its exploitation on any large scale. Lead, zinc and salt have also been worked in various places, but no longer. These earlier activities may, however, explain the remains of various earthworks, excavations or buildings which the inquisitive wanderer may notice in the remoter parts of the forest.

Not surprisingly, the Black Forest is also rich in health-giving mineral waters, as is reflected in the number of spa towns which still provide specialised treatment for various ills. Few readers are likely to make a point of travelling to Baden-Baden, Bad Liebenzell or Wildbad to take the waters, but the bottling of these spas' products is a major industry and they are to be found in restaurants all over Germany and, indeed, much further afield.

In several respects, the Black Forest is an ideal place for children. They are welcomed everywhere and frequently singled out for special treatment. It is very much an area for family holidays and, as such, considerable provision is made everywhere for the entertainment and enjoyment of all age groups. Naturally, the emphasis is on activities calling for a measure of physical exertion.

There are many splendid playgrounds (*Kinderspielplätze*), their equipment constructed, as one might expect, mainly of wood. Every centre of any size has one or more of them and even the tiniest village usually has a small play area. It is by no means unusual to find these attractions for children far from any habitation at all, deep in the woods or beside a small lake. Sometimes a little sign saying '*Waldspielplatz*' is the only clue to their presence.

Reduced prices for children are fairly usual in hotels and guest houses while most restaurants, including those on the motorways, have a special children's menu or will serve smaller portions for children on request. The family seeking a good, moderately priced holiday could hardly do better than select the Black Forest.

As is to be expected in an area where there are significant variations in altitude, there can also be great variations in the weather. The Rhine valley north of Basel is the warmest and driest part of Germany and this fringe of the Black Forest benefits accordingly. In the mountains the prospect of rain increases but during the summer months the chances of wet weather are certainly no greater than in other mountainous regions. Summer temperatures are, on average, significantly higher than in the British Isles and this is emphasised by the large number of outdoor swimming pools, not to mention the vineyards.

Thunderstorms can occur quite frequently in the mountains. Away from the Rhine, average winter temperatures are low enough to make winter sports a realistic possibility. From April onwards, the Black Forest is warmer than other parts of Northern Europe and remains so until about the end of October. In the Rhine valley, however, reasonably mild weather is likely to persist throughout the winter. There are invariably long periods of fine weather during the autumn which makes this the ideal season for walking holidays.

For the visitor from Britain, there are really only two practical methods of travelling to the Black Forest after the sea crossing — by rail or by car. If the journey is made by train, nearly all the main resorts may be reached without difficulty. The more remote parts require the use of a bus service, probably infrequent, for the final stages of the journey, and the rail traveller would do well to select his destination from the many towns and villages having a station. The motorist has the advantage of being free to choose his base from any spot which appeals to him and there is much to be said for having one's own transport available for general touring and excursions.

While other routes may also be used, the vast majority of rail travellers will proceed via London and then make the sea crossing from Harwich to the Hook of Holland or from Dover to Ostend. If the overnight sailings are used, most parts of the Black Forest can be reached by late the following afternoon.

Motorists travelling from Scotland or Northern England will find the North Sea Ferries services from Hull to Rotterdam or Zeebrugge (14 hours) very convenient. Dinner and breakfast are included in the fares on these routes. On the east coast too, there are the Felixstowe to Zeebrugge and Harwich to the Hook of Holland routes (7-8 hours) operated by P&O Ferries and Sealink respectively. South of the Thames there are 'long' overnight crossings from Sheerness to Vlissingen (Flushing) (about 8 hours) by Olau Lines and from Ramsgate to Dunkirk by Sally Viking on which, although the actual distance is short, passengers may remain in their cabins until about 7am in the outward direction.

Finally, there are crossings both day and night from Folkestone or Dover to Ostend and Zeebrugge (P&O Ferries), each taking about

4 hours. There are also, of course, many sailings on the traditional short sea routes from Dover and Folkestone but apart from Dunkirk and Calais, the Continental ports concerned cannot be regarded as ideal starting points for the journey to the Black Forest. Hook of Holland, Rotterdam, Vlissingen, Zeebrugge, Ostend and Dunkirk all have good connections into the European motorway system which takes one without any break to the fringes of the Black Forest. Distances from the various ports do not differ sufficiently to make this a factor in the choice of route. Baden-Baden, at the north end of the Forest, is about 713km (443 miles) from the Hook of Holland. Forty-five kilometres (28 miles) or 110km (69 miles) further are Freudenstadt and Freiburg respectively. There is a variety of motorway routes across the Low Countries but eventually one should cross the German border at Aachen and continue about 40km (25 miles) towards Köln (Cologne) to join the fine new A61 *Autobahn* which is much better than the older road east of the Rhine.

The transatlantic visitor will also find that his or her arrival in the Black Forest has to be completed by train or car. Arrival will probably have been by air at Frankfurt or at some other international airport and there is no difficulty then in reaching nearly all the main resorts by train. All the principal car hire firms have offices or agencies at the airports and the advantages of having one's personal transport for the duration of the holiday have already been mentioned.

Where, in the ensuing chapters, it is necessary to refer to distances or heights, the metric versions will be used, since these are what the visitor will find on signposts and maps. However, where appropriate, the imperial equivalents will also be given. Similarly, the local versions of place names will be used except where there is a well-established English version of the large cities or rivers. Incidentally, English is widely understood, particularly by younger people, who have often learnt it as their first foreign language.

In Germany, accommodation in private houses is widely available in tourist areas. Such accommodation will be recognised by a *'Zimmer frei'* (rooms available) sign at the roadside. Such rooms will invariably be found to be comfortable and spotlessly clean. The usual arrangement is 'bed and breakfast', and in this part of Germany the breakfast can be expected to be more substantial than the basic 'continental' and will perhaps include boiled eggs, cheeses, cold meat and a choice of breads. An advantage of using private accommodation is that one is more likely to have meaningful contact with local inhabitants than in larger establishments. It is fairly unusual for the private landlady to be able to provide an evening meal — the Germans often have their main meal at midday — but she will certainly know of a suitable inn or café.

Very good value can also be obtained in the village inns or in small hotels or pensions which will usually be able to provide an evening meal as well. Half-board or full-board arrangements may not be available in private houses and one usually has to select a hotel or pension for these or, alternatively, one of the numerous farm-houses offering accommodation.

Farm holidays are, in fact, very popular in the Black Forest and a book *Urlaub auf dem Bauernhof* (Holidays on the Farm), available from German National Tourist Offices (GNTO) overseas, lists hundreds of addresses. Such accommodation is good value and allows the visitor to become acquainted with the people and the country. Of course, for children it is ideal. (Remember their wellington boots and old clothes if they are to be allowed to participate to the full). Milking time on the dairy farms is popular and the youngsters will usually be allowed to 'help' in some way.

The book mentioned gives details of the activities of each farm and includes information on possibilities for riding, angling, skiing, etc, together with places of interest in the vicinity, distances to swimming pools and so on. Some of the farms are actually riding schools and others cater for unaccompanied children, usually from 10 years-of-age upwards. In vineyard areas, the information will often refer to wine-tasting in the house. Most of the farms have a common room where the family and guests can meet in the evening. Farm holidays are popular with both the Germans and their continental neighbours so the visitor may well find himself in a truly international gathering.

The Germans were pioneers of self-catering and there is a wide range of such accommodation in the Black Forest. Many farmhouses have one or more holiday flats built into the main building, while others have constructed a separate house for the purpose. Details of all these are to be found in the farm holiday book. There are also many holiday flats in and around the towns and villages. Most are in private houses and the proprietor usually lives on the premises. Lists are available from local tourist offices.

There is a growing number of holiday villages with self-catering houses or flats and with site amenities such as shops, restaurants and swimming pools, according to the size of the development. Some of these are run by religious or other institutions; a list of locations and addresses is given in the 'Useful Information' section of this book. The ferry companies also offer package holidays which include accommodation in holiday villages.

Camping or caravanning is the choice of many, and there are numerous sites to be found. Advance booking is essential for the summer months. There are also many youth hostels in the Black Forest and for these, too, advance booking at busy seasons is strongly recommended. Hostel-type accommodation is also available in around forty *Naturfreundehäuser*, while the *Schwarzwaldverein* has numerous *Wanderheime* along its routes. See the 'Useful Information' section for more details and addresses.

While there is no shortage of accommodation, it is not always easy to know what is available or where to get information. The GNTOs overseas will provide useful general information about any area and also accommodation lists for the main resorts. Alternatively, one can write direct to the Tourist Information Office (*Verkehrsamt*) of any place in which one is interested and ask for their accommodation lists. The material will invariably be more comprehensive than what is available in the overseas offices and will often include outlying villages. When writing to book accommodation, enclose an International Reply Coupon and expect to wait at least two or three weeks for a reply. Given an adequate command of the language, by far the most satisfactory thing is to telephone first — direct dialling is possible to all parts of Germany — and find out if the required accommodation is available. Incidentally, the farm holiday book includes references to the family's ability to speak English.

In general, there are no high season prices in the Black Forest, but there may be considerable reductions for the early and late season, commonly October or November until March or April. Places with winter sports potential often keep the same prices all year. A glossary of common terms and abbreviations encountered when seeking or booking accommodation is given at the end of this book.

Black Forest cooking is unlikely to offend the visitor's palate. Apart from boiled eggs, breakfasts are 'cold'. *Marmelade* is not marmalade but jam and the local honey is excellent. Lunch (*Mittagessen*) starts early; by noon on weekdays and as early as 11.30am on Sundays in restaurants, hotels and inns. Particularly good value is to be had on weekdays in the many modest inns which provide 'business' lunches. A sign announcing 'Gute bürgerliche Küche' (Good home cooking) is usually an indication that the establishment can be relied upon to provide a satisfactory and reasonably-priced meal. In some places there will be several set meals, sometimes shown as Gedeck I, II, etc on the menu (Speisekarte), the lowest priced first. The main course of meat or fish will usually be preceded by soup of the day (Tagessuppe) and sometimes followed by stewed fruit (Kompott) according to season. Cooked puddings or desserts are rarely found, but ice cream of some sort will usually be available as an alternative to the Kompott.

The main course at lunch or dinner will often be some sort of Schnitzel or Kotelett (chops or cutlets of pork or veal). In addition to the set meals, there will be separately priced dishes and many Germans choose one of these and have only the main course. Snacks of the open sandwich type with some of the many varieties of German sausage (Wurst) or cheese (Käse) with bread (Brot) or a roll (Brötchen) will be shown on the menu as Wurstbrot or Käsebrot or belegtes Brötchen mit ... One can also try Frankfurters or the rather similar Vienna sausages, often described as 'ein Paar Wienerle' (a couple of Viennas) or a substantial Bockwurst with mustard. There will be potato salad or bread with the sausages. Potatoes in many guises are popular but as an alternative one can try some of the delicious dumplings (Knödeln). Cooked green vegetables are rare and a side salad is more likely to be provided. Salat or Kopfsalat means lettuce; gemischter Salat means lettuce with cucumber, tomato, etc. The salad is always served in a dressing. Goulash and omelettes are often available too.

Afternoon tea becomes afternoon coffee (Nachmittagskaffee), taken in the Kaffeepause which can occur any time between 3 and 5 o'clock. It is an opportunity for indulging in a little pure gluttony among the cream cakes, fruit flans, pastries, etc. Most famous is the Black Forest cherry cake (Schwarzwälderkirschtorte). Portions of this and all other cakes are generous but even they can be supplemented by a large helping of whipped cream (Schlagsahne). Other specialities are Zwetschenkuchen (blue plums on a pastry base) in season, Käsesahnekuchen (creamy cheese cake) and Johannisbeerenkuchen (red currants on a sponge base).

The traditional drink at this time is coffee, which is fairly strong and with a little evaporated milk. This is not to everyone's taste and alternative beverages are tea (for which one has to use the evaporated milk), lemon tea (*Zitronentee*) or drinking chocolate (*heisse Schokolade*). Iced coffee (*Eiskaffee*) or iced chocolate (*Eisschokolade*) are refreshing drinks and there will be soft drinks, fruit juices or ice cream for the children. The usual German coffee cups are on the small side and it is preferable to ask for a pot of coffee (*Kännchen*) which will contain enough for two or more cups. Some establishments now only serve coffee in a *Pott* (a mug) which contains the same amount as a *Kännchen* but costs a little less. In the more fashionable resorts, the principal hotels or the *Kurhaus* or *Kurzentrum* may extend *Nachmittagskaffee* into a *Kaffeekonzert* and there may be a modest supplementary charge for the pleasure of an hour or so of light music with the coffee and cakes.

The evening meal is usually served from 6pm and much of what was said about the midday meal also applies to late dinner (*Abendessen*). The set meals will probably have disappeared, but an identical menu is likely to be available. Wine by the glass (0.2 or 0.25 litres) or $^1/_4$, $^1/_2$ and litre carafe (*offene Weine*) is readily available and is quite cheap, or one can enjoy a bottle of superior German wine. The prices displayed always include VAT (*Mehrwertssteuer*) and service (*Bedienung*), even if they do not say so. It is usual for the bill to be made out and the money collected by the waiter or waitress. While tipping is not necessary and not expected, most people wave away any small change left after paying the bill.

For the self-caterer, the advent of self-service shops has made the purchase of foodstuffs very simple. Each village has at least one small supermarket; the chains 'A & O', 'Edeka' and 'Spar', are among those most commonly found in this area. Larger supermarkets ('Aldi', 'Plus', 'Norma', etc) will be found in all the main towns. In addition, a baker's or butcher's shop will often have a small self-service area for general foodstuffs and drinks. Nearly all drink bottles, often including wine and plastic bottles, carry a deposit.

Fruit and vegetables are often found in street markets, or on individual stalls if there is no proper market. The butcher's shop (*Metzgerei*) is usually a place of cool and sparkling cleanliness. In addition to fresh meat, there is a bewildering display of sliced sausages (*Wurst*) and other cooked meats; for an assortment of different sorts of *Wurst* ask for *Aufschnitt*. A useful item, very popular with children, is *Fleischkäse*—literally meat cheese—a firm sort of pâté which can be sliced thinly for sandwiches or more thickly for frying.

There is no need for the self-caterer to carry a lot of foodstuffs from home because everything needed is readily available locally at very competitive prices. Those living on a dairy farm can buy milk very cheaply and have the pleasure of recalling or discovering how fresh pure milk really tastes. Needless to say, German quality and cleanliness controls are very strict.

Souvenirs from the Black Forest include the cuckoo clock. The traditional craft of clock-making still continues and the production of timepieces of every conceivable size and design is a major cottage industry. Today, many of the movements are mass produced but it is the attractive case which really sells the clock. At the lower end of the price scale a simple, spring-driven clock can be purchased very cheaply. A little more upmarket, there is an enormous range of weight-driven clocks for which one might pay between 40 and 120 marks. The largest and most expensive cuckoo clocks will cost upwards of 400 marks, for which sum one could acquire a truly magnificent example of the clock-maker's art.

In the ensuing chapters, an endeavour has been made to divide the Black Forest into areas which can be fitted into a logical touring pattern. Apart, perhaps, from the Baden Wine Road described in Chapter 1, each of the areas could be explored reasonably well by car from a single base but the Black Forest is best known for its walking possibilities and much has been done to encourage the walker to see the best of the countryside. Over a hundred years ago, Mark Twain wrote in glowing terms about the Black forest in *A Tramp Abroad*, having explored the region extensively on foot. The long-distance paths have been identified and marked by the *Schwarzwaldverein* (Black Forest Association), including such marathon hikes as the *Westweg* from Pforzheim to Basel, the *Mittelweg* from Pforzheim to Waldshut, the *Querweg* from Freiburg to Bodensee (Lake Constance) and several others. '*Weg*' means 'way', so the paths may be translated as West Way, Middle Way and Cross Way, etc.

The Association has marked about 22,000km (13,700 miles) of footpaths including some 7,000km (4,300 miles) of long-distance paths such as those mentioned above. Other routes have been marked by the local authorities or by tourist associations covering a particular geographical area. Inevitably, there is duplication of marking where, for example, one of the long-distance paths follows a locally marked one for a time; it is, therefore, a good idea to supplement the wayside markings by using a good map.

The 'Wanderkarte' series issued by Atlasco are very clear and easily followed. These are to a scale of 1:30,000 and the sheets covering the Black Forest can be readily identified by their distinctive yellow covers. In some popular resorts, the information office provides a map showing walks in and around the resort, some of which do not always appear on the more comprehensive maps. Such local walks are frequently marked by numbers rather than the more usual geometrical signs. The *Schwarzwaldverein* produces very good maps to 1:50,000 scale. Incidentally, the waymarking system used in the Black Forest has been highly regarded for many years and has been used as the pattern for marking footpaths in several other countries.

The motorist will often wish to use his or her vehicle to reach the starting point of a walk and will benefit from the many free *Wander-Parkplätze* (walkers' parking places) which have been established throughout the Forest. These provide good access to walks in the vicinity and each parking place has a map showing the various possibilities and an indication of the time required for each walk or the distance involved. All such walks can be completed in one day, the majority being less than 10km (6 miles). Some of the car parks are recognised by a distinctive blue 'P' sign with a pictogram of a couple of hikers, others by a rustic sign saying *Wander-Parkplatz* or *Wald-Parkplatz*. Car-park locations are clearly shown on the Atlasco maps.

The motorist also requires a smaller-scale map for his or her general movements about the Forest and those issued by the petrol companies will be found very suitable for this purpose. For example, Sheet 6 of the series issued by Aral covers the whole Black Forest at a scale of 1:400,000. The *Tourenkarten* issued by the same company are also recommended. These are to 1:200,000 scale and are designed for the tourist exploring the area. Sheets 13 and 16 cover the northern and southern parts of the Black Forest respectively. On the reverse of the sheets is a comprehensive catalogue of the various places of interest, etc. In addition to maps, there are many booklets obtainable locally giving detailed descriptions of walks. It will be easy for those with some knowledge of German to choose one which covers the part of the Forest they want to explore. These booklets complement the maps and sometimes prevent one missing a worthwhile feature or viewpoint.

A book of this size cannot give a comprehensive catalogue of Black Forest walks, but the chapters which follow include details of some which may be regarded as typical of the area.

1
THE BADEN WINE ROAD

North of Freiburg

The *Badische Weinstrasse* (Baden Wine Road) runs from north to south along the western fringe of the Black Forest and passes through almost all the important wine-producing areas. Most travellers, whether they come by road or rail, enter the Forest through this narrow strip and may find more of interest here than expected. The lover of good wine will certainly want to take time to sample the products of the great vineyards facing the river Rhine in this mild and dry part of Germany. The designated *Weinstrasse* is not quite continuous but sometimes doubles back on itself or is divided in order to embrace all the vineyards. For much of its length it follows the main road No B3, the principal route to the south before the construction of the nearby *Autobahn*. Road B3 enters the northernmost point of the Black Forest at Ettlingen just south of Karlsruhe and it is from here that the journey southwards commences.

Ettlingen, virtually a suburb of Karlsruhe, is a place of considerable interest, especially for those interested in architectural treasures. The Catholic parish church of St Martin incorporates the twelfth- to thirteenth-century tower choir and the high choir of 1459-64. The rest of the original building was burned down in 1689. The interior is now a plain, single space with some decorated wall recesses. The striking façade is divided by three large pilasters.

The *Rathaus* (town hall) dates from 1737-8 and was built to the plans of the Baden-Baden master stonemason, A. Mohr. The Roman period in this area is recalled by a copy of the Roman Neptune stone washed up from the river Alb in 1480 which has been incorporated

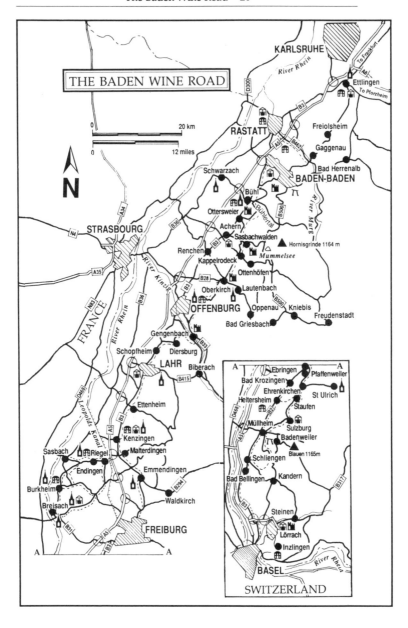

THE BADEN WINE ROAD

0   20 km

0   12 miles

N

KARLSRUHE

River Rhein

To Frankfurt

Ettlingen

To Pforzheim

Freiolsheim

Gaggenau

RASTATT

Bad Herrenalb

BADEN-BADEN

Schwarzach

Bühl

River Murg

Ottersweier

Achern

Sasbachwalden

Hornisgrinde 1164 m

Renchen

Mummelsee

Kappelrodeck

Ottenhöfen

Oberkirch

Lautenbach

OFFENBURG

Oppenau

Kniebis

Bad Griesbach

Freudenstadt

Gengenbach

Diersburg

Schopfheim

LAHR

Biberach

STRASBOURG

River Kinzig

River Rhein

FRANCE

Leopolds Kanal

Ettenheim

Kenzingen

Sasbach

Riegel

Malterdingen

Endingen

Emmendingen

Burkheim

Waldkirch

Breisach

FREIBURG

A   A

A   A

Ebringen

Pfaffenweiler

Bad Krozingen

Ehrenkirchen

St Ulrich

Heitersheim

Staufen

Müllheim

Sulzburg

Badenweiler

Blauen 1165m

Schliengen

Bad Bellingen

Kandern

Steinen

Lörrach

Inzlingen

BASEL

River Rhein

SWITZERLAND

in the wall. The *Schloss* is a fine building with four wings and was built during the years 1728-33. In the courtyard there is the Delphin-brunnen (dolphin fountain) of 1612 and, in front of the *Schloss*, the Narrenbrunnen (fools' fountain) which dates from 1549.

In 1727, the Margravine Sybilla Augusta of Baden decided to move from the official *Residenz* in Rastatt and base herself in Ettlin-gen. The old sixteenth-century *Schloss* there had been burned out during the Palatinate war of succession. It had been a gloomy building and Sybilla Augusta decided to replace the remains with the building seen today. The architect Michael Ludwig Rohrer had to work to her very firm ideas as to what the building should look like and the south wing became her living quarters, decorated in the formal baroque style. Finally, the complex was completed by the construction of a chapel, also in baroque style, which was the equivalent of three storeys in height.

Sybilla Augusta originated from Bohemia and was anxious to have some reminder of her homeland incorporated in the new building. The famous Bavarian painter, Cosmas Damian Asam, was commissioned to produce a ceiling and wall fresco cycle in the chapel, depicting the life and martyrdom of Johannes Nepomuk, the patron saint of Bohemia; the work was carried out in 1732. With the death of Sybilla's second son in 1771, the Catholic line also died out and the significance of the *Schlosskapelle* was extinguished by the new Protestant masters.

In Napoleonic times, the *Schloss* was used as a hospital; the chapel was desecrated and the altars were sold. The chapel became a place of worship again from 1840 to 1876, this time for the little Protestant community of Ettlingen. In 1871, a school for Prussian non-commis-sioned officers was established in the *Schloss*; it demanded ever more accommodation and eventually took over the chapel in which addi-tional floors were built. Large parts of Asam's wall frescos were whitewashed over and only the ceiling painting and a few other remnants remained.

After World War II, it was realised that the ceiling in the *Schlosskapelle* was the only remaining example of Asam's work in the area, the others in the Mannheim *Schloss* and in the Bruchsal Hofkirche having been destroyed. It was decided to restore the chapel, the undesirable additions were removed and it became a splendid little concert hall in 1954. Since then it has been the venue of the famous Ettlingen chamber music festivals, the restored work of Asam beautifully complementing the baroque music often performed there under the auspices of Süddeutscher Rundfunk (South German Radio and TV). The rest of the *Schloss* complex now houses the Albgau and Albicker-Museum as well as the tourist information office.

Incidentally, the word *Schloss* frequently describes a building which in English would be called a residential palace, whereas a castle in the sense of a fortress is a *Burg* in German.

Today, Ettlingen is an important centre of the paper-making trade, an industry which goes back here to the year 1452 when the oldest paper-mill in Baden first produced acceptable writing paper for government offices. In fact, the Chinese had discovered the art of paper-making some 500 years earlier but it had been a closely guarded secret which only trickled slowly westwards through the reports and souvenirs of early travellers.

A picturesque road runs southwards through the villages of Schöllbronn, Völkersbach and Freiolsheim and, after 18km, reaches Gaggenau, a town of about 30,000 inhabitants. Here the little river Murg is met for the first time. The source of this river will be visited in a later chapter, but for the moment, it is necessary to go downstream for a brief visit to the town of Rastatt, a rather larger centre than Gaggenau. The lower reaches of the Murg support a considerable paper-making industry, one of the specialities being the fine quality, thin paper used for printing bibles, etc. **Rastatt** may well be the gateway town for the traveller arriving by train, for it is here that one must transfer to the so-called *Murgtalbahn* (Murg Valley Railway) to go towards Freudenstadt. The pretty little river Murg winds its way westward through Rastatt on its journey to the Rhine. The motorist may also find that the Rastatt exit from the *Autobahn* is the most suitable for his destination and it would be a pity to hurry through without spending a little time here.

Margrave Ludwig Wilhelm created a town of remarkable spaciousness for the period and after his death in 1707, his wife Sybilla Augusta, who has already been mentioned, continued his ambitious plans. The centrepiece is the magnificent *Schloss* which was the first baroque palace of such size to be erected in Germany. The owner and his architect wished to bring the splendour of Italian *palazzi* and French *châteaux* (such as Versailles) to the Upper Rhine and they succeeded in creating this outstanding example of the art in 7 years. The central section is the *Residenz* which dominates the wings grouped around a large courtyard. The interior staircases are among the finest to be found in a baroque *Schloss*. In the north wing, the Schlosskirche Heilige Kreuz (palace church of the Holy Cross) is entered through a magnificent portal and the visitor will be struck by the interplay of light and colours, to which great importance was attached, as in many churches built about this time. In addition to the large fresco of the vault, there are numerous smaller ornamental panels. The high altar has a silvered wooden crucifix and is particularly distinctive.

The Kapelle of Maria Einsiedeln was consecrated in 1717 and is now separated from the *Schloss* by a busy roadway. Its rather plain decoration is significantly different in character to that of the *Schloss*. The Pagodenburg (1722) next to the chapel was inspired by the pagoda in the grounds of Schloss Nymphenburg in Munich. The *Marktplatz* (market square) was part of the original concept for the town and is dominated by the Stadtkirche (town church) of St Alexander, which was consecrated in 1764, and by the *Rathaus* of 1750. The high altar in the church should not be overlooked and three large fountains complete the baroque townscape.

There are three museums in, or close to, the *Schloss*. The *Heimatmuseum* (*Heimat* means homeland or regional) concerns itself mainly with local history, while the Freiheitsmuseum deals with the various freedom movements which have featured in the national history of the country and is also a memorial to those who have died in that cause. Lastly there is the Wehrgeschichtliches Museum — Germany's national war museum.

The Margravine Sybilla Augusta was also responsible for Schloss Favorite, 5km (3 miles) south-east of Rastatt at **Förch** near Kuppenheim. This was another link with Sybilla's homeland and an architect was actually brought from Bohemia to carry out the Margravine's wishes which she again expressed in no uncertain terms. However, the end result is delightful and reflects the owner's personality and charm. Built in 1710, this little baroque jewel now houses a fine collection of porcelain and antique furniture.

Excursions can readily be made from Rastatt to the ruins of two old castles which occupy fine vantage points. Altes Schloss Hohenbaden is quite near Baden-Baden and can be reached via the road from Gaggenau. Three kilometres (2 miles) to the west, Ebersteinburg has the advantage of having not only a splendid view over the Rhine plain, but also a very adequate restaurant and café.

The motorist using the A5 *Autobahn* between the Rastatt and Baden-Baden exits should stop at the Baden-Baden *Raststätte* (service area) to visit the unique *Autobahnkirche*. It is, of course, dedicated to St Christopher and was built to serve those using the motorway. It is a significant example of modern church architecture. The architect Friedrich Zwingmann and the artist and sculptor Emil Wachter have created a visual world embracing mankind's past, present and future. The church itself is in the form of a pyramid and the stained glass depicting the life of Christ makes an immediate impact upon the visitor as do the doors which are finished by an unusual enamel technique.

Between Gaggenau and Rastatt, the first signs of viticulture may be observed and these continue as road B3 is followed towards Baden-Baden where the *Weinstrasse* officially commences. **Baden-Baden** (population 50,000) is, of course, the classic spa and while it may lack the sparkle which it had in the days when it was frequented by the crowned heads of Europe, it remains an attractive town which may appeal to the less-active visitors in particular. It is served by the majority of the express trains on the main line to Basel.

Surrounded by hills and pine woods, Baden-Baden is a veritable sun trap and thus well-suited to the early or late season holiday. Royalty and oil sheikhs still frequent the elegant hotels which were built around the turn of the century. However, as the town is now the headquarters of the south-west German radio and television service, musicians, artists, journalists and the like from all over Germany are more likely to be one's neighbours. Baden-Baden is also the home of the oldest casino in Germany where, in earlier times, one might have rubbed shoulders with Kaiser Wilhelm I, Bismarck, Berlioz or Brahms. Today, well-heeled visitors from all over the world frequent the gaming rooms, where evening dress is still obligatory.

It was not, however, the attractions of the casino which gave Baden-Baden its position as an internationally famed spa. The reputation is due to the remarkable qualities of its healing thermal springs which gush out in the famous Friedrichsbad at a temperature of 69 °C, (156 °F) making them the warmest thermal springs in Europe. The Friedrichsbad was built in 1866; its modern counterpart, the Augustabad complex, includes gymnasia, a sun terrace and, on the uppermost of its seven storeys, an indoor swimming pool. The 'cure' is noted for its beneficial effects on sufferers from mental stress, heart and circulatory conditions. The area has been famed for the curative

Places of Interest In and Around Ettlingen, Rastatt and Baden-Baden

Ettlingen
Schloss
In town centre
Fine palace of 1728-33 with
fountains.

Schlosskapelle
Former palace chapel with
elaborately painted ceilings.
Converted to concert hall.

Albgau and Albicker Museums
Located in the *Schloss* complex.

Church of St Martin
Sections dating back to the twelfth
century.

Rathaus (1737-8)
In town centre.

Rastatt
Marktplatz
Huge market square with fountains,
dominated by the church of St
Alexander (1764) and the *Rathaus*
(1750).

Schloss .
In town centre.
The Schloss was the first baroque
palace of such size to be built in
Germany and with other buildings
of the period forms the focal point
of the town.

Freiheitsmuseum
History of national freedom
movements and memorial to
freedom fighters.

Wehrgeschichtlichesmuseum
National war history museum.
(Above museums are in or close to
the Schloss)

Schloss Favorite
In Förch 5km (3 miles) south-east
of Rastatt.
A fine exhibition of porcelain and
antique furniture in a baroque
palace (1710).

Baden-Baden
Römische Badruinen
Römerplatz, in town centre.
Ruins of Roman baths.

Brahms Museum
Maximilianstrasse 85, Lichtental
Some manuscripts and other items
connected with the composer.

Staatliche Kunsthalle
Lichtentaler Allee 8a, town centre.
Works of art.

Kloster Lichtental
Hauptstrasse 40, in town centre.
Religious works of art, especially
those connected with Cistercians.

Stadtmuseum
Küferstrasse 3, in town centre.
Collection relating particularly to
the history of the town.

Autobahnkirche
On the A5 Autobahn at Baden-
Baden *Raststätte*.
Modern church dedicated to St
Christopher.

Ruine Yburg
6km (4 miles) south-west of town
via Fremersbergstrasse
Outstanding viewpoint and marked
walks.

Mummelsee
24km (15 miles) along road B500
Charming mountain lake.

Schloss Favorite, Förch

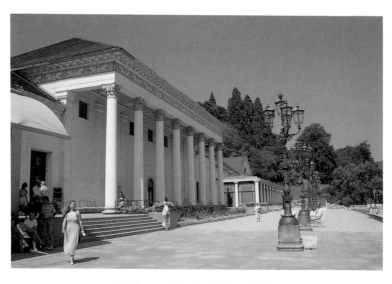

Kurhaus and casino, Baden-Baden

properties of the waters for more than 2,000 years, the Romans having carried out much development in the first 200 years AD. The ruins of the Roman baths are open for inspection from April to October.

Not much happened for some centuries after the Romans left but there was a revival of activity in the Middle Ages, especially after the illustrious Margrave Philipp I (1504-67) had taken the *Kur* from the distinguished Swiss physician Paracelsus, for the successful treatment of his rheumatism.

During this period, the thermal waters, welling up from a depth of 12-1500m (3,940-4,920ft) beneath the earth's crust, were led in channels through the alleys of the town for the steam to protect the inhabitants against the plague and cholera, though the level of success does not seem to be recorded. However, the turbulent times of the late seventeenth century did not leave Baden-Baden untouched and, when the town was sacked by the French in 1689, everything that would burn was set ablaze. Restoration took a long time and it was only after 1800 that the baths and healing streams became a significant part of the town's life again. Incidentally, the name really means Baden in Baden, and the present hyphenated form was adopted to distinguish it from numerous other 'Badens' throughout Europe. The town certainly revolves round its casino and the 'cure', but for the many visitors who are not attracted to these particular features, it is rich in well-kept parks, pleasant promenades and numerous buildings of historical or architectural interest.

The Lichtentaler Allee, a beautifully conceived sort of 'Rotten Row' close to the town centre, is a pleasant spot for a stroll. In addition to the Roman baths, there are no fewer than seven museums and art galleries in the town. Music lovers may enjoy exploring the archives of the Brahms Museum; others will find the religious works of art in the Kloster Lichtental of interest. (*Kloster* is another of those words which requires some explanation for there is no English word which exactly corresponds to it. It is a sort of omnibus German word meaning monastery, nunnery or convent. It seems to be used fairly loosely in describing religious buildings, even after their religious use has ceased.)

There are numerous possibilities for varied and attractive rambles within easy walking distance, such as in the idyllic Waldseetal with its trout pond, the climb to the 668m (2,191ft) high Merkur, or into the Wolfsschlucht (gorge) which provided Weber with the for a scene in his opera *Der Freischütz*. Six kilometres (4 miles) south-west of the town, the ruins of a castle called Yburg have splendid views of the countryside and make a worthwhile excursion. Beneath the Yburg is a *Wander-Parkplatz* with four short, round walks. The round walks based on the many *Wander-Parkplätze* need no detailed description as there is always a simple map at the parking place and each route is well-signed. The slight abbreviation *W-Parkplatz* will be used from now on.

Baden-Baden could be the place for an introductory Black Forest ramble of 14km (8$^1/_2$ miles) taking in the Ebersteinburg, which has already been mentioned. Start in the old town near the *Rathaus* and climb up the Staffelweg to the Neues Schloss for a view back over the town. Then follow the road for a few minutes until a marker stone points the way to the left along a shady footpath to the Altes Schloss, which can be reached comfortably in 1 hour. The extensive ruins date from the eleventh to fifteenth centuries and provide a broad vista over the Rhine plain.

Above the *Burgschenke* (inn), continue up through an arched gateway to the nearby Battertfelsen (rocks) and then follow the sign 'zum Oberen Felsenweg' and before long there is a view back over the castle ruins. When the path divides, do not take the left fork direct towards Ebersteinburg but keep to the right where it is possible to clamber up some of the many rocks and enjoy impressive views. These rocks are often used by climbers because they offer conditions seldom found in the Black Forest. The good track continues down some steps to a junction at the 'Hütte am unteren Felsenweg'. Here it is best to go along the route of (but not towards) the Engels - and Teufelskanzel (rocks — Angels' and Devils' pulpits), past some rather nice houses, direct into the village of Ebersteinburg. Go on to the ruin Alteberstein where there is a good outlook to the north.

From Ebersteinburg, go south beside the road towards Gern-sbach or Gaggenau and at the end of the bus lay-by, immediately after the sign 'Zum Krankenhaus', walk to the right through the wood to the nearby Engelskanzel. Retrace your steps for about 20m (65ft) and follow a path (yellow bar waymark) through the woods and past more rocks to reach the obvious Hungerbergweg. Turn towards Baden-Baden and, after passing the Steinwaldhütte, soon rejoin the outward route down to the Neues Schloss and return to the starting point.

Another splendid tour is along road B500, the *Schwarzwaldhoch-*

A café in Baden-Baden

strasse (Black Forest High Road), which runs from Baden-Baden to Freudenstadt, a distance of rather less than 50km (31 miles), and one can make this slight deviation from the *Weinstrasse* if the weather is good. After climbing a series of steep, serpentine curves out of Baden-Baden, the road follows the crest of a ridge at a height of around 1,000m (3,280ft) until it descends into Freudenstadt. There are superb views on either side if the weather is clear.

After passing through Geroldsau, 5km (3 miles) from the start, there is no place of any size on this road. Hamlets such as Plättig, Sand, Hundseck and Unterstmatt are hardly noticeable unless one wishes to stop for a meal at one of the various hotels. One then reaches the large hotel at **Mummelsee** (*See* means lake) and may be astonished at the car parking space provided. The lake, 1,028m (3,372ft) above sea level, nestles at the foot of the 1,164m (3,820ft) Hornisgrinde in a delightful woodland setting. There are rowing boats for hire and an Old Father Neptune character tells the legends of the lake.

One story, recorded by the Jesuit Athanasius Kircher in his book of 1678, warns that any person throwing stones into the lake places his or her life in danger. Kircher tells how a Margrave from Baden came here with members of his court, including some religious advisers, and threw certain consecrated objects into the water. The reason for this action is not explained but a horrible monster suddenly emerged from the depths and chased the whole assembly from the shores. For seven days, the most violent storms imaginable raged around the spot. Needless to say, today's representative of the underwater world is a rather more benevolent character.

Apart from the summer scenery and the possibilities of walks along this ridge, the area also provides for winter sports; the settlements of Ruhestein, Alexander-Schanze and Kniebis are all devoted to skiing and associated activities. In fact, this area is at its busiest on fine winter weekends and what might have seemed in summer to be excessive car parking provision, is now filled to capacity as skiers converge upon the area from all directions. Both skiers and winter walkers make for the Vogelskopf 1,053m (3,454ft), the Schliffkopf 1,055m (3,460ft) and the Pfälzer Kopf 1,013m (3,322ft). There are also the less popular areas away from the main ski-runs where ramblers can soon find themselves totally isolated.

Down in the Rhine valley, there will be the first signs of spring while up here on the ridge, winter sports are still in full swing and the snow ploughs are still engaged in the task of keeping the roads clear. It is a delight on a cold winter's day to go into one of the many hostelries along the High Road for a bowl of warming soup or a glass of *Glühwein* (mulled wine) before continuing the outdoor activity. (A programme of winter sports package holidays is available from the German National Tourist Offices.)

The little resort of **Seebach** is not far from the Mummelsee, just off the ridge to the west on the road to Ottenhöfen. This is a popular place with nature lovers who can readily reach the various nature conservation areas along the *Hochstrasse*. Seebach and Ottenhöfen are both good starting points for a fairly strenuous ramble to the summit of the Hornisgrinde which is behind the Mummelsee. After Kniebis, the road descends towards Freudenstadt, which is to be visited in a later chapter.

The way must now be retraced to Baden-Baden to pick up the *Weinstrasse* again. In this area, the *Weinstrasse* never follows any one road for long but meanders to and fro in the best of the vineyard scenery. **Bühl** is reached 16km (10 miles) from Baden-Baden. The octagonal *Rathaus* tower and the nineteenth-century church of Saints Peter and Paul are worthy of inspection. The baroque church (1765) in the suburb of Kappelwindeck should also be seen.

A very worthwhile excursion can be made north-westwards from Bühl to **Schwarzach**, a distance of some 9km (5$^1/_2$ miles), where the former Benedictine Klosterkirche is to be seen. In the days long before the Rhine was as disciplined as it is today, a monastic cell was founded on an island in the river. Because the river changed its course or flooded new areas so often, the settlement had to move to firmer ground on the east bank in AD826.

Another move became necessary around 1200 when the present site was chosen. Following a fire, the present church was built in the then current Romanesque style in about 1220. The abbot allowed himself to be guided by influences from the *Klöster* at Hirsau and Gengenbach as well as from Alsace across the Rhine. Considering the resources available at the time, the resulting three-naved, cross-form basilica was a remarkable achievement.

In 1724, following periods of war and poverty, Peter Thumb, the distinguished architect and builder from the Austrian Vorarlberg region, was given the task of rebuilding the *Kloster* complex and improving the church. The interior was re-finished in the baroque style which was in vogue by then. The mighty high altar, now in the south transept, was built in 1752 by a Rastatt craftsman named Eigler. The choir stalls and the organ over the entrance are both eighteenth century, the latter having been supplied by the Strasbourg organ builder, Johann Andreas Silbermann.

In 1967, work started on a renovation of the church to remove some of the later additions and restore it to the more strict original form. The completion of this work has resulted in a church which is both dignified and exceedingly pleasing to the eye. Many of the eighteenth-century buildings survive and make the area around the church a pleasant backwater which certainly justifies the short diversion from the *Weinstrasse* or the *Autobahn* for a visit.

There is a fine ramble of 12km (7¹/₂ miles) from the Oberbühlertal up to the *Schwarzwaldhochstrasse* and back, taking in the wild and romantic Gertelbach waterfalls on the way. Just past the Hotel Schindelpeter, a little road goes down to the right to a car park in the valley. From there, follow the blue diamond waymark up the valley past the Café Waldhorn. The climb up steps and landings beside the waterfalls begins 20 minutes after passing the Restaurant-Café Gertelbach.

It takes about half an hour to reach the top of the falls, where there is a fork in the path. The waymark should be followed to the left to reach the imposing rocks, the Wiedenfelsen, in about 10 minutes. There is a hotel of the same name, immediately opposite which there is a sign 'Paradiesweg' pointing in the direction of Plättig. Follow the signs to gradually turn northwards and reach the Hotel Plättig on the Black Forest High Road in about half an hour. At the end of the car park, obey the sign 'Zur Hertahütte' but when the broad track goes right after about 5 minutes, keep straight on (sign 'Felsenweg'), climbing through the impressive labyrinth of the Falkenfelsen (rocks) to reach a good viewpoint at the Hertahütte. You will have been walking for some 2¹/₄ hours.

Retrace steps towards the Falkenfelsen but now take a right fork past the massive Brockenfelsen. Just before reaching a wide track from Plättig, go down to the right at a sign saying 'Wiedenfelsen über Paradiesweg'. Then, almost immediately, on the edge of the wood, there is another sign indicating the way back down to the Bühlertal. This is along the so-called Briefträgerweg (postman's way). After a sharp left curve with a barrier and the sign 'Steinbruch' (quarry), leave the main track and climb up a woodland path marked with a blue spot and the number '10'. On reaching the first houses, go briefly right and then left down the road to the starting point. Total walking

Schwarzach, near Bühl

time for this circuit is around $3\frac{1}{2}$ hours.

Returning to the *Weinstrasse* and continuing in a southerly direction, one reaches the ruins of Burg Altwindeck with a viewpoint back towards Bühl and over the Rhine valley. There is a *W-Parkplatz* at the castle with three round walks. The Burg Windeck hostelry lets a few rooms and there is a comfortable restaurant which is closed on Tuesdays. (Nearly all hotels and inns in Germany close on one day each week. This is the so-called *Ruhetag* or rest day.)

The *Weinstrasse* has wandered off to the vineyards in the Bühlertal (*Tal* means valley) east of the town but it comes down to touch Ottersweier briefly on main road B3 before returning to those behind Achern. In Achern itself there is a small museum which includes a collection of agricultural implements. However, it is only open on Sunday afternoons and not at all in January. The hotel Götz Sonne-Eintracht in the Hauptstrasse specialises in frogs' legs cooked in white wine and venison dishes in season. A modern railcar travels on the private Achertalbahn (Acher Valley Railway) which runs the 11km (7 miles) from Achern to Kappelrodeck and Ottenhöfen. However, on alternate Sundays from May to September, it is also possible to travel over this line in a carriage which may be 100 years old, hauled by a diminutive steam locomotive built at the turn of the century.

At Sasbachwalden, on a minor road east of Achern, there is a *W-Parkplatz* with five round walks. The walker will enjoy the splendid mixed woods with their many chestnut trees. **Sasbachwalden** is well-worth seeing anyway. It enjoys the title *Blumendorf* (flower village) and was picked out over twenty years ago as the most beautiful parish in the whole of Baden-Württemberg. It is now protected by a conservation order and when the flower-decked window sills of the old and new timbered houses are seen in summer, it is clear why the village achieved such renown.

The Brigittenschloss and the Burg Hohenrode (both eleventh-century) occupy fine vantage points and, in clear weather, the granite hillocks provide a distant view of the tower of Strasbourg cathedral and of the mountain chain of the Vosges (Vogesen in German). The two little rivers, Sasbach and Brandbach, meet in the village and one can follow the course of the latter up through the rocky ravine called Gaishölle where there are many little waterfalls. The famous *Spätburgunder* wine grapes are among those grown around the village with the greatest success.

Meanwhile, the *Weinstrasse* has reached the village of **Kappel-rodeck** which is in a delightful situation; Rodeck castle was built in the twelfth century. It is here that the Verein für Familienerholung in Deutschland (Assocation for Family Holidays) has one of its attractive self-catering villages. A little further on, Oberkirch (17,000 inhabitants) is reached and here the *Weinstrasse* crosses another of the named roads, the *Freundschaftstrasse* (Friendship road) running from Strasbourg across the Rhine to Freudenstadt and beyond. There are two *W-Parkplätze* near the main road (the B28) in the vicinity of Oberkirch. The first, called Moos, can be reached via the turning to Kalicutt and has five round walks of between 3 and 8km (2 and 5 miles). The other is in Hubacker and can be reached over the railway bridge there. It too, has five walks, in this case of 2 to 6km (1 to 4 miles). Oberkirch is also the starting point for one of the marked long-distance paths, the 100km (62 miles) *Kandelhöhenweg*, which will be mentioned again in a later chapter.

Oberkirch is popular with wine connoisseurs who come to enjoy the local Renchtal wines — this is the commercial and cultural centre of the Upper Rench valley. The holiday visitor is well-catered for. There is a magnificent open-air swimming pool with sauna and solarium, the pleasant town gardens have a concert pavilion and there are children's playgrounds, as well as an animal enclosure. Tennis courts are also available and the ever popular mini-golf may be played.

The *Altstadt* — the old town centre — has been painstakingly restored and many of the streets are now for pedestrians only. The *Verkehrsamt* has produced a free, pocket-sized guide to the historic buildings and places of interest and the visitor should certainly make a couple of hours available for exploration of this charming old place. There is also ample accommodation in all categories.

Oberkirch lies right on the boundary between vineyards and forest. Downhill, into the Rhine valley, the vines appear to go on creating a gentle landscape as far as the eye can see; uphill to the east, the tree-clad slopes mark the start of the forest proper. The ruins of Schauenburg, high above the town, seem to be there to protect the idyllic scene. As the journey continues, this is a picture which will be constantly repeated.

There is a station at Oberkirch on the little branch line from Offenburg or Appenweier to Bad Griesbach so although the vineyards are soon left behind, it is appropriate at this stage to continue a little further up the Rench valley to the end of the line. Despite the presence of the railway and the rather busy B28, this is an entirely charming valley and the journey up it, especially by train, is one which can be recommended.

The village of **Lautenbach** is less than 4km (2¹/₂ miles) eastwards along the Friendship Road and has the Gothic pilgrimage church Maria Krönung (coronation of Mary) which was consecrated in 1493. Its origin can be traced back to a fourteenth-century pilgrimage. Two additional bays and the tower were added in 1895-7. The interior is lavishly decorated and has a net vault. A large lectern is supported by four columns and dates from 1488 while the Gnadenkapelle, from 3 years earlier, is where the sixteenth-century wooden image of the Blessed Virgin was kept. These are both noteworthy features, as are the pictures in the choir altar (1483 and 1510-20) and the fifteenth-century stained-glass windows. The choir stalls are the original ones from the time the church was built.

Just past Lautenbach, a minor road to the left leads to the tiny spa of Bad Sulzbach but the main road continues through pleasant scenery to reach the *Luftkurort* of **Oppenau** (population 3,000) in about 6km (4 miles). This little town, now slightly industrialised around the station, was developed by the Prämonstratensian monks from nearby Allerheiligen during the period from 1299 to 1319. Much of the place was later destroyed by fire but it was rebuilt in the years up to 1617 by a master builder named Schickhardt. Local history is on display in the *Heimatmuseum*.

From Oppenau, a minor road leads up through the Maisachtal and through Maisach to the little spa of Bad Antogast. Even today this is a pretty remote spot but the Romans discovered the healing springs here nearly two thousand years ago, making this the oldest of the several spas in this vicinity. A great peace reigns here and the visitor, whether he or she is taking the *Kur* or on holiday, will remain undisturbed by the noises usually associated with modern life.

This is perhaps the point at which to explain some of the terms used to describe the German resorts. A *Bad* is a spa at which curative treatment (the *Kur*) is based on the properties of thermal springs; a *Kurort* is also a place where treatment is available; a *Luftkurort* is a place where the air is particularly beneficial and a *Heilklimatischerkurort* bases the *Kur* on the healing properties of the climate generally. At a *Kneippkurort* the water treatments of Sebastian Kneipp are adopted. An *Erholungsort* specialises in recreation, recuperation and convalescence while a *Ferienort* is a general holiday resort.

Back on the B28, as it climbs towards the *Schwarzwaldhochstrasse*, is the double spa resort of **Bad Peterstal-Griesbach**, a well regarded convalescent centre. The mineral springs in Peterstal were also discovered in early times and the first documentary reference to what was then called 'St Peter im Tal' dates from 1290. The therapeutic qualities of the waters are valuable in the treatment of heart trouble, circulatory diseases, rheumatism, etc and the first spa hotel opened in 1584.

In order to protect the early aristocratic guests, a citizens' militia was founded and today the historic costumes of the little army are a great attraction at the various festivals in the Rench valley. Peterstaler Mineralwasser is excellent for table use and is bottled and exported all over the world. One would not, however, drink water from the associated sulphur spring for pleasure, although it is still used for medicinal purposes. The springs in **Griesbach** were discovered at about the same period, the first *Kurhaus* was built in 1579.

The bottling plant for the Griesbacher Mineralwasser is a short distance from the entrance to the valley of the Wilder Rench which leaves the main road at the east end of the village. There is a drinking

Places of Interest In and Around Bühl, Achern, The Rench Valley and Offenburg

Bühl
Rathaus (Town Hall)
Unusual octagonal tower.

Church of Saints Peter and Paul
Fine nineteenth-century building.

Baroque Church (1765)
In Kappelwindeck 3km (2 miles)
south-east of Bühl.

Burg Altwindeck
4km (2¹/₂ miles) south-east of Bühl.
Views of the Rhine valley.

Former Benedictine Klosterkirche
In Schwarzach 9km (5¹/₂ miles)
north-west of Bühl
Romanesque church (1220) with
later baroque treatment. Fine
organ.

Achern
Sensen and Heimatmuseum
Berlinerstrasse 31.
Local relics with a collection of
agricultural implements.

Achertalbahn
Steam railway from Achern to
Kappelrodeck and Ottenhöfen.

Sasbachwalden
First floral village of Baden-
Württemberg.

Brigittenschloss and *Burg Hohenrode* (Eleventh-century)
Splendid viewpoints above village.

Renchen
Memorials to famous writer J.J.C.
von Grimmelshausen (1622-76)

Oberkirch
Altstadt
Well-restored old town centre with
half-timbered houses.

Zum Silbernen Stern
North-east of town centre near

church in Gaisbach
Traditional hostelry once owned by
J.J.C. von Grimmelshausen.

Schauenburg
Castle ruins above town, with
excellent views.

Lautenbach
Maria Krönung
Gothic pilgrimage church (1493).
Lavishly decorated interior.

Offenburg
*Catholic parish church of the Holy
Cross*
Consecrated in 1791. Splendid
high altar and other furnishings.

Rathaus (1741)
Hauptstrasse
Baroque Town Hall with striking
façade.

Königshof (1717)
Hauptstrasse
Another building with a fine
baroque façade.

*Former Franciscan Monastery
Church*
Lange Strasse
Beautifully maintained baroque
church with fine Silbermann organ
and furnishings.

Ortenberg
Schloss Ortenberg
4km (2¹/₂ miles) south-east of
Offenburg
Ruins of twelfth-century castle
rebuilt around 1840 in 'English'
style.

Gengenbach
Medieval town in Kinzig valley
11km (7 miles) from Offenburg
Many half-timbered houses,
fountains and former *Klosterkirche*
with baroque tower.

The Rench valley

fountain outside the little factory where the passer-by can sample the water. The traditional local costumes are often worn at weddings and other festivities in Bad Griesbach. The tiny St Antonius Kapelle can be reached by a path which goes up the hillside opposite the modern *Kurhaus*. From there one can wander gently upwards to the *Sprungschanze* (ski-jump) and there are open-air tennis courts close to the top of this, found by following signs for 'Tennis-Hütte'.

This resort in the popular Rench valley has excellent visitor facilities including indoor and outdoor swimming pools and a wide range of accommodation with many *Ferienwohnungen* (holiday flats). On the first Saturday in August the Summer Nights Festival is held, with illuminations and fireworks. There is also an easy and exceptionally picturesque walk of $4^1/_2$ km ($2^3/_4$ miles) between the two parts of the resort.

At Griesbach station, go round behind the buffer stops and turn left, parallel with the line. Beyond the station area the path goes down to the bank of the river Rench — the waymarks to follow read 'Renchtalweg'. After a short while, the river and path pass beneath the railway under a fine arch. If one looks back from time to time, there are pretty views. On the outskirts of Peterstal, turn right over the river, cross the main road and go under the railway again to climb rather steeply up the slope the other side of the valley. After a short distance, turn left to follow a path through the woods along this slope with views down on to Peterstal. Watch for the sign 'Bahnhof' and turn left down the hill to Peterstal station.

The Wine Road route must be rejoined in Oberkirch but before going further south, it would be a good idea to follow the Rench valley a few kilometres down to **Renchen**, a little town on the B3, more concerned today with its breweries and timber workshops than with the tourist trade. However, the visitor will soon note that it is quite an attractive place and some of the surrounding villages are very pleasant indeed. The most famous son of Renchen is Johann Jakob Christoffel von Grimmelshausen (1622-76) the noted chronicler of the Thirty Years War, who told the story mainly through the adventures of his anti-hero, Simplicius Simplicissimus.

Grimmelshausen had a varied if not very long life, serving often in the rôle of writer or secretary to various military units. He came to Offenburg in 1649 after one period of service and married the 22-year old daughter of a cavalry sergeant-major from Saverne in Alsace and, as a result of this union, adopted the Catholic faith. He settled in Gaisbach on the outskirts of Oberkirch, where he was the official in charge of the Schauenburg properties but, perhaps partly because of his change of faith, his masters came to distrust him and he was dismissed. He then leased a fine manor-house and converted it to a wine hostelry called Zum Silbernen Stern (the Silver Star), an identity which the charming building beside the Gaisbach church has retained to this day.

Grimmelshausen was born and is buried in Renchen where he was the village mayor for the last 9 years of his life. An obelisk was erected in 1879 at his final resting place near the church; it looks more like a war memorial of the period with its stone palm branches and wreath of oak leaves. A more modern memorial is the bronze fountain cast by Giacomo Manzu of Rome and presented by one Dr Franz Burda (of the extensive Burda magazine empire) in 1977. Further reminders of the writer are to be found in the Renchen restaurant Zum Bären (the Bear) where one room has been named the Grimmelshausen-Stube. His *Adventuresome Simplicissimus* was first published in 1668 and Simplicissimus has been adopted as the title of a German satirical periodical published in Munich since 1896.

The *Weinstrasse* winds down from Oberkirch towards Offenburg, into the heart of the vineyards. **Durbach** (population 3,700) is an important vineyard village with several hostelries serving good food which is complemented by the local wines. In particular, the tastefully decorated Gasthaus 'Zum Ritter', at the foot of Burg Staufenburg, is noted for its cuisine with Baden specialities — it has a Michelin 'star' — and wine from its own vines.

Staufenburg castle was originally built in the eleventh century. It was destroyed in 1689 and a new building was erected on the site in the nineteenth century. The Duke of Edinburgh is occasionally here as the guest of the Duke of Baden, who is the present owner of Staufenburg castle, much of which is normally open to the public. There are some rather good half-timbered houses in the main street, along which there is a pretty little river. In summer the bridges are a blaze of colour with boxes of flowers along the balustrades. Look out for some fine traditional farmhouses in the vicinity. For the guest there is fishing, tennis and mini-golf at hand.

Offenburg (population 50,000) is yet another fringe town, standing, like Rastatt, astride a Black Forest river flowing westwards to the Rhine. The river Kinzig has come through the beautiful Kinzigtal from Freudenstadt. Offenburg is a stopping place for many of the trains on the main line south to Basel and is also an interchange station for trains up and down the Rhine valley, into the Rench valley, and over the Rhine to Strasbourg (half an hour). It forms the western extremity of the *Schwarzwaldbahn* (Black Forest Railway) which runs through the Kinzig and Gutach valleys eastwards to Donaueschingen, with many trains going through to Konstanz on the Bodensee (Lake Constance). There are also many bus routes to outlying villages. All this makes it an ideal centre for the traveller reliant upon public transport.

Offenburg itself has numerous places of interest and the first-time visitor would do well to arm him- or herself with the English language guide and town map obtainable free from the *Verkehrsamt* at Gärtnerstrasse 6, just behind the Hauptstrasse. The Catholic parish church of the Holy Cross, with its dominant three-storey tower, was erected under the influence of the Vorarlberg architectural school. After a period of building lasting nearly 100 years, it was

Church of the Holy Cross, Offenburg

consecrated in 1791. The splendid high altar was created by Franz Lichtenauer in 1740 and the left side choir houses a Renaissance crucifix dating back to 1521. The Protestant town church in the Hauptstrasse has an ornate steeple and was built in neo-Gothic style between 1857 and 64.

At the south end of the Hauptstrasse are several places of interest in close proximity. The baroque *Rathaus* of 1741 has a fine façade; above the balcony are the town coat of arms and the Austrian double-headed eagle, reflecting the allegiance of the town at the time of its construction. Opposite, in the little square called Fischmarkt, the painted front of the Hirsch Apotheke has many amusing features; the lion fountain outside dates from 1599.

The old coaching inn 'Hotel Sonne', next to the *Rathaus*, dates back to 1350 but, like nearly everything else in the town, it was completely destroyed at the hands of the French in the great fire of 1689. It was reconstructed almost at once and is, therefore, the oldest existing hotel in Offenburg. The courtyard where the horses were changed now serves as the hotel car park and the former stables are now garages and store rooms. Inside there is a fine baroque staircase and the main public rooms have magnificent tiled stoves which are still in regular use, although today they are supplemented by modern central heating. A small picture is a reminder that von Grimmelshausen was a guest here at one time.

Immediately after the 'Sonne' is the Landratsamt or Königshof, a fine baroque building with a very ornamental façade. It was built in 1717 under the instructions of the Margravine Sybilla Augusta, of whom mention has already been made, and it now houses the police headquarters. Nearby, in the centre of the street, is the Ursula Column, one of several modern sculptures in the town. It was created in 1961 by the sculptor Emil Sutor and was a gift from Dr Franz Burda, who is an honorary citizen. St Ursula is the patroness of the town and is said to have appeared on the walls in 1638 to ward off an attack by the troops of Duke Bernhard of Weimar.

At the other end of the town, not far from the station, the former Franciscan monastery now houses a girls' school. It too was rebuilt after the great fire of 1689. The beautiful baroque church has a massive wooden altar, a Silbermann organ and carved choir stalls. In St Mary's chapel there is a late-Gothic wooden Madonna. The church is attractively decorated inside and should be included in every visitor's itinerary. Access is through the entrance hall, beyond which there is a wrought iron screen with a bell-push. One of the girls acts as doorkeeper and, upon being summoned, will open the gate in the screen for the visitor to pass through into the church itself. There is no charge.

This only represents a small selection of the places of interest in a compact town. Most of the Hauptstrasse (main street) is a spacious pedestrian zone lined with departmental stores and other shops. The accommodation in the town itself is almost entirely in the hotel category. There is a pleasant little park outside the walls alongside the river Kinzig and this leads into the Bürgerpark where the *Freibad* and *Hallenbad* are situated. The Stadtwald (town forest) just west of the town has several parking places, one of which is adjacent to a *Trimm-Dich* (keep fit) circuit. There are many pleasant walks through the woods; the visitor without his or her own transport can walk from the town centre (a detailed description of the route in English is available from the *Verkehrsamt*) to the far side of the Stadtwald and back in about 4 hours, or make the journey one way by bus.

Offenburg, like other towns of its size, can pose car-parking problems. Although most of the Black Forest towns which the visitor will visit are comparatively small, narrow streets, markets and agricultural activities can contribute to a significant traffic problem. The casual motoring tourist is advised to leave the car on the outskirts rather than face the harassment of trying to park in the centre.

Since starting the journey down the *Weinstrasse*, the visitor has had ample choice of fairly short walks, mostly demanding no more than modest effort. For those who require something more exciting, a 5-day ramble is organised by the Verkehrsampt Offenburg, Gärtnerstrasse 6, 77652 Offenburg. The tour, called the '*Fröhliche Weinwanderung*' (merry wine ramble), starts in Baden-Baden. It follows the Ortenauer Weinpfad (Ortenau Wine Path), more or less parallel with the *Weinstrasse*, by way of Unterbühlertal, Sasbachwalden, Kappelrodeck, Oberkirch, Offenburg and Gengenbach to Diersburg.

The walkers travel light, their luggage being forwarded between the good hotels used by the organisation. Walking time is between 4 and 6 hours each day, leaving ample time to sample the various wines along the way. The total distance to be covered is about 100km (62 miles) and the terrain traversed does not exceed the 'moderately strenuous' category. The route is full of interest; the vineyards as well as picturesque castles and historic towns are visited en route.

Not every walker will wish to commit him- or herself to the whole of the ramble mentioned but a most pleasant 1 day walk of 16km (10 miles) along the *Weinpfad* can be started in Offenburg. Go south from the *Rathaus* along the Hauptstrasse and at the end turn left through the rose garden until reaching the end of Lange Strasse. Here, in a fine

group of trees, is a memorial to Carl Isenmann who set Ludwig Auersbach's poem *O Schwarzwald, o Heimat* to music.

Go forward over the railway bridge and cross the road to go to the right along Ortenberger Strasse for about 700m (765 yards) to the junction left to Fessenbach. Follow this road for about 1km ($^1/_2$ mile) and about 200m before the first houses of Fessenbach turn right onto a surfaced track rising slightly for about 500m (547yd) to reach the *Weinstrasse*. Cross this road and go straight ahead into Senator-Burda-Strasse, past a *Kloster* and the vineyards and estate house of Dr Burda. Then turn sharply right into the heart of the vineyards, following the Ortenau Wine Path (bunch of grapes waymark) along surfaced roads until Schloss Ortenberg is approached.

The castle is now a youth hostel and the experimental station for vine cultivation in the Ortenau district. Turn left 150m (164yd) before the castle and continue through the terraces until, descending slightly, one passes through a pair of former gate pillars marking an estate boundary. Keep to the left here and almost at once turn back to the right, up through woods and before long on to an unsurfaced track which goes round the top of a quarry. Continue down towards the hamlet of Büchen and then follow waymarks '5', which pass mostly through woods, until coming out into the vineyards of Ohlsbach, which is the village below. Ahead will be seen a little red-roofed chapel called Maria im Weinberg, built as recently as 1985 by the Karl Wacker family in fulfilment of an old vow. Visit the chapel and then walk straight down into the village.

It will have taken $2^1/_2$ to 3 hours from Offenburg so this is a good place to stop for refreshment in one of several hostelries. Leave Ohlsbach via Weissenbachstrasse to the Waldcafé, past the recreation area to footpath No 1. The route forks to the right above the cemetery down via 'Holzer Eck' to the Reichenbach school. Cross the valley road and continue past the sports field to the few houses at a corner called Sanktis Klaus and turn right. Continue on the path parallel with the road as long as possible but eventually walk on the road itself down into Gengenbach past the Geschwister-Scholl-Schule and into the old town through the Oberer Tor. The total time from Offenburg is 5 to 6 hours. There is a reasonably frequent train service from Gengenbach station back into Offenburg and buses are also available.

From Offenburg, the *Weinstrasse* now swings up into the Kinzigtal, following the north bank of the river to reach the village of **Ortenberg** in 4km ($2^1/_2$ miles). The impressive Schloss Ortenberg overlooks the valley and occupies the site of a twelfth-century castle. It was reduced to ruins when this part of the country was overrun by French soldiers in 1678, suffering the fate of many similar fortifications which originally guarded the valley entrances. The rubble lay around until 1840 although much of it was removed to be used as building material by the local population. However, funds were then made available for the building of a new 'English' style castle which, after many changes, eventually became the youth hostel and experimental station which it is today.

The *Schloss* provides a wonderful viewpoint. Immediately below

*The town hall,
Gengenbach*

*The main square,
Gengenbach*

are vineyard slopes and the village; towards the Rhine are extensive orchards and the city of Offenburg with its housing and industrial areas, while across the Rhine, the distant tower of Strasbourg cathedral may perhaps be seen.

In another 7km (4 miles), **Gengenbach** is reached; an immediately attractive, medieval town which makes a pleasant overnight stop or a longer stay. The centre of the walled town makes visitors feel as if they are back in the Middle Ages. The market place is surrounded by delightful timbered houses, and a fountain is a reminder that until 1803 this town had 'free' status; it had bought itself out of obligations to local dukes and sundry other noblemen and owed allegiance only to the crown. The nobility frequently used this as a means of raising capital when times were hard, but all such 'arrangements' were finally cancelled by law in 1803. Roman remains have been found in the area and a Benedictine Kloster was founded here in the eighth century. The building itself, rebuilt in 1695 after a fire, today houses an educational establishment.

The former Klosterkirche, now the main church of Gengenbach, has a fine baroque tower but the garish interior decor is somewhat disturbing. The writer and folklore researcher Ernst Sutter lived here in the house 'Zum Löwen' which now, appropriately, houses the *Heimatmuseum*. It is through Sutter's efforts, ably supported by the *Bürgermeister* of the day, that the historic townscape has remained unsullied by obtrusive advertisement hoardings and the like, to charm us today. This delightful little town has an air of sparkling cleanliness, with carefully restored buildings and a riot of flowers, making it a much photographed place. It is a centre of pre-Lenten festivities when the masked fools take over the town.

Leaving Gengenbach, one travels back down the other side of the river on road B33 towards Offenburg, but before then the *Weinstrasse* leaves the main road to turn south through the vineyard villages of Zunsweier and Diersburg to rejoin road B3 at Schopfheim. This main road is now followed for some 40km (25 miles) but the unchanging landscape and succession of villages devoted to the wine industry does not provide very much new interest.

There are few walking opportunities along this section of the route. However, Lahr, a town of about 36,000 inhabitants, has a *W-Parkplatz* which is the starting point for a walk through the vineyards and around the Schutterlindenberg, a modest hill with a splendid outlook. The Protestant church in **Lahr**, the former St Peter's Church,

stands on a site where there has been a religious building of some
kind since the eighth century. The former collegiate church in the
same town was spoiled by unsympathetic restoration work in the
middle of the nineteenth century but a choir from the original
thirteenth-century building has survived.

The *Neues Rathaus* has a beautiful colonnaded hall in the upper
storey. It was originally built in 1808 as a town house for the Lotzbeck
family. There are late baroque, rococo, classical and Biedermeier
houses in the town, one of the most important being the Stoessersches Haus (1783) at No 41 Kaiserstrasse. The Geroldsecker Museum
is in the Storchenturm which is all that remains of the *Burg* which
Walter von Geroldseck built in 1250.

Road B415 runs eastwards from Lahr through the Schuttertal
and, after a couple of kilometres, it reaches the little village of
Kuhbach which contains a sight worth seeing in its tiny old church
of St Gallus. It was built about 1300 and has the remains of medieval
wall paintings in the choir. At some later date the original tower was
removed, probably because it was unstable, and it was replaced by
the pretty little turret seen on the roof today. Used for some time for
school children's services only, the church authorities now seek to
obtain financial support from the state in order to protect and
preserve this historic building and restore it to its original use as a
cemetery chapel. Twelve kilometres ($7^1/_2$ miles) south-west of Lahr
between the *Autobahn* and the Rhine, there is the leisure centre called
Europapark Rust which has many attractions for children.

Ten kilometres (6 miles) south of Lahr, it is necessary to leave the
main road for a kilometre or so to visit **Ettenheim** (population 8,000).
This is a former place of residence of the Prince-Bishops of Strasbourg. A brief visit here would be particularly rewarding; there is an
imposing baroque church, splendidly flanked by a number of attractive Renaissance and rococo buildings.

If the picturesque road is followed for a further 6km (4 miles)
beyond Ettenheim, one reaches **Ettenheimmünster** which is situated in grand rambling country with at least four *W-Parkplätze* within
2km ($1^1/_4$ miles) of the village. The first of these is reached 1km ($^1/_2$
mile) up a road which goes south for 1km before reaching the village
and has three round walks. Near the *Kloster* at the west end of the
village, take the Lautenbachstrasse for 1km to a parking place with
a marked walk of 8km (5 miles). A kilometre past the *Kloster* and at
the east end of the village, a minor road goes due east alongside a

stream to a car park with a round walk of 4.5km (3 miles).

Yet another easily accessible *W-Parkplatz* is on the main road beyond the village close to the first sharp bend of the zig-zag road which climbs into the hills and has numerous further opportunities for *parken und wandern* along the next 8km (5 miles). This is an area which will be dealt with in more detail in a later chapter.

Kenzingen, 10km (6¹/₄ miles) south of Ettenheim, has the typical oval layout of many towns in this area which were planned by, or in imitation of, the towns founded by the dukes of the Zähringen dynasty in the twelfth century. This delightful little town — the population is only about 8,000 — presents a medieval face to the world and it is not easy to detect that many of the buildings were, in fact, only built or rebuilt following a disastrous fire in the nineteenth-century. However, the seventeenth-century building styles were faithfully reproduced so that the new and old blended together harmoniously.

The *Rathaus* was built in 1550 and there are three pretty fountains nearby, typical again of the 'Zähringen' towns. At No 20 Alte Schulstrasse, the Verbande Oberrheinischer Narrenzünfte (Association of Upper Rhine Fools' Clubs) has a colourful exhibition of the artefacts of the Alemannic *Fasnet* — masks and costumes as well as 230 life-size 'fools' figures. The parish church of St Laurenzius was built about 1275; it has wall paintings dating from about 1300 and some viewable sixteenth-century gravestones.

Because so much of Black Forest folklore, particularly the pre-Lenten *Fasnet* or carnival celebrations, is bound up with the Alemannic origins of much of the population, some words of explanation may not come amiss. There is a distinct Alemannic dialect which crosses national and ethnic boundaries and is to be found in Alsace, in German-speaking Switzerland and in the Vorarlberg of Austria as well as in the south-western corner of Germany which includes the Black Forest.

All this results from the history of the Alemannians, which goes back to the third century. About that time, tribes known as the Sueben (or Sweben) banded together with others as the *'alle Mannen'* (all men), and this was the title by which they were known until about the year 1000. In AD213 they started to move against the Roman garrisons on German soil and, 47 years later, finally succeeded in ending Roman domination. From the year 1000, the term *Alemannen* ceased to be used in German speaking regions but was

Places of Interest In and Around Lahr, Ettenheim and Kenzingen

Lahr
Neues Rathaus (1808)
Former family house. Colonnaded hall in upper storey.

Stoessersches Haus (1783)
Kaiserstrasse 41
One of several fine town houses representing the baroque, rococo, classical and Biedermeier styles.

Geroldsecker Museum
In the Storchenturm
All that remains of the castle of 1250.

St Gallus' Church
In Kuhbach, east of Lahr town centre. Built about 1300; medieval wall paintings.

Europapark Rust
12km (7¹/₂ miles) south-west of

Lahr
Modern family leisure centre.

Ettenheim
'Baroque' town with church and attractive Renaissance and rococo buildings.

Kenzingen
Typical Zähringen dynasty town.

Rathaus (1550)
Three attractive fountains nearby.

Exhibition of masks, costumes, etc of 'Fasnet'
At Alte Schulstrasse 20

Parish church of St Laurenzius (about 1275)
Several items of interest with wall paintings from about 1300.

adopted in the Latin languages as the general name for the whole German area. This has persisted until today as in Allemagne (French) and Alemania (Spanish).

The great dialect poet, Johann Peter Hebel (1760-1826) re-awakened interest in the old language and in the unity of the people able to converse in it. The old customs and language are now safeguarded by several dedicated organisations and the museum in Kenzingen is a fine place in which to find out more about this interesting background; a visit there is especially rewarding.

Continue following road B3 to Malterdingen, where it is necessary to leave it and turn west towards Riegel; here the Leopoldskanal connecting Freiburg with the Rhine is crossed. Ahead there is a fantastic conglomeration of vineyards on the hill, or rather cluster of hills, called the Kaiserstuhl. This is a volcanic hump rising abruptly from the Rhine plain to a height of 557m (1,827ft), encircled by a loop of the Wine Road and dotted with numerous small communities, all working feverishly to produce what they claim are the best wines of the *Weinstrasse*. One thing is certain; the remarkable climate experienced here does give them a very good chance of achieving their aim.

Riegel is the starting place for a leisurely journey in the *Rebenbummler*, a train — complete with well-stocked wine bar — which potters through the vineyards to Breisach. In the *Rathaus*, which dates from 1784, there is an exhibition of finds from the area, principally from Roman times. The baroque St Martin's-Kirche is also worth seeing.

Going round the Kaiserstuhl in an anti-clockwise direction, one soon reaches the very attractive little town of **Endingen**, its fine towers straddling the road. This is an excellent place for an introduction to rambling on the Kaiserstuhl, for not only is the *W-Parkplatz* the starting point for round walks of 2-10km (1-6$\frac{1}{4}$ miles) but there are five further parking places on the circular footpath network. With Breisach, Burkheim and Endingen represent the urban element of the Kaiserstuhl.

The Gothic and baroque citizens' houses of Endingen fit comfortably into a townscape with charming squares and streets. The main public buildings are of a high quality; the early Renaissance *Kornhaus* (1417), the old *Rathaus* (1527) in Gothic and baroque and the new *Rathaus* in rococo style are grouped around the market place with its *Ratsbrunnen* (fountain) in the centre of the town. Architectural styles from late-Romanesque to that of Louis XVI are incorporated in the Peterskirche while St Martin unites Gothic elements from the fourteenth century with nineteenth-century replicas. There is a *Gnadenbild* (miraculous image) of the weeping Mother of God. A recommended short ramble is to the Katharinenkapelle on the Katharinaberg 492m (1,615ft) — a distance of 8km (5 miles) there and back.

The Katharinenkapelle may also be visited during a rather more ambitious, circular walk of 15km (9$\frac{1}{2}$ miles) starting in the village of Oberbergen, and taking in a good selection of Kaiserstuhl scenery and several fine viewpoints in an area that is not so dominated by the vineyards. Leave Oberbergen by the church on the road to Kiechlinsbergen and, after about 15 minutes, reach the first big serpentine curve and look for a path to the right near the 100m stone '4'. This leads up to the Waldparkplatz 'Auf dem Eck' and from here the waymark of the long-distance Querweg Schwarzwald-Rhein (red diamond on yellow ground) can be followed eastwards. The path goes gently up and down with pretty views and, in about 1 hour from the 'Eck', the Katharinenkapelle 492m (1,615ft) is reached, with the first view to the north.

There is a kiosk here where it may be possible to buy drinks but apart from this, provisions for the whole tour should be carried. Go down to the right following signs 'Eichelspitze-Neunlinden-Totenkopf' and in 15 minutes, on the grassy ridge called Schönebene, there are views left to the Black Forest and right to the Vosges across the Rhine. From the slopes of the Eichelspitze 500m (1,640ft), can be seen the Naturschutzgebiet Badberg which lies to the right. The Parkplatz Vogelsang is soon reached and this marks the start of a climb through woods to the Neunlinden tower at 555m (1,820ft) which may be ascended for an even better vista.

Leave the north-south way in the dip between here and the television mast on the nearby Totenkopf, and follow a path marked by a green spot until you return to the starting place in 45 minutes. Although no great altitudes are attained, the undulating nature of this walk means that there is a total climb of more than 500m (1,640ft) and this should be borne in mind when planning the outing. Because of the exposed nature of much of the route, this walk is not recommended during stormy or very hot weather.

The next place of interest is **Sasbach** on the banks of the Rhine. The ferry which formerly provided the link across the river to France was replaced by a temporary Bailey bridge after the war. After many years of service, this has been replaced in its turn by a fine, modern road bridge, the frontier formalities being on the French side. The natural river here is bypassed by the Rhine-Rhône Canal in France which is used by all through shipping traffic, leaving the noble Rhine to become a rather forlorn lagoon with boats for hire and steamer trips. Pictorial displays near the riverside car park describe the history and progress of the canalisation.

Throughout its length, the *Weinstrasse* is identified by special signs at junctions and from time to time by small plaques bearing the symbol of a bunch of grapes. The section round the Kaiserstuhl is no exception and there is no difficulty in following the route. There are several *W-Parkplätze* along the way but the similarity of the vineyard landscape does not make this very attractive walking territory — it is more suited to mechanised touring. Although the Kaiserstuhl may

Places of Interest on the Kaiserstuhl and in Emmendingen

Riegel to Breisach
Railway with historic steam train,
Rebenbummler

Endingen
Attractive town with fine towers.

Kornhaus (1617)
Early Renaissance style.

Altes Rathaus (1527)
Gothic and baroque

Neues Rathaus
Rococo style.

All these buildings grouped around
the *Ratsbrunnen* (fountain) in the
town centre.

Churches of St Peter and St Martin
Both buildings combine a variety of
architectural styles.

Sasbach
Rhine bridge to France. Boating on
the river.

Bischoffingen
Protestant church
Excellent wall paintings.

Burkheim
Rathaus
Renaissance building comple-
mented by timbered houses.

St Pankratius-Kirche
Wall paintings and stained glass.

Schwendi-Schloss
Mighty Renaissance ruin.

Niederrotweil
St Michael's Catholic Church
Very impressive late-Gothic high
altar. Important wall paintings from
about 1500.

Achkarren
Museum of vine culture

Breisach
Minster with outstanding high altar.
Oldest parts from about 1200.
Views over Rhine.

Oberschaffhausen
Church of St Alban
Outstanding fifteenth-century
frescos.

Emmendingen
Parish Church
Fifteenth-century altar.

Alten Friedhof (Old cemetery)
Graves of Goethe's sister Cornelia
and the aviator Carl Friedrich
Meerwein.

Heimatmuseum
Housed in former *Schloss*
Town history and memorabilia of
Goethe and works of painter, Fritz
Boehle.

Rathaus (1729)

Museumbahnhof
Wolfratsreuter Strasse
Small collection of historic rail
vehicles.

Endingen, on the Kaiserstuhl

not be ideal for general rambling, it is an area of great significance to geologists and naturalists who find much here to stimulate their various interests.

Abandoned quarries are a rich source of finds for the amateur mineral collector and have been described by one writer as providing a window on earth history. The geological diversity also gives rise to variety in the flora and fauna; unusual species are found in quantities rarely seen in Germany. Of the fifty-five types of orchids known in the Federal Republic, no less than thirty-three are to be found on the Kaiserstuhl. Birds and butterflies more common in a Mediterranean environment can also be found here.

The visitor wishing to see a selection of the many places of interest on the Kaiserstuhl could hardly do better than to follow the 40km (25 miles) *Weinstrasse* circuit and what follows could provide the basis for a suitable itinerary.

Continuing southwards parallel with the Rhine, the visitor will pass through many pleasant vineyard villages and may often be tempted to stop and take photographs or sample the local wine. The very fine wall paintings in the Protestant church in **Bischoffingen** include scenes from the childhood and suffering of Christ, with portrayals of the prophets and apostles.

Burkheim stands lovely and romantic on a spur of the Kaiserstuhl running towards the Rhine and is dominated by the mighty Renaissance ruin of the Schwendi-Schloss. The town has some fine timbered houses and a Renaissance *Rathaus*. In the St Pankratius-Kirche, the vault under the late-Gothic tower has evangelical symbols from the mid-sixteenth century, with St Michael and the martyrdom of St Ursula in the windows.

A stop should certainly be made in **Niederrotweil** to visit the Catholic church of St Michael where the late-Gothic high altar is an outstanding work by an anonymous master craftsman known only by his initials, H.L. The altar depicts the coronation of Mary who is flanked by St Michael and John the Baptist. The inner panel reliefs include St Michael with a balance for weighing souls, the fall of the damned and the beheading of John the Baptist. The wall paintings in the choir date from about 1500 and show Christ with the four evangelical symbols and St Michael again, while the side walls have the figures of the apostles and scenes from the New Testament. The paintings represent the start of important fresco cycles in the churches of the Kaiserstuhl.

Achkarren is a typical wine village in an excellent location. Nearby is the Schlossberg 352m (1,155ft), with the ruins of Höhingen castle. At the foot of the south-west corner of the Kaiserstuhl is the little town of Breisach with Neuf Brisach across the Rhine in France. The main road (B31) eastward from Breisach is the *Grüne Strasse* (green road) and this runs west to east from the Rhine to the Bodensee (Lake Constance).

The Minster in **Breisach** occupies a commanding position with a fine view. Despite having survived many wars and political upheavals, the church, which is dedicated to St Stephan, had to be completely rebuilt after World War II. This was done so skilfully that it is impossible to distinguish between parts which are original and those which are of modern construction. For practical purposes, the building which can be admired today is that which dates from about 1200, when the nave, transepts and east towers were built. The choir and the west bay date from 1300-30 while the vaulting, sacristy and interior furnishings are fifteenth-century. The addition of the choir made the *Münster* into a hall church.

Rebuilding in the fifteenth century accentuated the Gothic elements and each of the symmetrical towers has a Romanesque and a more elaborate Gothic section. In addition, a North Italian influence can be detected in the Romanesque nave. The late-Gothic choir screen (about 1500) and the monumental fresco by M. Schongauer in the west hall are of note but the most valuable interior fitment is the famous Breisach altar, another work of that master known simply as H.L. It dates from 1523-6 and the Madonna appears on the central shrine between God the Father and Christ. The martyrs Stephan and Laurentius can be seen on one side panel and the town's patrons, Gervasius and Protasius, on the other. Their bones are in a silver shrine in the church treasury.

From Breisach, the circuit of the Kaiserstuhl is continued by travelling north-eastwards through Ihringen, a wine community with a history documented back to AD962. Fruit trees grow here as well as vines and it is a favourite place to visit in spring when they are in blossom. The outwardly homely little church of St Alban in **Oberschaffhausen** is the place where the artistic pinnacle of the early wall paintings was reached. The frescos were created between 1477 and 81 and the portrayals are the most extensive in the region of the Kaiserstuhl. The realistically carved *Pestkreuz* (plague cross) above the altar is most impressive. It is also worth making a final stop in the village of **Eichstetten** which has some fine timbered houses and a bridge dating from 1556.

The first-time visitor may have been surprised by the vastness of the Kaiserstuhl vineyards and a few words about the wines of the area may not come amiss. It is not known exactly when viticulture was started on the Kaiserstuhl and the nearby sunny slopes on the east side of the Rhine. It seems probable that the Romans were responsible for introducing the vines but the first documentary evidence on the subject does not appear until the eighth century. The traveller who has been following the Wine Road may have become aware by now of the great variety of wines produced. This is due mainly to the number of grape varieties used but is also influenced by the nature of the ground in which they are grown, the varying climatic conditions from place to place and the methods employed by the various growers.

There are eight classic grapes and numerous new crosses; of the former, the *Riesling* is widely grown and produces an elegant white wine. The *Ruländer* is also very common and from it comes a fiery wine with a fulsome bouquet. A light, slightly prickly wine comes from a *Ruländer* mutation known as *Weisse Burgunder* while earthy wines, with almost a hint of rose-scent, stem from the *Traminer* and *Gewürztraminer* varieties. However, it is the *Müller-Thurgau* which is grown most extensively and produces a light wine with a hint of nutmeg which should be drunk young. The *Silvaner* grape, on the other hand, is not as widely grown as it used to be. The *Gutedel* is only grown in the Markgräflerland south of the Kaiserstuhl and produces grapes for dessert as well as for wine.

So much for white wines; the growers claim that the wine made from the grapes of the blue *Spätburgunder* is the finest red wine in the world. Newer grape varieties which may be found on bottle labels include *Scheurebe, Nobling, Huxel* and *Bacchus*. The visitor will find plenty of opportunities for tasting and buying wine. The signs to look for are *Weinproben* (tastings) and *Weinverkauf* (sales); many vineyards and wine co-operatives have facilities for tasting on weekdays (only in the morning on Saturday). One should not expect wine from these sources to be appreciably cheaper than in the supermarkets but the prospective purchaser will have a greater variety from which to choose and the satisfaction of trying before buying. The previous notes may give him or her a little help in deciding what to taste.

A selection of addresses for tastings and sales which are readily accessible from Freiburg is given in the Useful Information section of this book. Wine festivals take place from about the end of June (Freiburg) through into September. The visitor here during the wine harvest should certainly try the new wine, with which it is the custom to eat warm onion-cakes.

Leave the Kaiserstuhl area by continuing to Teningen just beyond the north-south *Autobahn* A5. Rejoin the main route of the *Weinstrasse* (B3) and turn right towards **Emmendingen**. Here it is worth pausing to visit the parish church and inspect the *Flügelaltar*. This is a carved altar piece in three sections with folding wings, dating from about 1470, although the church itself is nineteenth century. In any event, Emmendingen is a good centre with excellent tourist facilities and provides a suitable base for exploring the area. Goethe was particularly fond of this district and wrote about it in glowing terms. His sister Cornelia lived and died here; her grave can be seen in the *Alten Friedhof* (old cemetery), which is also the resting place of the German flying pioneer Carl Friedrich Meerwein.

The former *Schloss* was the *Residenz* of the Margraves of Baden and now houses the *Heimatmuseum* which deals with the history of

The town centre of Emmendingen

the town and has memorabilia of Goethe and works of the painter, Fritz Boehle. The *Rathaus,* dating from 1729, and the eighteenth-century town gate are also worth seeing. The nearby Hochburg is one of the best preserved castles in the area. The *Weinstrasse* continues as the B3 towards Freiburg and soon becomes a very busy highway leading into the city centre.

South of Freiburg

Freiburg is described fully in a later chapter and the city can be bypassed by using the *Autobahn* between the Freiburg *Nord* and *Süd* junctions, resuming exploration of the Wine Road south of the city on road B3 at Ebringen. The vineyard route soon leaves the main road and saunters off past Pfaffenweiler to the little town of Ehrenkirchen.

The *Weinstrasse* may be left here for an excursion 4km (2$^1/_2$ miles) to the south-east of Bollschweil where there is an entrance to a narrow, steep-sided valley. The little river Möhlin can be followed through this to the hamlet of **St Ulrich**, a further 4km away. This picturesque journey is worthwhile in its own right but there is a bonus at St Ulrich in the rich stucco work of the baroque church of the former Benediktinerkloster, another work of the Vorarlberger, Peter Thumb. A Romanesque font can also be seen; this was formerly in the parsonage garden and is now to be found inside an ornamental gate just to the left of the church.

The next place of interest is **Staufen**, at the entrance to the Münstertal. This little town has a folk and costume museum worthy of a visit. The old Gasthaus 'Löwen' (Lion) has tales of the legendary Dr Faustus and even a Faust room to substantiate them. The death of this mysterious character is colourfully portrayed on the front wall of the 'Löwen' where there is a brief description of the event. The area around Staufen was already settled in prehistoric times from which there have been some interesting finds indicating early defensive works.

Already, in AD770, there was a documentary reference to the place but the formal founding of the town only took place in 1280. Later inhabitants had to put up with the plague, famine and witch-craft as well as the warlike activities of their neighbours, who were often anxious to get access to the silver mines in the Münstertal. The ruins of the Staufenburg are now surrounded by vineyard slopes. It was erected to discourage this pillaging but the castle was burned down in 1632 by the Swedes, who then went on to plunder the town. In the period 1689-90, the French virtually pulled the town apart and set it on fire. Later, the French Revolution and World War II both left their marks and it is clear that the beautiful façade of the *Rathaus*, built in 1546, is only there today because of painstaking restoration after all these damaging events.

Even before receiving its charter, this was an important settlement on one of the main routes eastwards into the Forest and the little man on the octagonal market fountain is a reminder of the market rights once held here. The late-Gothic church of St Martin is worth seeing and there is an international music festival each summer. On the south-eastern outskirts of Staufen along the Münstertal road, there is a camping and caravan site popular with English-speaking visitors, and a pleasant but unheated open-air swimming pool nearby.

In the village of **Grunern** near Staufen, at the vineyard of the Koeppler family, there is a private museum which has an interesting collection of historic tools and equipment associated with wine-making. The vineyard has been owned by the same family for seven generations but some of the items on display go back to the sixteenth century. The most impressive item is the 4m (13ft) high and 10m (33ft) long *Torkelbaum* (wine press) with massive stone weights bearing the date 1578. This machine was in use pressing the local grapes until after World War II.

After Staufen, the *Weinstrasse* divides, the left fork leading to the village of **Sulzburg**. In fact, it rather likes to think of itself as a 'town', having received its town charter as far back as 1250. It has not grown much since and has the distinction of being known as the tiniest town in the state.

Sulzburg is a surprise, for here in this quiet valley — the Sulzbachtal — is a spot with more than its fair share of historical associations. There is little traffic as there is no way out of the valley beyond the village and the road finally peters out after a few kilometres. The visitor, therefore, has peace to explore the charming market square with the colourful centuries-old houses around it. Here there is the mining museum of Baden-Württemberg, although mining activities in the area have long since ceased. Knowledgeable campers speak highly of the camping place at the *Alte Sägemühle* (old sawmill) beyond the village. Through the camp site, one can reach the gold-lettered gateway at the entrance to a Jewish cemetery, a very old burial place which served a wide area and is still kept in remarkably good order. The visitor may also learn of other Jewish associations with Sulzburg and can see the restoration work done on the synagogue which was built in 1823.

In contrast to their Austrian neighbours, the Margraves of Baden were kindly disposed towards the Jewish communities and this is reflected in the numerous Jewish cemeteries and places of worship throughout the former state of Baden. The charming little church of St Cyriak was originally built in 1510 but has been virtually rebuilt on several occasions.

In a sheltered spot, a little way past the camp site, is a natural woodland swimming pool fed by crystal-clear mountain streams and surrounded by a spacious playing and sunbathing area. Going on up the valley, the visitor comes to the Waldhotel at Bad Sulzburg, surrounded by tall pine trees. This, in fact, is just about all this miniscule spa has to offer. There are useful parking areas here and at the swimming pool, which provide the rambler with access to 100km (60 miles) of marked paths around the valley. From 20 to 22 August each year, there is an event called *Weinkurtage*, a word which cannot really be translated but refers to three days devoted to festivities

Places of Interest South of Freiburg

St Ulrich
Church of former Benedictine Kloster
Beautiful baroque church by Peter Thumb.

Bad Krozingen
Historic Keyboard Instrument Collection
Housed in the *Schloss*.

Staufen
Gasthaus Löwen
Fine old inn with Faust room and tales of Dr Faustus.

Museum of Wine Presses and other Equipment
At the vineyard of the Koeppler family in Grunern.

Sulzburg
Landes-Bergbaumuseum
Former silver mine. Underground tours for visitors.
Relics dating back to the eleventh century.

Jewish Cemetery
Very old, well-kept resting place.

Synagogue
Built in 1823 and now restored.

Heitersheim
Schloss (sixteenth- to eighteenth-centuries) and baroque Chancery (1740)

Badenweiler
Roman bath ruins
Very well-preserved remains in the Kurpark.

Schloss (1811)
Former *Residenz* of grand dukes of Baden.

Bad Bellingen
Gasthaus 'Schwanen' (1716)
Baroque hostelry in the old village.

Lörrach
Museum am Burghof
Medieval history of town.

Burg Rötteln
3km (2 miles) north of Lörrach near road B317.
Impressive ruins and fine views.

Inzlingen
Wasserschloss Reichenstein (1563-4)
6km (4 miles) south-east of Lörrach. Charming moated palace now serving as the *Rathaus*.

associated with the grape. Regional food specialities are served, accompanied by wine and music, in the historic cellars around the Sulzburg market place. The sleepy village today has a population of no more than 1,700, although it is said that, in their heyday, no fewer than 500 people were employed in the mines alone.

The distance from Sulzburg to Müllheim is only about 15km (9

*Staufen with
Schlossberg*

*Markgrafenbad,
the centre of spa
treatment in
Badenweiler*

miles) but before reaching the latter town, bear to the left to visit the distinguished spa resort of **Badenweiler**. Compared with the better-known Baden-Baden, it is a rather reticent sort of place. It is peaceful and quiet, mainly because traffic is not permitted to enter the streets of the little town (population 4,000) except for access to the hotels, etc. As with Baden-Baden, this is a resort much favoured by prominent international personalities, but here they are rarely seen, favouring a domicile with friends or in private villas hidden from the curious by flower-covered walls.

The town, with its parks and villas, occupies a sunny slope which falls towards the Rhine and there is a wide vista of vineyards and orchards to charm the eye. The Celts already knew of the thermal springs here but the first bathing complex was that developed by the Romans during the first century AD. There is a saying that where the Romans came they built and where they built they bathed — that is certainly true here. A holy place was declared and a temple was erected to honour the favours of the spring goddess Diana Abnoba. Badenweiler is proud to possess the best preserved Roman bath ruins north of the Alps and the visitor is able to get a very clear idea of the ancient Roman bathing customs.

The ruins have been integrated into the *Kurpark* and the modern (1874) Markgrafenbad was built on the pattern of the Roman original and is the centre of spa treatment today. There is nothing left of the medieval bath installations although there is little doubt that these did exist. A castle of the Zähringer dynasty was built in 1122 on the remains of a Roman fort but this was destroyed in 1678 by French troops under General Mélac. All that is left is the fine view from the ruins. The *Schloss* was the *Residenz* of the grand dukes of Baden. It was built in 1811 by the court architect Friedrich Weinbrenner for the Grand Duchess Stefanie, an adopted daughter of Napoleon. Hilda, the last grand duchess, died here in 1952.

The Protestant church (1897) is worth seeing and has the earliest German representation of the 'dance of death' (1413) in the choir. The Catholic chapel was built in 1862 in the Byzantine style. Many well-known names feature in the catalogue of those who have come to Badenweiler for their health. They include the Russian dramatist Anton Chekhov and the American writer Stephen Crane, both victims of tuberculosis and both of whom died here. The relatively new *Kurhaus* — an entertainment centre rather than a place for medical treatment — is a remarkable piece of modern architecture.

The resort has a daily programme of walks, with leisurely local strolls in the mornings and more energetic rambles in the afternoons, often to vineyard villages where there is wine-tasting.

The Wine Road divided at Staufen, the right fork going down towards Bad Krozingen and through Heitersheim where it rejoined the B3. **Bad Krozingen**, one of the trio of south Black Forest spas, is comparatively modern and, as at Bad Bellingen, its thermal springs were revealed during a vain search for oil. It was in 1910 that, at a depth of 500m (1,640ft), the hopeful oilmen struck water instead of oil and a new spa was born. What is more, the water was found to have properties similar to those at the 2,000-year-old, third member of the group, Badenweiler. Over the years, a very pleasant and well-kept spa complex has grown up on land which, until the turn of the century, was no more than fields and meadows.

The so-called *Schloss* was built in 1579 for the priory of St Blasien and today houses a collection of some fifty historic keyboard instruments. The collection belongs to Frau Klaraliese von Gleichenstein, one of whose predecessors, Ignas von Gleichenstein, appears in the annals of musical history as a friend of Beethoven. The instruments are kept in working order and each month a concert is given in the Gobelin tapestry-hung hall of the *Schloss*, where the music of previous centuries is played and wine and food is served. The little Glöcklehofkapelle (court chapel) has frescos which date from around the eleventh century or even earlier.

Heitersheim, a little south of Bad Krozingen on the B3, deserves a brief mention. Although having less than 4,000 inhabitants, it was granted its town charter in 1810. This little town sparkles with cleanliness and has an impressive Hauptstrasse — a charming baroque street — with its several old *Gasthäuser*, including the 'Löwen' and the 'Krone', with the 'Ochsen' round the corner in Eisenbahnstrasse.

Heitersheim may lack the natural landscape of some other places along the *Weinstrasse* but this is more than compensated for by the historic buildings which go to make up the town on the little river Sulzbach. In 1428 it became the seat of the grand prior of the Order of the Knights of St John. The *Residenz* was gradually converted into an imposing palace with mighty walls and vast courtyards which has become a landmark of the town, an honour it shares with the parish church erected in 1825. The palace houses the Johanniter and Malteser Museum but even if this is not visited, a stroll through the courtyards is very pleasant. On the third Wednesday in each month there is a guided tour of the whole complex.

The two Wine Road routes both touch Müllheim but then continue on their separate ways as far as Schliengen. **Müllheim** (population 13,000) is only 8km (5 miles) south of Heitersheim. It is a busy border town with an important crossing over the Rhine to French Alsace. There are a number of good hotels but, for the general holidaymaker, some of Mullheim's satellite villages such as Britzingen, Feldberg or Hügelheim, would be more pleasant places to stay in, rather than the town itself which is at the junction of two busy roads. Facilities in the area include an open-air pool heated to 24 °C (75 °F) by thermal water.

Seven kilometres (4 miles) further on, **Schliengen**, with its stately baroque houses and interesting *Rathaus*, invites a short stop. The nearby moated palace, Wasserschloss Entenstein, originated in about 1400 but was extensively rebuilt in the sixteenth century. It stands in a park laid out in the so-called 'English' style. A *Weinlehrpfad* (vineyard nature trail) starts at the Winzergenossenschaft (wine-growers' co-operative) building.

The main road is now left for a quieter route closer to the Rhine for the final 24km (15 miles) of the named road to its end at Weil am Rhein, just 6km (4 miles) from the centre of Basel. The *Weinstrasse*, the railway, the *Autobahn* and the Rhine are confined to an ever narrowing strip and there is a temptation to hurry on. However, if time permits, the traveller should meander through the many delightful villages which lie to the east between the main road and the mountains, or spend some time in the well-appointed modern spa of **Bad Bellingen**, close to the Rhine.

As already hinted, this resort has a history similar to that of Bad Krozingen a little further north. In 1955, oil exploration was taking place near the sleepy and homely little village of Bellingen. Once again, when the trial bores reached a depth of about 500m (1,600ft), the drillers struck water. The oil men left the site in disgust and Herr Ruf, the *Bürgermeister* (mayor) of the day, did not have too much difficulty in persuading his council to take over the well for the benefit of the community. By the following year, the place was known as 'Bad' Bellingen, even though the facilities for guests were extremely primitive at first. But the water, shooting from the depths at more than 38 °C (100 °F), proved to be very effective in the treatment of certain ailments and it was not long before patients, especially from nearby Basel, were making their way here in considerable numbers.

The years of development are now long past and Bellingen today has nothing to fear from comparison with its older neighbours. Needless to say, all the facilities one expects in a modern resort are to be found here. In the old village, the baroque Gasthaus 'Schwanen' (1716) makes a worthwhile stop for a drink or a meal. Near the Rhine, just south of Bad Bellingen, is a little place called **Blansingen** which has a Romanesque church with a late-Gothic choir, restored in 1955, and superb wall paintings from about 1440. The Swiss border and the city of Basel lie ahead. The towns of Weil am Rhein and Lörrach, reached before the frontier, are both mainly industrial centres within the orbit of Basel itself.

Lörrach was a favourite place of the dialect poet Johann Peter Hebel who was a teacher at the Pädagogium here from 1783 to 91. A monument has been erected in his memory and the Hebel society is based here. St Fridolin's church was built in the district of Stetten, in 1821-2. Inside, the neo-Classical lines are broken by J. Wilhem's stucco imitation of the late baroque style. The west tower dominates the exterior. The tower of the Protestant Stadtkirche was built in 1514 but everything else was rebuilt in 1815-7. The result is quite pleasing; there is a classical hall inside with a gallery supported by Doric columns. On the other hand, four of the pillars in the Catholic parish church of St Peter are in concrete relief — an unusual use of a modern material.

The Museum am Burghof (*Heimatmuseum*) gives the history of the town and of nearby Burg Rötteln. There are seventeenth- to twentieth-century paintings, sculptures, prints and maps as well as displays showing domestic interiors of former centuries. The museum is partly housed in a former cooper's workshop. In the town there are several beautiful fountains built of white limestone from Solothurn in Switzerland.

The imposing ruins of Burg Rötteln can be found about 3km (2 miles) north of Lörrach near road B317, and from here the way up to the castle is clearly signed. The oldest parts, including the keep, are Romanesque but many important sections were added in the period up to the sixteenth century. It is another fortress which was destroyed in 1678 when the French overwhelmed this part of the world. Rötteln commands the finest viewpoint in the lower Wiesental. However, the charming moated palace, Wasserschloss Reichenstein, is still intact and is situated in the little town of **Inzlingen**, about 6km (4 miles) south-east of Lörrach and virtually on the Swiss border. The palace was built in 1563-4 and now serves as the *Rathaus*. The stucco coats of arms on a ceiling of the upper floor are reminders of the Reichenstein family's history.

The *Badische Weinstrasse* then, is a route of considerable interest which is very largely associated with the wine industry. From a layman's point of view, one vineyard is very much like another — a determined effort to explore the road from end to end could become boring. The visitor is advised to combine part of the *Weinstrasse* with some of the other areas covered in later chapters: two sections being particularly suitable; the first at the north end, between Baden-Baden and Offenburg, and the other the Kaiserstuhl. Of course, all the towns and villages have their wine festivals, mostly between the last week in August and the end of September. This is the time to visit the *Weinstrasse* if eating and drinking, together with music and general jollity, have an appeal.

2

VALLEYS OF THE NORTH

Pforzheim to Freudenstadt

A pleasant road leads eastwards from Ettlingen (see Chapter 1) towards Pforzheim. After a few kilometres, it divides in Busenbach, the right-hand fork going southwards towards Bad Herrenalb through the Albtal. That route will be explored later but, in the meantime, continue east through the villages of Waldbronn, which is a *Luftkurort* with thermal bath, Langensteinbach, Ellmendingen and Dietlingen. The road crosses numerous streams carrying water down from the northern hills towards the Rhine at Karlsruhe. After about 20km (12$^1/_2$ miles), **Pforzheim** is reached. It has a population of 97,000 and lies on the northernmost fringe of the Forest.

The city boasts the title 'Gateway to the Black Forest' and in many ways it is justified, for it has excellent road and rail connections. On 23 February 1945, the city was devastated by the Allied forces and an estimated 80 per cent of the buildings was destroyed, including many historical sites which are now remembered only in name. The Waisenhausplatz, now a large par park, was formerly the site of an orphanage which had been housed in an old Dominican monastery. Apart from the name, all that remains of this historic building are some remnants of a wall, preserved near the river Enz. The Enz is one of two formerly important northern Black Forest rivers, the other being the Nagold, which meet here to continue as the Enz until finally disappearing into the Neckar north of Stuttgart.

Until the beginning of this century, rafts of logs from the forests up-river were floated down the Enz and Nagold to Pforzheim, where they would be combined into larger units to continue their journey northwards. The last timber raft went down the Enz in 1913 and this mode of transport was never revived after World War I. However, the floatage of timber on these rivers had been the principal factor in the economy of Pforzheim for about 300 years.

Together with buildings, the old town walls and their towers disappeared in the destruction of 1945; this and other rubble provided sufficient material to raise the general level of streets in the town by about 2m ($6^1/_2$ft). Today a spacious modern city has risen from the ashes. Pforzheim is the home of an important gold and jewellery trade, the secrets of which are jealously guarded by the firms engaged in this work. The Technical Museum of the jewellery and clock industry in Bleichstrasse may be visited, but most visitors might be better to see the *Schmuckmuseum* (Reuchlinmuseum) in the *Stadtgarten* (town park) where there is a worthwhile collection of examples of the jeweller's art through the centuries or the Schütt exhibition of precious stones and jewels.

The museum is actually part of the cultural centre which also houses the town library and a lecture hall. The name comes from that of a famous son of Pforzheim, Johannes Reuchlin (1455-1522). He was a contemporary of Martin Luther (1483-1546), many of whose ideas he shared, if not with such obvious fervour. Johannes Reuchlin was a humanist and is famed for his work as a Hebraist and as a statesman.

Close to the *Hauptbahnhof* stands the Protestant Schlosskirche of St Michael. All but the outer walls were destroyed in the bombing of 1945 but it was rebuilt in exemplary fashion in the years 1949-57. Building originally began in 1225 and the reconstructed church faithfully portrays the style of that period, with a fine porch and rose window on the south gable. The rest of the building is early-Gothic; the massive collegiate choir is significantly higher than the nave and has outstanding stellar vaulting. The church contains the wall-tombs of the Margraves of Baden-Durlach, for whom St Michael's has been the funerary chapel since 1535.

At the Protestant parish church of St Martin in Altstädterstrasse, there is an interesting portal in the west tower porch which has survived from the Romanesque basilica. On the tympanum, symbolic figures depict the Threat of Evil to Mankind and its salvation through the Church. The choir of 1340 has late-Gothic wall paintings with the Last Judgement, Sheltering Mantle of the Virgin Mary and saints (1430-50). The *Heimatmuseum* at the west end of the long Karl-

Friedrich-Strasse (No 243) has a collection which includes scientific instruments and goldsmiths' tools.

A pleasant walk through the *Stadtgarten* leads to Kupferhammer, where the little river Würm joins the Nagold and where a restaurant is now housed in a smithy and sawmill dating from 1663. Kupfer-hammer has one of the ten *W-Parkplätze* in and around Pforzheim. This one has three round walks but, more importantly, it is the starting point for three long-distance paths, to Basel, Waldshut and Schaffhausen, as well as for a nature trail into the Erzkopf, an *Erhol-ungsgebiet* or recreation area. Despite the ravages of war, there is still much of interest to see in Pforzheim but its gateway role has the greatest significance for the tourist. The countryside meets the town on all sides and the shortest of excursions leads into areas of the utmost beauty and tranquillity.

Continuing south-eastwards, the river Würm may be followed from Kupferhammer to the little town of Würm where a delightful alpine garden has been laid out and has become a popular goal of summer excursionists. A little later, the Gasthaus Liebeneck is reached, formerly the water mill belonging to the castle of the same name, the ruins of which are hidden in the woods above.

A stiff, 15 minutes' climb will bring the visitor up to the castle and the effort is certainly worthwhile. Such well-concealed castles are rare and one could be forgiven for thinking that this might just have been the original retreat of the Sleeping Beauty. The reality is less romantic for this was one of the haunts of the robber-knights who preyed upon travellers and merchants passing along the valley below. In this case, they received their just deserts, for, in the war with the French, the castle was captured by the troops of General Mélac in 1692 and robbed of the valuables found there.

Not far away, a little up a side valley, may be glimpsed yet another castle, Burg Steinegg. This is a much more extensive com-plex which, perhaps because of its location, remained more or less intact until the 1840s. Then the state of Baden decided to turn the place into a factory to provide employment for the local populace. This had been done with some success in a number of disused monastery buildings following the 1803 Secularisation. However, the idea did not appeal to the owners, the Lords of Gemmingen, who removed the roofs, took out the doors and windows and left the elements to take their toll. After World War II, youth groups from Pforzheim worked together to create a hostel in part of the buildings

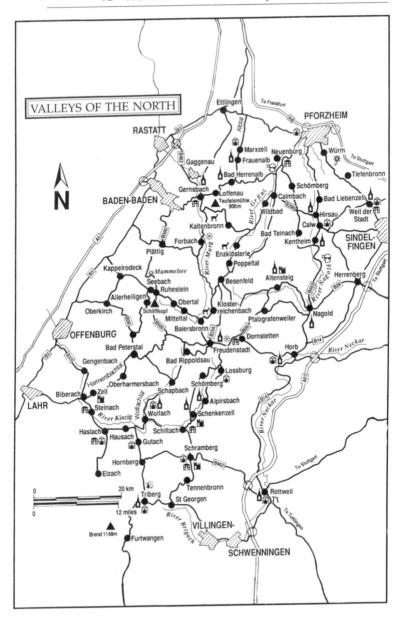

VALLEYS OF THE NORTH

still in reasonable repair.

The village of **Tiefenbronn** (population 3,500) lies about 2km ($1^1/_4$ miles) across the valley and has in its Catholic parish church of St Maria Magdalena, a remarkable altar painting, the only known work of one Lukas Moser, which bears the date 1431. The church itself is a Gothic basilica dating from around the same time.

Continuing through the Würm valley, **Weil der Stadt** is reached about 20km ($12^1/_2$ miles) from Pforzheim. This little town with its towers and gables is a medieval gem, an exciting discovery in rural surroundings yet only a dozen miles from the centre of sprawling Stuttgart. The famous astronomer, Johannes Kepler (1571-1630), was born here in the house at Keplergasse 2 which is now the Kepler-Museum. A monument to the great man is in the market place, where one of the fountains has the figure of Emperor Karl V.

The *Rathaus*, dating from 1582, is a fine building with arcades which has survived almost unchanged. The Catholic parish church of St Peter and St Paul has a west tower which not only dominates the church, but has become the emblem of the town. The architect Albertin Jörg incorporated the twelfth- and thirteenth-century east towers when he rebuilt the church, this work being completed in 1492. The choir, which has stellar vaulting, was added in 1519, and the Renaissance tabernacle in 1611; the interior was partly redecorated during the baroque period. The *Stadtmuseum* is to be found at No 12 Marktplatz and there is a Narrenmuseum (Fools' museum) at Stuttgarter Strasse 60 which is occasionally open. One of the old defensive towers, the so-called Storchenturm, is no longer visited by the storks although the locals are always hopeful that the birds will return some day.

The river Würm has its sources beyond the Black Forest boundary but the visitor prepared to travel another 10km (6 miles) or so in this direction could spend an hour or two in the large town of **Sindelfingen**. Here, the former canonry church of St Martin is a basilica with a nave, two aisles and no transept, which was consecrated in 1083. It was authentically restored in 1933 and in 1973-4. The arches and pillars show Lower Saxon influence, the apses that of Lombardy. The Romanesque strapwork of the west door should be noted as should a late-Gothic relief slab dating from 1477.

The *altes Rathaus* is from the following year and is connected to the Salzhaus of 1592. Both buildings are half-timbered as are several others in the town. The *Stadtmuseum* has interesting collections

Places of Interest In and Around Pforzheim and The Würm Valley

Pforzheim

Schlosskirche of St Michael
Near the station
Parts dating from 1225. Extensively rebuilt after World War II.

Parish church of St Martin
In Altstädterstrasse
Romanesque and Gothic. Wall paintings from 1430-50.

Heimatmuseum
At Karl-Friedrich-Strasse 243
Collection includes scientific instruments and goldsmiths' tools.

Schmuckmuseum
(Reuchlinmuseum)
In the *Stadtgarten* close to town centre.
Outstanding collection of jewellery.

Kupferhammer
Short walk south from *Stadtgarten*
Restaurant in seventeenth-century smithy and sawmill. Nature trail.

Würm
Alpine garden

Gasthaus Liebeneck and castle ruins
The *Gasthaus* is the former water mill of Burg Liebeneck.

Tiefenbronn
Burg Steinegg
Partly ruined castle now a hostel for young people of Pforzheim.

Church of St Maria Magdalena
(1430)
Gothic basilica with notable altar painting (1431).

Weil der Stadt
Charming medieval town, birth-place of astronomer Johannes Kepler (1571-1630)

Kepler Museum
In the house at Keplergasse 2, where the famous astronomer was born.

Rathaus (1582)
A fine building which has hardly been changed over the centuries.

Church of St Peter and St Paul
(1492)
Towers from twelfth and thirteenth centuries.
Some interior baroque treatment.

Stadtmuseum
At Marktplatz 12

Storchenturm
An old defensive tower.

 dealing with town history while the Haus der Donauschwaben is a museum housing the central collection and library of the Swabian Danube.

The next route to be explored starts along the valley of the river Nagold from Kupferhammer. Bad Liebenzell, Hirsau, Calw, Nagold

Hirsau

and Horb are small towns along the lesser of the two routes south from Pforzheim (road B463) and it is convenient to consider them collectively in the order that the traveller entering by the Pforzheim gateway will reach them. All except the last lie on the pretty river Nagold; Horb is on the Neckar. Similarly, all are served by the Pforzheim-Freudenstadt railway line except Horb, which has a direct link with Stuttgart. **Bad Liebenzell**, only 24km (15 miles) from Pforzheim, provides a favourite excursion for the citizens of the big cities of Karlsruhe and Stuttgart who find it ideal for a couple of hours in the spa centre known as the Paracelsusbad, a walk in the woods or a climb up to the castle (1363) for coffee and cakes in the clean air.

Bad Liebenzell boasts a large camping and caravan site close to the outdoor heated swimming pool with its exciting waterchute. During the summer months there are frequent concerts in the *Kurpark* but there is an admission charge unless one is staying in the area and holding a *Kurkarte*. In earlier years the river Nagold had a history of serious flooding and, on a few houses in Bad Liebenzell and other towns in the valley, old high-water marks may be seen.

Bad Liebenzell station is the starting point for a modest ramble of 10km ($6^1/_4$ miles) which includes the attractive Monbachschlucht (ravine) and is suitable for warm days. Leave the station northwards, following the bank of the river Nagold for about 45 minutes to reach Monbachtal. Turn right by the kiosk here, following the signs up along a little stream, cross the mini-golf area and then climb up through the ravine for about 45 minutes. A junction is reached where there are many signs; the red square with letter 'L' should be followed steeply upwards to the Monakam 541m (1,775ft).

Pass the church and the school-house to reach the edge of the woods nearby. Go briefly to the left then follow the signs to the right on a field path which soon joins a steep forest track. In a good 15 minutes, the road by the markers 'Layle' and 'Hehren' will be reached. The forest track continues to drop and the return to the starting point at Liebenzell station takes barely 45 minutes from Monakam. Because of the terrain through the *Schlucht*, good footwear and a degree of sure-footedness are necessary on this walk.

Hirsau, 4km ($2^1/_2$ miles) further along the road, is one of the most significant places in terms of south German culture and the train traveller has an advantage over the motorist here in having a splendid view of the ruins of the famous Benedictine Kloster and the hunting castle of Duke Ludwig of Württemberg in the Kloster precincts.

The cultural history of Hirsau goes back to AD770 when workers from Kloster Lorsch in Hessen erected a house here which soon, however, fell victim to the repeated floods. Then, in AD830, a small group of monks founded a cell here which was dedicated to St Laurentius. In the eleventh century, this developed into the Benedictine monastery and the monks set out from here on their missions to found a number of other religious houses on the pattern of that at Hirsau. Religious life in the building ceased at the time of the Reformation in 1534 and Ludwig then built his castle in the grounds. Both were destroyed by French troops under General Mélac in 1692 but, after nearly 300 years, the remains are still worth a visit. The only part of the *Kloster* which survives intact is the north-west tower, the so-called Eulenturm (owl tower) built around 1100.

One should not leave Hirsau without seeing the St Aurelius Church, a triple-naved basilica dating from 1071, the only remaining building pre-dating the monastery. From the outside the church appears more like a barn and it was, in fact, used as such for many years. However, in 1955 the restoration of the church was begun and now worshippers stand again in the dark interior between the Romanesque columns.

Another 2km (1^1/$_4$ miles) upstream is **Calw** (pronounced Kalb), the principal town in this valley and the home town of the writer Hermann Hesse (1877-1962). He was very fond of Calw and wrote that although his travels had taken him to beautiful towns in all sorts of situations; in the mountains, on the coast and in the countryside, there was none to compare with Calw, 'a little old Swabian Black Forest town.' Several old buildings are evidence of the one-time importance of Calw in the international textile trade. It was also a centre for timber floatage on the Nagold and the town derived much of its prosperity from these two diverse activities. Today the interest of the visitor may be caught by the many reminders of Hermann Hesse, mainly collected in the old house which serves as the folk-museum

In recent years, the old town centre in Calw has been transformed by adoption of an imaginative pedestrianisation scheme. Most of the fine, half-timbered houses around the Marktplatz and elsewhere have been renovated and, where appropriate, provided with a discreet plaque outlining their history. The majority were erected

Calw

following the great fire which devastated the town through the action of the French troops in 1692. The *Rathaus* of 1673 had its upper storeys added in 1726 and the fine market place fountain was erected in 1686.

The oldest building in Calw is the tiny Gothic St Nikolaus chapel, built above the middle pier of the old Nagold bridge in the fourteenth century. Near the door are two niches in which one might expect to see biblical figures portrayed. In fact, the statues are of a man in medieval dress unrolling a bolt of cloth and of a *Flösser*, a man responsible for floating timber down the river, thus reminding the visitor of the two most important economic influences in the history of Calw. The stained-glass windows portray prominent citizens with their coats of arms.

It is worth pausing in **Kentheim**, three kilometres (2 miles) south of Calw, to visit one of Germany's oldest churches, dating from the ninth century. Shortly after Kentheim, the road from Bad Teinach and Zavelstein comes down from the west. The tiny health resort of **Teinach**, with no more than about six hundred residents, has been known for its mineral springs since the fourteenth century. It was the

Calw market

summer residence of the former Dukes of Württemberg and the building of hotels only dates from the eighteenth and early nineteenth centuries. Whether for health reasons or otherwise, this is a place where the visitor should be able to unwind in peaceful surroundings. There is the usual range of resort facilities on a modest scale, including a *Freibad* heated to 24°C (75°F). The Bad Teinach spring water is bottled and distributed widely as table water.

The valley is dominated by the imposing ruins of Burg Zavelstein, another castle which succumbed to the attentions of General Mélac's troops in 1692. One can walk from Bad Teinach to **Zavelstein** in about 45 minutes. Zavelstein claims the distinction of being the smallest town in Baden-Württemberg but the reader will note that it is not the only such claimant. Despite having only about five hundred inhabitants, it is a town as distinct from a village, having been granted *Stadtrecht* (town status) in 1367 by Count Eberhard II in recognition of the protection given him in the castle when fleeing from his enemies.

Around Easter time, the fields of Zavelstein are ablaze with the colour of thousands of crocuses and the area is much visited in the spring for this reason. How the bulbs came to be here in the first place is not really known but one theory is that they were introduced in Roman times to provide saffron flavouring.

Returning to the valley, continue the remaining 23km (14 miles) to **Nagold**, an important transport centre and a town with more industrial activity than is usual in the Black Forest. Fortunately, the important main road (B28) which crosses the Forest on its way eastwards from Strasbourg towards Munich, now bypasses the town and the tourist is unlikely to notice the industry as he wanders through the old streets with their many fine timbered buildings. Standing near the bypass, and worth a visit, is the eighth-century Remigiuskapelle with its fourteenth- and sixteenth-century frescos. It is also worth finding the *W-Parkplatz* at the Schlossberg where the round walk is, in fact, a nature trail.

If one were to follow the river now, one would turn a complete half-circle to find oneself heading north again and eventually turning towards Freudenstadt. However, that is not the intention and the valley is left to follow the road 15km (9 miles) south to **Horb** where the Neckar flows north from its source near Schwenningen. Horb is a pleasant little town with a number of timbered houses and some interesting paintings on the *Rathaus*. The collegiate church, with an

attractive coloured altar-piece and a pretty baroque organ, is sufficient reward for the modest climb. Interest along this route from
Pforzheim has mainly centred upon the charming little towns.
However, a pleasant 12km (7$^1/_2$ miles) excursion from Horb lies
eastwards along the Neckar valley to Schloss Weitenburg, which
dates from 1585. There are good views over the valley and the quiet
hotel of the same name provides an opportunity for a leisurely meal.

The main road south from Pforzheim, B294, follows the valley of
the river Enz and is pretty for most of the way through this fairly
sparsely populated area. Reached after a few kilometres, **Birkenfeld**
is an *Erholungsort* surrounded by forest and in nearby **Gräfenhausen**
the Wehrkirche (a fortified church) has early Gothic frescos. Twelve
kilometres (7$^1/_2$ miles) from Pforzheim, the houses of the little town
of Neuenbürg are crowded into the narrow strips on either side of the
river, which has to make a wide sweep around the Schlossberg above
the old town. Through traffic no longer has to negotiate the old
streets but passes beneath a spur of the Schlossberg through a short
tunnel. The town was rebuilt after seventy houses had been destroyed in a disastrous fire in 1783. On the Schlossberg today, there
is a Renaissance *Schloss* of the fifteenth to sixteenth centuries which
houses the local forestry office but, unfortunately, the interior cannot
be visited. An earlier *Burg* on the site was destroyed in the Thirty
Years' War. This area around the *Schloss* is a protected nature reserve
and the visitor can see the many exotic trees which have been
planted. The former *Schloss* church of St George — earlier a Gothic
building — was altered in 1557. The decoration includes early
fourteenth-century wall paintings which were only revealed in 1952.
The Protestant parish church is a neo-classical building with a rare
pulpit altar.

Schwann, six kilometres (4 miles) westwards, is a tiny village on
the hill road from Pforzheim to Dobel. Gasthaus Hirsch is noted for
its good value meals with large portions, and home-made *Wurst* may
be purchased in the adjoining *Metzgerei*. Above the village, near the
Schwann observatory, the Hotel Adlerhof has a restaurant, a café,
and splendid views over the countryside. Although quite a modern
building, it is furnished in a rustic style.

Ten kilometres (6 miles) further on at Calmbach, the river divides, the main road following the minor leg known as the Kleine
(little) Enz while a lesser road follows the Enztal proper and leads to
the little spa town of **Wildbad**. Apparently, the waters here were

Places of Interest In and Around The Nagold and Enz Valleys

Hirsau
Ruins of Benedictine Kloster and Duke Ludwig's hunting lodge.

St Aurelius Church
Triple-naved basilica dating from 1071.

Calw
Heimatmuseum
Local and regional items, especially reminders of writer Hermann Hesse.

St Nikolaus Chapel (fourteenth-century)
Stands on old Nagold bridge.

Kentheim
Ninth-century church
3km (2 miles) south of Calw. One of the oldest churches in Germany.

Nagold
Remigiuskapelle
Just south of town, near bypass (road B28). Eighth-century chapel with important frescos.

Horb
Collegiate Church
Painted altar and baroque organ.

Heimatmuseum
In Neckarstrasse. Mainly items of local interest.

Excursion from Horb:
Schloss Weitenburg, 12km (7$\frac{1}{2}$ miles) east along Neckar valley. Sixteenth-century Schloss, with good views and pleasant hotel.

Neuenbürg
Schlossberg
Fifteenth-sixteenth-century *Schloss*
Interior not open to the public. Nature reserve with exotic trees.

Schloss Church
Originally Gothic. Fourteenth-century wall paintings.

Wildbad
Spa
Thermal springs up to 40°C and outdoor pool open all year.

Funicular railway to Sommerberg, 836m (2,743ft)

Kaltenbronn
15km (9 miles) south-east of Wildbad in direction of Gernsbach. Particularly beautiful woods in summer. Deer park.
Unique moorland plateau around Hohlosee and Wildsee

Enzklösterle
Red-deer park and nature trail.

Poppeltal
5km (3 miles) south of Enzklösterle.
Source of river Enz.
Giant summer 'toboggan' run.

Half-timbered houses in Horb

Carved signpost in Calmbach

discovered not by the
Romans, who developed
so many spas, but, according to legend, by a lone hunter who
shot and injured a wild boar which fled
through the forest. The hunter caught up to find it
bathing its wounds in a hot spring, thus giving justification for the
name Wildbad. Records show that the spa was founded in 1367; the
thermal spring here has a temperature of up to 40 °C (140 °F), having
come from a depth of about 1,000m (3,280ft). Each year it gives forth
$1^1/_2$ million litres (330,000 imperial gallons) of healing water which
is used in the treatment of, among other things, rheumatism and
accident injuries.

In winter, the snow and the thermal bath provide a novel combi-
nation for skiers. After winter sports on the Sommerberg above the

town, a long swoop down to the very doors of the thermal bath, a quick trot across the snow and into the steaming water, one can relax in comfortable warmth while breathing the clear winter air. There are many good hotels and inns to provide for the needs of the visitor in both summer and winter. There is a camp site nearby and plenty of places for modest strolls but there are no designated *W-Parkplätze* in the immediate vicinity.

Wildbad is the terminus of a branch line from Pforzheim and a funicular railway will carry one swiftly from the centre of the town up to the Sommerberg, the summit of which is at a respectable 836m (2,743ft). In earlier times, the town was much favoured by the nobility, especially the princely houses of Württemberg, of whom the baths are a constant reminder.

Today, anybody with sufficient resources can visit the Graf Eberhard-Bad and bathe in the tub that has been used by, among others, Czar Nicholas of Russia, Kaiser Wilhelm I, the Rothschild brothers and Count Bismarck. If this does not appeal, there is no shortage of other attractions for the visitor and it is also worth taking a stroll along the pleasant shopping streets which front both sides of the Enz. Then on, perhaps, into the Kurpark at the end of the town for easy walking or by the funicular to the Sommerberg, where there are many near level paths through the woods for summer or winter exercise. The Sommerberg skiing area can also be reached easily by the same means.

Wildbad is the second stop on another hotel-based walk similar to that described in Chapter 1. Whereas the earlier walk centred on wine, this one, named *Auf Spätzlespfaden*, (*Spätzle* is a kind of dumpling, a favourite dish of this region), is more concerned with its gastronomic delights. It starts in Bad Herrenalb and calls at several places on the *Badische Bäderstrasse* (the spa road). Seven hotel nights are included and luggage is transferred from place to place. The total distance is around 90km (55 miles). (Information in this case from the Herrenalber Reisebüro.)

On the fifth day of this walk, one of its highest points will have been reached — the very attractive *Heilklimatischer Kurort* of **Schömberg**. This is at an altitude of around 650m (2,130ft) on the ridge between the Nagold and Enz valleys. Here one is away from major roads in a resort which does not appear to have developed too rapidly but which has an excellent choice of good accommodation in all grades. The visitor who is staying will find a full measure of peace and quiet; he or she will be able to explore many kilometres of woodland paths starting virtually at the door of the hotel or guest house. There is a heated swimming pool with a giant chute which will entertain the youngsters for hours, and a *Hallenbad* with artificial waves.

Past Wildbad, the valley varies in width but there are no large settlements — merely single farms, hostelries and sawmills. At the Christophshof, a farm just before the turning to Kaltenbronn, there is a large camp site. From here the visitor is urged to make a side excursion up to **Kaltenbronn**, situated at about 900m (2,950ft) on the ridge between the Enz and Murg valleys. If there is enough time, the ascent can be made on foot through the attractive pine woods where the ground is carpeted with bilberries. There are six or seven car parks near the top, three of which — called Seeloch, Wildsee and Schwarzmis — have marked, round walks of 3.5-7km (2-4 miles).

In winter this is a popular skiing area, hence the car parking provision, but in summer the paths can be used to visit a unique nature conservation area around the Wildsee and the Hohlosee. This is a moorland plateau and at first sight, the tiny lakes appear to be of little interest. However, the processes of nature have caused a large area which was once open water to gradually become a spongy mass supporting a variety of wild life and plants more suited to a tundra environment.

The water up here derives entirely from rain or snowfall and, because of the ground conditions, cannot readily drain away. After the Ice Age, small ponds gradually increased in size, then reeds took a hold around their edges and sphagnum started to spread and form a mossy blanket over the area. Sphagnum dies from beneath but grows quickly above so the surface gradually became ever thicker with the lower parts now turned to peat. Gardeners will know of the water-holding property of sphagnum and this is what has given this area its unusual character. Alongside the lakes, walkways have been formed from old railway sleepers and the unwary visitor who steps off, quickly discovers, to his or her discomfort, just how much water is held in the moss. This environment cannot support much tree life except for silver birches and some pines, nor are there fish to be found in the waters. Other similar moors in the northern Black Forest have been destroyed by drainage, peat cutting or afforestation but fortunately this one was placed under protection in the early part of this century and so has survived.

Not far from the Hohlosee there is a 28m (92ft)-high tower, from which an extensive view may be obtained in all directions. Detailed walking directions are unnecessary here. Follow the very adequate signs from the car park opposite the *Kurhaus* and reach the plateau after about half an hour's fairly steep climb; a circular route taking in the Hohlosee and the tower (Hohloturm) could be completed easily in 1$\frac{1}{2}$-2 hours.

Kaltenbronn is actually an outlying part of Wildbad but appears to consist of little more than the *Kurhaus* (hotel, restaurant and café), a forester's house and the former hunting lodge of the Grand Duke of Baden. The *Kurhaus* is a comfortable rural hostelry and the restaurant is noted for its venison and other game specialities; there is also a deer park across the road.

Back in the Enztal, 12km (7$\frac{1}{2}$ miles) from Wildbad, is the resort of **Enzklösterle**. This is described as a *Luftkurort*; a place which is recognised as having particular climatic qualities due to its altitude and geographical situation, qualities considered to be helpful to sufferers from certain health problems. Already a summer holiday centre, it has also developed quickly in recent years into a first-class winter sports resort. There are many kilometres of footpaths for summer walks and there is a red-deer park through which the visitor may be conducted personally by the forester. The deer park has a *W-Parkplatz* with a woodland nature trail and four round walks. Five kilometres (3 miles) further on, at **Poppeltal**, one reaches the source of the Enz, surrounded by dark, stately pines. Nearby, there are signs to the *Riesenrutschbahn*, a long summer bob run and a popular venue for holidaymakers, especially family groups. There is a large, free car park. Originally, *Riesenrutschbahn* was the name given to the long wooden chutes constructed to enable the foresters of bygone days to slide the timber down the hillsides to the nearest waterway suitable for floatage.

The road leaves the valley to rejoin the B294 shortly before the village of Besenfeld. The remaining 21km (13 miles) into **Freudenstadt** are not of outstanding interest. However, this town, with a population of 19,700 is a bustling little place and a popular goal for visitors to the northern part of the Forest, for whom it is a delight to wander through the arcades which surround the main square with their miscellany of attractive shops. Incidentally, visitors from the United Kingdom compose the second highest number of foreign guests here.

Protestant church in Freudenstadt

Freudenstadt is the highest northern Black Forest town, lying at around 735m (2,415ft), and its sub-Alpine climate and near fog-free atmosphere have made it a suitable place for numerous clinics and nursing homes. It is not a 'spa' in the accepted sense of the word but it is an officially accredited *Luftkurort*. Surprisingly, Freudenstadt was founded in 1601 by Duke Friedrich I as a home for miners. Minerals, particularly silver, had been won in this area since at least the thirteenth century but it was to develop the industry and fill his coffers that Friedrich decided to supplement the local labour with experienced silver-miners brought from Austria. The present town plan mainly stems from that time.

Looking at Freudenstadt today, one can only wonder what possible military significance the town centre can have had for it to have been almost destroyed by Allied bombing on 16 and 17 April 1945. As a result of these bombings, picturesque though the town centre undoubtedly is, almost all the buildings are of post-war construction. The town church at one corner of the square is beautifully restored, a remarkable L-shaped building with an identical tower at each end and two naves at right-angles to each other. In providing for the segregation of the sexes in earlier times, it was arranged that the men and women could not even see each other. Both parties, however, could hear the sermon, from one central pulpit at the point where the naves converge. There is a valuable sixteenth-century crucifix near the pulpit and other precious relics to be found in the church include a carved lectern dating from about 1150 which came from the *Kloster* in Alpirsbach, and a font, also from the twelfth century, which may have originated in Hirsau.

At the opposite corner of the square stands the town hall, which has a tower with a wonderful panoramic view over the town and the surrounding countryside. The splendid modern *Kurhaus* is the place where much of the entertainment can be found. Tea dances are popular and concerts are given by the spa orchestra and by visiting artists. All the usual facilities of a holiday resort are available including a heated *Freibad* and a *Hallenbad*. The Panoramabad is a fun swimming centre for the whole family with six water chutes, fountains, a hot whirlpool, and a mother and toddler pool. There is also a solarium gallery with fifteen sun beds. As well as this, visitors are welcome at Freudenstadt's nine-hole golf course.

The town lies at the junction of several important roads but most through traffic is now diverted from the centre by a recently built bypass. Parking, which has been a headache for years, is now alleviated by the opening of an underground park for over four hundred cars beneath the part of the huge central square which forms the market place, close to the town hall. The forest marches uncompromisingly up to the very edge of the town and there are 150km (93 miles) of footpaths to be found in the so-called Parkwald, the biggest nature reserve in Germany. In Freudenstadt one can join the ten-day ramble called '*Auf der Fährte des Rothirsches*' (roughly translated; 'On the track of the red deer') organised by the Kurverwaltung between April and October. Included in the itinerary is a large part of the ridge along which the *Schwarzwaldhochstrasse* runs.

Baiersbronn, which lies 7km (4 miles) north of Freudenstadt, is also served by the branch line from Rastatt. Here the river Murg makes a sharp left-hand turn after flowing south-eastwards from its source on the Schliffkopf in order to make its way in precisely the opposite direction and join the Rhine near Rastatt. Like Freudenstadt, Baiersbronn is a *Luftkurort* and in this case the air is said to be particularly suited to those with respiratory conditions.

There is no great outward similarity between the two towns, for there is no magnificent central square here nor any very coherent pattern of shopping streets. Baiersbronn, in fact, is made up of a number of individual hamlets which straggle some way into the many side valleys which open out here into the main valley. This is a good starting place for excursions on foot or by car, while the railway makes for easy access, northwards into the Murgtal or southwards to Freudenstadt and the Kinzigtal.

Baiersbronn lies on the Black Forest Valley Road (*Schwarzwaldtälerstrasse*) and is now making a new name for itself as a skiing resort with a chairlift to the 730m (2,394ft) Stöckenkopf. The long-established skiing resorts along the Black Forest High Road are also within easy reach. The Valley Road, which started in Rastatt, continues to Freudenstadt and to Wolfach, some 50km further south.

Before leaving this area, one can visit the official source of the little river Murg and then go on to the summit of the Schliffkopf. The starting point for this 11km (7 mile) walk is at the *W-Parkplatz* in Buhlbach at the end of the road which leaves the main Ruhestein road at Obertal, 6km (4 miles) from Baiersbronn. This point can be reached by bus and the walk to Buhlbach adds about 2km (1$^1/_4$ miles) to the start of the ramble.

The Murg proper has been created by the confluence of the

Rotmurg and the Rechtmurg close to the road junction at Obertal and it is the Rechtmurg which is to be followed. Motorists, having parked in the *W-Parkplatz*, must go back along the road for about 400m ($^1/_4$ mile) to cross the river by a little bridge. The track is marked with a red spot, but very shortly a small road is joined and a turn to the right is taken. From here the marking is red 'T'; almost immediately the road divides, both branches having the same marking. The left fork runs higher up the hillside through the tiny settlement of Unterer Sand, while the right fork stays closer to the river and climbs more gently. After about 3km (2 miles) the routes reunite to cross back over the river. There is a hut here — one of several passed in the course of this walk — which provides useful shelter in the event of a sudden shower. Turning left along one of the marked paths of the *Schwarzwaldverein* (blue diamond) one now commences to climb up towards the *Schwarzwaldhochstrasse*, described in Chapter 1. It should be mentioned that the whole of this ridge is a nature conservation area (*Naturschutzgebiet*) in which it is forbidden to interfere with the plant life.

The forestry road, which has been followed since the hut, stays close to the Murg and having crossed the now tiny stream for the last time, ends close to the source about 1.5km (1 mile) from the hut. This is a good spot for rest and refreshment, for the steepest part of the climb is yet to come. Those not wishing to continue should retrace their steps to the hut and follow the direct track along the other bank of the river to the car park, making a total distance of about 7km (4 miles).

To continue to the summit, it is necessary to go back across the final bridge, pick up the blue diamond marking again, and follow this for 400m ($^1/_4$ mile) until the main road is reached and crossed. Still following the signs, now climb to the summit of the Schliffkopf, at 1,055m (3,360ft), before continuing in a north-westerly direction to another splendid viewpoint. From here one can see the mountains of the middle and south Black Forest, the Vosges, Strasbourg cathedral and, in the most favourable conditions, the Swiss Alps.

Nearby, the track divides and the left fork (red diamond) would, in another 3km (2 miles), bring one to Ruhestein for a return to Obertal or Baiersbronn by bus. Returning on foot to Buhlbach, however, the right fork is followed to recross the main road and descend to a junction of half a dozen forest roads or paths known as Roter Schliff. The way lies along the second turning to the right to

Places of Interest In and Around Freudenstadt, Baiersbronn and The Valley of the Northern Alb

Freudenstadt
Stadtkirche
Church of unusual L-shaped
design.
Lectern from 1150, sixteenth-
century crucifix and other valuable
relics.

Stadthaus (Town Hall)
Views from tower.

Panoramabad
Fun swimming centre for all the
family with chutes, fountains and
whirlpool.

Parkwald
On the fringes of the town. Said to
be the biggest nature reserve in
Germany, with 150km (93 miles) of
footpaths.

Baiersbronn
Stöckenkopf
730m (2,394ft) hill, 1km ($\frac{1}{2}$ mile)
from Baiersbronn with chairlift.

Mummelsee
20km (12$\frac{1}{2}$ miles) north-west on
Schwarzwaldhochstrasse B500.
Charming mountain lake. Boating.

Schliffkopf
15km (9 miles) west on

Schwarzwaldhochstrasse B500.
Views over Forest, to Strasbourg
and the Alps.
Nature conservation area.

Allerheiligen
20km (12$\frac{1}{2}$ miles) east on
Ruhestein to Oppenau road.
Waterfall and ruins of Kloster
founded in 1196.

Deer Enclosures
At Sankenbachtal, Klosterreichenbach, Schönegrund and Langenbach.

Marxzell
Albtal Transport Museum
Collection includes early vehicles
from Alb Valley Railway.

Frauenalb
Ruins of Benedictine Kloster
Church (1727)

Bad Herrenalb
Ruins of Kloster and Church

Loffenau
Important hang gliding centre on
the Teufelsmühle 906m (2,972ft).
Look-out tower.

descend fairly steeply and soon follow a small river, the Wolfach.
After about 2km (1$\frac{1}{4}$ miles) this joins the Murg, and Buhlbach is
reached after 1.5km (1 mile). This walk is suitable with or without a
car and even a visitor dependent upon public transport will find no
difficulty in reaching the starting points of walks in this area. There

is a multitude of marked paths in the vicinity of Baiersbronn itself and the tourist information office will be able to give details of conducted rambles either starting from the centre or using public transport.

Deer are quite numerous in the Forest and wild boar are also to be found. Both are difficult to see in their natural habitat and in many places enclosures have been constructed so that they may be observed and preserved at the same time. Most of these enclosures are accessible at all times without formality. The signs to look for are *Saupark* or *Wildgehege*. There are several deer enclosures in and around Baiersbronn; the nearest is that in the Sankenbachtal, a pleasant 3.5km (2^1/$_4$ miles) stroll from the centre. Others are to be found in the Ailwald at Klosterreichenbach, 4.5km (3 miles) away, in Schönegründ, 9km, (5^1/$_2$ miles) away, and through Schönmünzach to Langenbach, 24km (15 miles). Exact locations vary from time to time and it would be advisable to check with the *Kurverwaltung* before setting out.

Another interesting excursion from Baiersbronn is to **Allerheiligen**, on the road between Ruhestein and Oppenau. There is a very fine seven-stage waterfall, beside which a steep stairway descends from the parking place near the main road. Here too, are the ruins of the Kloster Allerheiligen which was founded in 1196 and burnt down three times — in 1470, 1555 and 1803 — after being struck by lightning, if one can give credence to such a remarkable history of disaster. The few buildings which survived the last fire are now used as a forestry office and a *Gasthaus*.

From Ettlingen, the visitor without his or her own transport can take the little train for the 20km (12^1/$_2$ miles) or so through the Albtal to Bad Herrenalb. This valley is often described as the *nördliches* Albtal for there is another of the same name in the southern part of the Forest. Soon after leaving Ettlingen's industry, one is in a genuine Black Forest atmosphere with densely packed pine trees and, in some places, pleasant meadows beside a merry little river.

When **Marxzell** is reached, it is worth pausing to visit the church of St Markus (1772-82) with its colourful sandstone tower. Across from the Marxzeller Mühle Hotel, there is the little Albtal Transport Museum which has an interesting collection of vehicles, including some early ones from the Alb Valley Railway.

As the journey progresses, the ruins of the *Kloster* at **Frauenalb** soon come into view. Nuns of the Benedictine Order were already resident here in the twelfth century. In 1727, the famous architect Peter Thumb was responsible for the design of a church whose two towers still stand. Some parts of the main aisle also survived a devastating fire in 1853 but the religious establishment itself had been disbanded 50 years earlier as part of the Secularisation process. The extensive ruins are in stark contrast to the traditional spa hotel, the 'König von Preussen' (King of Prussia) which is nearby. The monastery garden has three terraces and usually a colourful display of flowers and shrubs.

Frauenalb seems almost to live in the past but **Bad Herrenalb**, the most important place in the valley, has developed into a modern *Kurort* with a wide range of facilities for guests convalescing after illness or just seeking relaxation from the trials of everyday life. The monastery at Herrenalb was also founded in the twelfth century to complement nearby Frauenalb. Both establishments were wealthy and the monks had the privilege of calling themselves *Herren* (gentlemen). Their lives were occupied solely with religious observance, in great contrast to the hard-working lay brothers.

In the fifteenth century, the religious zeal of the gentlemen monks began to cool and they started to take interest in more earthly pleasures. There was, for example, Abbot Georgius Trippelmann. He had certainly encouraged the revival of life in the Catholic establishment following the doldrums of the Reformation but he did not conduct himself with the expected monastic virtues. In the end, two of his monks complained to higher authority that, among other misdemeanours, the Abbot 'consorted with a female person'. As a result, Trippelmann had to lay down his abbot's staff in 1555; perhaps he had the last laugh though, for he married the lady in question! If one sits in the porch of the former Klosterkirche, two meditating monks can be seen standing in niches to the right. Are they, perhaps, praying for the soul of the sinning Trippelmann? Of the church itself, only the choir of 1427 and its side chapel remain. An exhibition of the history of the monastery and a collection of handmade roof tiles can be seen in the *Heimatstube* of the *Kurverwaltung* building on Saturdays from 10am to 12noon.

Herrenalb is at the convergence of seven little valleys. About 5km (3 miles) along one of these, to the north-west, is the little village of **Moosbronn** which has a pretty baroque church. Here, in 1626, the glass-maker Franz Kunard and his sons established the first *Glashütte* (workshop) in this district. Several others were to follow but as they relied on large quantities of wood for their processes, they fell into disuse when the nearby forests were felled and had to be re-established elsewhere, nearer new supplies of the essential commodity. In those days, transport of timber for any distance without a convenient waterway was a virtual impossibility.

There is a road from Bad Herrenalb to Gernsbach, in the neighbouring Murg valley, which passes through the *Erholungsort* of **Loffenau** (population 2,500). There are some half-timbered houses and several old water mills are within walking distance. The nearby Teufelsmühle has a deceptive name, for it is not a mill at all but a 906m (2,972ft) high mountain with a lookout tower. This is the principal hang gliding centre in the northern Black Forest and the school here prepares the fliers for international certificates of competency.

A walk of 12km (7^1/$_2$ miles) can be started in this area at the *W-Parkplatz* Talwiese in the upper Gaistal, 4km (2^1/$_2$ miles) south of Bad Herrenalb. This is a varied ramble for sure-footed walkers and begins at the Raststätte Talwiese along the so-called Brudes-Weg, marked by blue diamond and the number '11'. Climbing continuously through the wood, the Hahnenfalzhütte is reached in about 45 minutes and, after a few more minutes' climb, the long-distance *Westweg*, with its red diamond waymark, is encountered at Langmartskopf. However, the sign to follow remains the blue diamond and there is a notice 'Zur Teufelsmühle'. Some fine, long-distance views enhance this section and the highest point of the walk, at 942m (3,018ft), is soon passed.

Continue towards the Teufelsmühle which has an observation tower at 906m (2,972ft) that can be climbed for even better views into the Enz and Murg valleys and to the mountains along the *Schwarzwaldhochstrasse*. The nearby Gasthof provides rest and refreshment but it is closed on Tuesdays.

Commence the return descent by following route number '43', still marked by the blue diamond, along a little road at first but then bearing left towards a good viewpoint, continuing from here to follow the waymarks steeply down to the Grosses Loch. Thereafter, path '43' leads to the right and there is a sign 'Herrenalb'. But take care — after just 5 minutes, leave the '43' and now follow '44' and the signs 'Zur Plotzsägemühle'. First of all, follow this for about 200m (217yds) along a little road and then turn right, down through the woods until the old sawmill on the river Alb is reached. Refreshments are available here at weekends.

Alb Valley Railway at Bad Herrenalb

The mill is at 540m (1,650ft) and the whole descent will have taken about 1 hour. Now go uphill for a short while on a little road; follow the *Naturfreundehaus* sign and pass the *Spechtschmiede* (refreshments) up to an open area. Take the level road 200m (650ft) to the right and into the wood in order to get back to the starting point at Talwiese.

Rastatt (see Chapter 1) is left in a south-easterly direction to follow the *Schwarzwaldtälerstrasse* (Black Forest Valley Road) through the valleys of the rivers Murg and Kinzig. Schloss Favorite is passed on the outskirts of Rastatt and the road goes on through Kuppenheim and **Bad Rotenfels**. The latter has a baroque church and a thermal spring delivering water at 34°C (93°F). The B462 is joined and **Gaggenau** is reached in about 7km (4 miles).

By Black Forest standards, this is quite an industrialised town and there was an ironworks here as early as the seventeenth century. The first *Glashütte* was established in the eighteenth century and these activities continued to flourish through the nineteenth and into the twentieth centuries. Now the most geologically and scenically interesting of all the northern valleys truly begins. This is especially true of the section from here to Raumünzach in which there are several interesting small towns and villages as well as numerous places to *parken und wandern*.

Gernsbach, only 5km (3 miles) from Gaggenau, should be singled out for special mention — a town of old timbered houses and medieval fortifications. An impressive fountain graces the pretty market place, and the Renaissance *Rathaus*, originally the home of a Gernsbach merchant, should not be overlooked. The Liebfrauen-kirche, the oldest church in the town, dating from 1378, is noted for its fine windows and an artistic altar. The railway traveller from Rastatt to Freudenstadt can enjoy a constantly changing scene as the train winds its way up the valley, frequently crossing and recrossing the river.

Two kilometres ($1^1/_4$ miles) upstream on a rocky outcrop is Schloss Eberstein (1150). The Schloss-Restaurant is worth visiting but, apart from this, the inner courtyard of the palace has a crucifixion group (1464) which originated in Kloster Herrenalb. Four kilometres ($2^1/_2$ miles) from Gernsbach, the road from Kaltenbronn descends into the valley at **Weisenbach**, an *Erholungsort* which is in a good rambling area with ready access to the Kaltenbronn upland already described. Here the valley is a little wider and the river bank is lined with attractive houses.

The pretty church is prominent on a small hill and was built in 1845 in the colourful local sandstone. The cultivation of vines is not possible any further up the valley than this and from now on the scenery changes dramatically. The traveller will note the several large paper mills in the narrow valley bottom, this being one of the most important areas for the production of newsprint in the Federal Republic.

Forbach is 14km (9 miles) from Gernsbach and is worth a stop for the benefit of the photographer. The covered wooden bridge is outstanding; it was built originally in 1778 and roofed with Canadian red cedar shingles. At 40m (131ft), it is the longest bridge of this type in Germany. The Catholic parish church with its two neo-Roman-esque bell towers is in a picturesque setting too. The Murg has been dammed between Forbach and Raumünzach to form a 600m (650yd)-long lake and at Raumünzach a road leads westwards up a steep, twisty road to another man-made lake. This is the Schwarzen-bach-Talsperre, about 4km ($2^1/_2$ miles) distant, where a popular recreation area has been created.

It was difficult to find space in this part of the valley for road and railway alongside the river and the line often cuts through rocky outcrops by means of short tunnels. For a long time, the Baden State Railway from the north had its terminus at Raumünzach for this was the frontier with Württemberg; the traveller then had to find his way 10km ($6^{1}/_{4}$ miles) to Schönmünzach where the Royal Württemberg railway took over for the remainder of the journey into Freudenstadt.

Before arriving in that town, the *Luftkurort* of **Klosterreichen-bach** is reached. There was once a monastery here which had been founded by the monks from Hirsau. Part of the west wing, the bath house and a tower survive. The restored Klosterkirche has two early Romanesque towers which date from the eleventh century. The *Kloster* garden is beautifully maintained and there is a modern outdoor swimming pool. In the nearby Ailbachtal there is one of the deer enclosures suggested as an excursion from Baiersbronn.

Before going further south, it is worth making a tour towards the east in order to explore the upper part of the Nagoldtal. A picturesque road goes south-east at first from Besenfeld for about 7km (4 miles) to Erzgrube, a name which recalls the seventeenth- and eighteenth-century iron-ore mining in this area. One of the countless streams originating near Besenfeld is the official source of the Nagold which turns east at Erzgrube and almost immediately enters the Nagoldtalsperre, two man-made lakes constructed between 1965 and 70. The dams are respectively 11.5 and 32.1m (38 and 105ft) high and the total length of the lakes is some 3km (2 miles). This has become another favoured recreation area, with water activities and an extensive network of footpaths around the lakes.

The little *Erholungsort* of Kälberbronn is just a few kilometres to the south. The valley road can be followed in a generally westerly direction for the 8km (5 miles) to **Altensteig** where the old town clings precariously to the steep slopes on the north flank of the Nagold. The old castle dominating the skyline dates from the thirteenth century and the attractive rococo church nearby dates from the eighteenth. The little church in **Altensteigdorf** was built around 1200 and contains some beautiful wall paintings. Altensteig is one of the most photogenic towns in the northern part of the Forest and although it does not lie directly on one of the main tourist routes, it is well worth a visit.

From Altensteig, the rather busy B28 continues down the valley and soon passes near the *Luftkurort* of **Berneck** where the many facilities for the visitor include a *Hallenbad* and a heated *Freibad*. The

Thirteenth-century inn, Gernsbach

main road continues through the attractive landscape and passes through the *Erholungsort* of Ebhausen before the final descent into Nagold, which was visited earlier in this chapter. To return towards Freudenstadt, turn right upon reaching the B463 and, after about 2km ($1^1/_4$ miles), turn right again into a pretty road going eastwards and signposted Pfalzgrafenweiler.

At **Haiterbach**, an *Erholungsort* just south of this road, there is the ruin of Mantelberg castle with a 30m (98ft) high tower. **Egenhausen**, also just off the through road, is reached about 14km (9 miles) after leaving Nagold. It is a little market town and makes a peaceful base, equally ideal for exploration of the immediate vicinity or for excursions further afield. The church has some interesting early-Gothic wall paintings. Altensteig is only a few minutes' journey to the north.

The important *Luftkurort* of **Pfalzgrafenweiler** is about 8km (5 miles) further on. This is a summer and winter resort with several attractive satellite villages grouped around it. The total population of the area numbers only some 4,000. Close nearby, another *Luftkurort* consists of the twinned communities of **Waldachtal** and **Lützenhardt**, which also have a group of surrounding villages. The

Places of Interest In and Near The Murg and Upper Nagold Valleys

Gernsbach
Old timbered houses and medieval fortifications.

Liebfrauenkirche (1378)
Fine windows and artistic altar.

Schloss Eberstein (1150)
2km (1$\frac{1}{4}$ miles) south.
Good restaurant.

Forbach
Covered wooden bridge (1778)
Longest example of this type in Germany.

Catholic parish church
Two neo-Romanesque bell towers.

Klosterreichenbach
Remains of former Kloster
Restored church (*Klosterkirche*)
with early Romanesque tower.

Nagoldtalsperre
7km (4 miles) to the east.

Man-made lakes 3km (2 miles) long.
Recreation area.

Waldachtal-Lützenhardt
Old sawmill
Has biggest mill wheel in Black Forest.

Altensteig
Picturesque medieval town on steep hillside.

Thirteenth-century castle and eighteenth-century rococo church

Church (1200)
In Altensteigdorf
Beautiful wall paintings.

Dornstetten
Outstanding old town centre. Many half-timbered houses, late-Gothic church and old fountain.

Heimatmuseum is worth a brief visit and an inspection of an old sawmill which has the biggest mill-wheel in the Black Forest, is recommended. At **Heiligenbronn** there is an old *Wallfahrtskirche* (pilgrimage church) which may be visited.

Finally, nearing Freudenstadt, the little town of **Dornstetten** (population 6,000) should on no account be missed. It has had 'town' status since 1276 and is thus about three centuries older than Freudenstadt, by which it is now rather over-shadowed. Silver and lead used to be mined here but these activities have long since disappeared. Many beautiful half-timbered houses line the main street and market place and complement the elegant late-Gothic church of St Martin. The fountain in the market place is almost 500 years old.

South of Freudenstadt

The *Tälerstrasse* south of Freudenstadt is road B294 which was the main route out of Pforzheim. The Kinzig valley is now the one to be followed. As all the principal places in the 70km (44 miles) of the Kinzigtal can be reached by train, this is a particularly suitable area for the visitor without his or her own transport.

Only 8km (5 miles) from Freudenstadt, the small, modern *Luftkurort* of **Lossburg** makes no claim to architectural splendour or historic assocations. But it does have a fine climate and quite a lot of attractions for the twentieth-century holidaymaker. Accommodation ranges from the traditional old Gasthof 'Bären' (The Bear) to simple bed and breakfast accommodation and self-catering flats, mostly in modern houses. There is a splendid heated swimming pool with grassy slopes for sun-bathing and a children's play area. There is also a *Hallenbad* (indoor pool); an open-air pool is usually called a *Freibad* — *beheiztes Freibad* if it is heated, as most of them are . A more natural bathing place may be called a *Waldbad* but this may equally be just a *Freibad* which happens to be in the woods. Other names such as *Schwimmbad* or *Schwimmhalle* are also used.

Near the outdoor pool at Lossburg, there are tennis courts and a small *Kurpark* where band concerts take place during the summer months. Lossburg has a good musical reputation and the brass band of the *Musikverein* is well thought of. The Schwarzwaldmuseum (Black Forest Museum) houses a comprehensive collection of objects from the Kinzigtal including a number of unusual Black Forest clocks.

Alpirsbach, a busy little town with useful shopping facilities, is one of the places in which the Benedictine monks founded a monastery on the pattern of Hirsau and the Klosterkirche (1125) still dominates the town. If it appears to be somewhat unbalanced, this is because a planned second tower to match the present one was never built. The church has much of interest and in the summer season is used as the venue for popular serenade concerts. There are a number of impressive half-timbered houses and the stately *Rathaus* (1566) is well-worth inspection. Many cosy hostelries offer the traveller a wide choice of meals or just a drink and a snack. Alpirsbach is yet another *Luftkurort*, noted for the mild climate experienced in its steep-sided valley. There are three *W-Parkplätze* in and around the town with nine round walks in pretty surroundings.

Schenkenzell stands at the junction of the Kleine (little) Kinzigtal with the main valley and is consequently somewhat more open and airy than Alpirsbach. The ruins of the Schenkenburg, 1km ($^1/_2$ mile) south of the town, provide a modest excursion while a tour or a walk in the peaceful and beautiful Kleine Kinzigtal should not be missed. One could start from the *W-Parkplatz* at the edge of the town on the road leading into this valley (signposted Reinerzau) and take one of the three walks shown on the map there. Alternatively, one could continue northwards up the valley and, after about 7km (4 miles), take the minor road on the left to Berneck, which should not be confused with the Berneck in the Nagoldtal that has already been mentioned.

After parking beyond this hamlet, continue forward less than 0.5km ($^1/_3$ mile) to reach the south end of a *Stausee* (reservoir). Following waymarks '21', there is a fine 5km (3 miles) ramble right round this man-made lake. The motorist may go on up the main valley to Schömberg and choose one of several routes for a modest round tour. This Schömberg is a village and not to be confused with the resort of the same name mentioned a little earlier. Nevertheless, it is the focal point of six marked walks of varying grades but presenting little difficulty.

Another interesting excursion in this area is that to the remains of the former nunnery at Wittichen. From Schenkenzell one travels a few kilometres up the valley of the Kleine Kinzig and at Vortal leaves the Reinerzau road in favour of a more westerly one leading up into the hills. This is part of the long-distance *Wanderweg* from Gengenbach to Alpirsbach and, if followed in this direction, would eventually allow one to drop down to Schapbach in the Wolfach valley.

The nunnery at **Wittichen** was founded in 1324 and, among the other difficulties experienced over the centuries, managed to survive the Reformation in the Upper Kinzig valley in 1540. Only with Secularisation in 1803 was the life of the abbey ended; the last abbess, Antonie Schmitt of Kaltbrunn died in 1840. Some of the church vestments made by the nuns are still to be seen in the old baroque church. In the cool, quiet interior one could be in another world unless, that is, one has come on a modest bus tour from Schenkenzell for a guided tour of the nunnery, or happens to be there when an excursion arrives.

On the hill to the east above the *Kloster*, there are a few remains of a castle called Wittichenstein. It was built to protect the numerous silver and cobalt mines that once existed here, traces of which may

Alpirsbach church

The river at Schiltach

A narrow street in Schiltach

also still be found. A mine called Sofie is reputed to have produced the best silver in the whole Kinzigtal.

Schiltach also stands at a junction of valleys, this time the main Kinzigtal and the Schiltachtal running south to Schramberg. A photographer's paradise, with a beautiful unspoilt market place surrounded by tall, timbered houses, it is a riot of colour in the summer months, almost every window ledge bearing a box of vivid geraniums or petunias. The *Rathaus*, built in 1590, carries colourful pictorial reminders of calamitous fires and floods which have destroyed the town in the past. In the market place there is a beautiful fountain of red sandstone (1751) on the column of which is a double-tailed lion, a creature which also appears on the town's coat of arms.

Schiltach's important strategic position means that it has been inhabited for a very long time. Indeed, Roman troops were stationed here to secure a route between the Rhine and the Danube. Excavations near the Brandsteig pass have revealed parts of the Roman settlement and Roman gold coins, including one with the likeness of Emperor Trajan (53-117), have been found in the vicinity of the town. Today, Schiltach is a *Luftkurort* with well under 4,000 inhabitants; a delightful base for those seeking a peaceful holiday without the trappings of the more fashionable resorts.

It is worth leaving the Kinzigtal briefly in Schiltach to drive the 9km (5$^1/_2$ miles), to **Schramberg,** one of the most important towns in the Black Forest, primarily resulting from its flourishing watch and clock industry. There is no settlement in the valley between these two towns except for a few isolated farmhouses and an occasional sawmill. Just before entering the town, an imposing rocky barrier of granite known as the Rappenfels can be seen. The ruins of the Burg Schilteck, built around the year 1200, stand opposite. Five valleys meet in Schramberg, but the place is still cramped because the steep and wooded valley sides give little scope for expansion. Towering above the town, the Burg Hohenschramberg dates from 1457 and is one of five medieval fortresses surrounding Schramberg. There is a significant production of good quality furniture here, and Schramberg pottery should not be overlooked by those seeking a worthwhile gift or souvenir. The Junghans family founded the clock business in 1860 and the visitor should inspect two fine examples of their craftsmanship: the decorative clock in the town museum and the complicated astronomical one at the *Rathaus*.

The clock in the museum, which is almost 5m (16ft) high, was built as an example of the work of the Junghans' factory for display at the Paris exhibition in 1900. The art work consists of themes from the Old and New Testaments, including a sequence of moving scenes depicting the sufferings of Christ. The *Rathaus* clock, built in the factory of Philipp Horz in Ulm, and installed here in 1913, shows a ✳ full astronomical calendar made up of twelve different functions. Visitors can obtain a free explanatory booklet in the information office situated in the *Rathaus* immediately beneath the clock.

This is perhaps the place to make reference to the history of clock-making in the Black Forest, for not only in Schramberg but in nearby towns such as Hornberg, Triberg and Furtwangen this activity has long played an important part in the rural economy and still continues to do so. In the seventeenth century, settlements were established deeper and deeper into the forests but this resulted in great poverty and deprivation, because of which trade came to a virtual standstill.

The plentiful timber led first to a charcoal burning industry and later to glass-making. Glass carriers conveyed the products across Europe on their backs and it is thought that one of them brought a primitive clock back from Bohemia which aroused great interest. The forest inhabitants pondered over the possibilities of this new idea and soon contrived to make simple timepieces using the materials readily available — wood, stone and glass. The wooden cog-wheels all had to be cut by hand. Some examples of these early clocks may be seen in the clock museum in Furtwangen.

Later came metal for the mechanisms, at first imported from afar but in 1787, Leopold Hofmayer succeeded in setting up a brass foundry in Neustadt. The painted clock faces of the early timepieces were succeeded by artistically carved cuckoo clocks, the better ones having complex musical movements. Coming right up to date, the mechanical parts are often now replaced by modern quartz electronic movements but the traditional 'Black Forest clock' appearance is still often maintained.

There is an adequate selection of eating places in Schramberg. The hotel-restaurant 'Hirsch' (stag) in the Hauptstrasse (closed for four weeks July / August, from 2pm Sunday and all day Monday) has a pleasant restaurant and selection of specialities including home-made pies, loin chops 'Florence' and Swabian roasts. Table reservations are advisable.

South of Schramberg, followed by the road towards St Georgen, is the so-called upper Schiltachtal or Bernecktal. The ruins of the eleventh-century Burg Falkenstein (one of the many with this name in Germany) are surrounded by dark pines. There are many stories of the treacherous deeds centred upon this castle in the eleventh century, in the course of which both Duke Ernest of Swabia and his friend Count Werner of Kyburg met their deaths. The road climbs to the plateau where the sunny summer resort of **Tennenbronn** has an attractive setting. From 1500 until 1902, this village was politically and denominationally divided, with one half belonging to Catholic Austria and the other to Protestant Württemberg.

In winter, Tennenbronn is a popular centre for *Langlauf* or cross-country skiing. The time when downhill skiing was the only way of enjoying the sport has long since passed, especially in the Black Forest. Indeed, there are none of the lengthy *pistes* which generally characterise the Alpine ski resorts. On the other hand, cross-country skiing is very much at home in this terrain — there are few resorts in the Black Forest's higher altitudes which do not have the appropriate facilities and there are many specialist ski schools. There are *Langlaufloipen* (marked tracks to be followed by cross-country skiers) nearly everywhere and they range from modest circular routes round a resort to lengthy tours for which it is necessary to arrange overnight accommodation away from one's base.

The great advantage of cross-country skiing is that it can be a family activity in which all members can participate regardless of their degree of proficiency. Several places are mentioned in this book in this connection and those wishing to try this sport for the first time might well write to these for details of what is available, including any 'package' holiday offers. Two words of warning though; the winter walker should avoid the *Loipen*; the summer walker should not assume that because a *Loipe* is marked on the map, it is necessarily a route along which he or she may walk. Walking routes are separately waymarked.

Continuing eastwards on the B462 from Schramberg, one would come, in 24km (15 miles), to the town of Rottweil which lies at the south end of the picturesque Neckar valley road from Horb. With 24,000 inhabitants, **Rottweil** is an important centre, right on the fringe of the Black Forest and there are fine views through the streets towards the Schwäbische Alb, another area of outstanding beauty to the east. The Heiligkreuzmünster (Holy Cross Minster) has altars and a crucifix of particular interest. The fourteenth-century

Places of Interest In and Around The Upper Kinzig Valley, Schramberg and Rottweil

Lossburg
Schwarzwaldmuseum
Clocks and other items from the Kinzigtal.

Alpirsbach
Klosterkirche (1125) and former Kloster.
Numerous relics of note. Serenade concerts in summer.

Rathaus (1566)

Schenkenzell
Schenkenburg
1km ($^1/_2$ mile) south.
Ruins of typical hilltop castle.

Church and remains of former Nunnery (1324)
At Wittichen, 4km ($2^1/_2$ miles) north-west.

Schiltach
Colourful market place with impressive timbered houses.

Rathaus (1590) with interesting murals.

Beautiful sandstone fountain (1751).

Schramberg
Stadtmuseum (Museum fur Sozial- und Technikgeschichte)

In town centre. Social and technical history. 5m (16ft) high decorative clock and many other treasures.

Rathaus
In town centre. Remarkable astronomical clock.

Ruins
Ruins of five castles around the town on the heights between the valleys.

Rottweil
Heiligkreuzmünster
Dating from fifteenth and sixteenth centuries with some older sections. Interesting altars and crucifix.

Kapellenkirche Unserer Lieben Frau (fourteenth-century)
Tower and rich stone sculpture.

Lorenzkapelle
Museum with art collection and late-Gothic sculptures.

Wolfach
Rathaus with painted façade and Fürstenberg palace (1631)

St Laurentiuskirche (sixteenth-century)

Glass Museum
Glass-blowing demonstrations.

Kapellenkirche has a noteworthy tower and stone carving said to be the best of its period; the Lorenzkapelle is now a museum housing a fine art collection. The old town centre is very attractive; there is a

Roman bath to be visited and an open-air exhibition of modern art.

Back in the Kinzigtal, the final 10km (6^1/$_4$ miles) of the officially designated Valley Road lead to **Wolfach**, where several typical valleys come together. The painted *Rathaus* and the Fürstenberg Palace (1631) are worthy of inspection, together with the sixteenth-century church of St Laurentius. During World War II it was intended that the Schlosskapelle should provide office accommodation but it actually became a prison. It was later used as stables and during the French occupation from 1945 it became a coal store! It was restored by local tradesmen in 1965. Although this pleasant little town is not developed on tourist lines to the same extent as, say, Lossburg, there is plenty of accommodation, including a camp site, and there is a fine outdoor swimming pool.

As has already been noted, glass-blowing is another typical Black Forest craft and here in Wolfach there is a fine example of a *Glashütte* where one may see the skilled craftsmen at work, admire the results and, in the associated museum, be taken through the 2,000 year history of glass-making. The extensive shopping area includes a year-round 'Christmas' shop where every possible type of decoration may be purchased. The *Heimatmuseum* houses a good collection of minerals, splendid crystals beautifully worked into a multitude of geometrical forms. There is a natrium-calcium-sulphur spring in the *Kurgarten* whose waters are claimed to be beneficial for stomach and intestinal disorders.

From Wolfach, a side valley follows the river Wolfach in a northerly direction towards Freudenstadt and the *Schwarzwaldhochstrasse* at Kniebis. From its name, one might imagine the Wolfachtal, or Wolftal, as it is sometimes called, to be a way through rough country where wolves had lurked in the past. The reality is quite the contrary as it is a remarkably beautiful valley throughout. After Oberwolfach, the valley is sparsely populated for about 10km (6 miles) — just the occasional farmhouse or tiny settlement where the valley widens a little. A twisty road climbs away to the left to Bad Peterstal and Griesbach, already described in Chapter 1. The valley road then enters the resort of **Schapbach**, now united with **Bad Rippoldsau**, 10km (6^1/$_4$ miles) further on. For all that, the population numbers little more than 3,000 so the place is hardly overcrowded. Traditional costumes are still worn sometimes in Schapbach.

The big farmhouses in the area are sometimes called *Zinken* and their underpart and doorways are built out of the local red sandstone, an unusual feature in the Forest. Ample provision is made for the accommodation of the holiday visitor and many facilities are available for those coming to 'take the waters' as there are numerous mineral springs here. Much of the output is bottled and exported as table water. In the *Kurmittelhaus* the facilities include a *Hallenbad* and a *Freibad*, both heated to 30 °C (86 °F) by the natural waters. There is also a heated *Freibad* for more general use, all the other leisure appointments expected of a modern resort and a camp site which is open all year round.

From the hamlet of Vorseebach, 3km (2 miles) north of Schapbach, a narrow road climbs up through a mysterious landscape where elves and goblins are said to live and where ancient superstitions abound, to the Glaswaldsee 839m (2,748ft) above sea level. There are three parking places as one approaches the little lake with access to nine circular walks ranging from 2.5 to 11km (1^1/$_2$ to 7 miles). The lake and surrounding countryside are in a *Naturschutzgebiet* (nature conservation area). At Klösterle, as one is approaching Bad Rippoldsau, a church with two towers appears to bar the way but the road divides, the right hand fork climbing steeply out of the valley to Freudenstadt and the left hand one to Kniebis near the point where the 'Wolf' river has its source.

The journey through the Kinzigtal brings one, 4km (2^1/$_2$ miles) from Wolfach, to the road running due south into the Gutachtal, probably the best-known of all the Black Forest valleys and the opportunity for yet another side excursion. In 20 or 30km, the Gutachtal offers a selection of everything that the visitor may consider to be genuinely 'Black Forest'. Not least, the traditional costumes of the area, with the women's red *Bollenhut* being the most distinctive feature. Throughout the Forest, the tourist will be offered dolls dressed in a sort of traditional garb with a red *Bollenhut* and this has become perhaps the most familiar worldwide symbol of the Black Forest. However, it should be remembered that it is only at home in the area of the Gutachtal and that other areas have their own equally significant, if less flamboyant, costumes.

The *Bollenhut* is difficult to make and is therefore stored most carefully when not being worn. An Italian straw hat is treated with plaster so that it becomes snow white (and very heavy). The fourteen red woollen balls or pompoms are made exactly according to tradition and fastened to the hat in the correct numbers and positions. The finished article weighs some 1.5kg (3lbs). By the way, not all the

Oberwolfach

Procession through the streets of Wolfach

Wayside shrine in Wolfach

*Wrought iron sign and
window boxes in Wolfach*

woollen balls are red — the hats
of the married women are
adorned with black ones.

There is an open-air mu-
seum in the village of Gutach which
consists of a collection of typical farmhouses
from all over the Forest. These have been re-assembled here,
complete with their furnishings, implements and vehicles. The original farm on the site was apparently the Vogtsbauernhof, which is still
standing and from which the museum rightly takes its name, since
this is the most imposing of all the houses.

It is possible to start a fairly strenuous ramble of 14km (8¹/₂ miles) in the centre of Gutach by the 'Krone' where there is ample parking space. Leave the village by the Sulzbachweg opposite and follow the blue diamond waymarks. After the Café Höflihof there is a big farm and a sign points uphill to 'Zum Michaelsberg und Farrenkopf'. The route is now well-marked and mostly shady and in about 1¹/₂ hours one reaches the Hasemannhütte on the summit of the Farrenkopf 789m (2,588ft). Refreshments are available here at weekends and the view makes the climb worthwhile.

The route now continues southwards on part of the long-distance *Westweg* whose red diamond should be followed on an undulating path to Büchereck, reached in about 45 minutes. Now the road coming up from Elzach must be followed downhill for about 20 minutes when, just past the second *Hütte*, a waymarked path will be seen coming up from the right. Go 50m (54yd) further and then leave the road to join a pretty, unmarked track going left. Follow this round great curves, first to the left, then to the right, after which it becomes the surfaced little road down the Sulzbachtal, past several pictur-esque farmhouses back to the starting point.

Next is **Hornberg**, a tiny town which impresses initially with a feeling of spaciousness, although this may not be confirmed by closer acquaintance with the place. There is plenty of good, fresh air in this favourite holiday centre in a deservedly popular valley. An eleventh-century castle provides a splendid view over the town — the church, with murals dating from the sixteenth and seventeenth centuries, is worth a visit. There is also a short course on mushroom culture available nearby.

The so-called Black Forest Railway, now part of the Deutsche Bundesbahn (German Federal Railway) runs through the Gutachtal. The panoramic delights of this line deserve to be sampled and even the motorist should forsake his car and make the train journey over the most spectacular part of the route from Hornberg to St Georgen and back. Indeed, the Black Forest offers the railway enthusiast several exciting possibilities for indulging in his or her hobby and none is more exhilarating than the *Schwarzwaldbahn*. This runs from Offenburg in the Rhine valley to Donaueschingen on the eastern fringe of the Forest, a distance of some 85km (53 miles).

It was long thought that the technical problems involved in constructing such a line were so great as to make the project imprac-ticable. However, detailed planning was started in 1862 with five possible routes in the starting list. In the end, it was decided to build the line through the Gutachtal despite the difficult terrain. For example, between Hornberg and Sommerau (today a journey of no more than 27 minutes), the line would have to overcome an altitude difference of 448m (1,460ft) in a straight line distance of only 11km (7 miles), and this through the notable Triberg granite. To do this, it was first proposed to introduce *Spitzkehren* which meant the altitude could be attained by a series of zig-zag movements. Such an arrangement persists today in the Andes and did, until recently, in Australia on the main line westwards from Sydney, where it is kept in operation as a museum piece.

The far-sighted railway pioneer Robert Gerwig realised that such cumbersome operations would soon prove unacceptable and he was responsible for the two great double horseshoes which the trains traverse to this day. Much of this section is in tunnels — in fact it has thirty-six of the thirty-nine on the whole line. Between the rapidly succeeding tunnels, the bewildered passenger catches tantalising glimpses of the spectacular scenery on either side. Gerwig was also responsible for building the tunnels big enough to take a double track even though only a single line was laid when the railway opened in 1873. Traffic developed quickly and the second track was laid piecemeal between 1888 and 1921.

Gerwig was later put in charge of the construction of the St Gotthard line in Switzerland and eventually returned home to become the general director of the Baden State Railways. So great was the impact of the new railway on the the territory through which it passed that, to this day, many places include 'Schwarzwaldbahn' in their postal addresses.

Soon after leaving Hornberg, the valley, which has hitherto been open and light, becomes narrow, dark and rocky, remaining so until **Triberg** is reached. The town is enclosed by the high mountains and a natural attraction is the famous Triberg waterfall, said to be the highest in Germany. There is a safe but somewhat exhausting walkway up beside the fall. This natural spectacle can, however, be seen with less expenditure of energy by taking the service bus in the direction of Schönwald and alighting at the stop known as 'Wasserfall' to follow the walkway downhill back to the town. In this busy resort of some 7,000 inhabitants, there is ample accommodation for the traveller but the town's restricted outlook makes it more suitable, perhaps, for an overnight stop only.

A traditional thatched farmhouse near Hornberg

Several large wood-carving shops, including the so-called 'House of a Thousand Clocks' make this a good place for the determined souvenir hunter. The *Heimatmuseum* in Triberg is held in high regard with its displays of costumes and clocks. An unusual exhibit is a relief model of the *Schwarzwaldbahn* complete with trains, the result of three years work by A. Fehrenbacher from Schramberg.

There are few really old buildings in Triberg for the town was almost completely destroyed by fire in 1826. All the same, there are a few sights of interest worth seeking out. The old *Amtshaus* (public office) with its timbered façade exposed in 1925 is one of these. Another is the simple *Rathaus* with its surprising council chamber decorated with beautiful carvings by the local craftsman, Karl Josef Fortwängler.

On the upper edge of the town, the interesting pilgrimage church known as Maria in der Tanne also survived the blaze. Already in

Hotel with window boxes in Triberg

Triberg waterfall

1645, there was a little chapel here with an altar painting of a miracle-working Madonna. The name is said to stem from the fact that someone had fastened the miraculous image to a *Tanne* (fir tree) in 1644. The picture was missing for some years but it is said to have been rediscovered by Austrian soldiers in 1692 when they suddenly heard singing as they were passing the tree.

The present church was built between 1699 and 1702 in order to accommodate the increasing number of pilgrims. The high altar, now incorporating the famous picture, was created by the sculptor, Anton Joseph Schupp from Villingen. He was also responsible for the side altars and the pulpit. Margrave Ludwig Wilhelm, who has been mentioned earlier, presented the artistic altar base in 1706. A memorial tablet of the citizens of Villingen (1715) is particularly interesting as it is the only known full picture of eighteenth-century Villingen. Triberg's modern spa centre is set in delightful gardens and embraces a concert hall, reading rooms, television room and a café with sun terrace.

The road divides at Triberg, the left fork going towards St Georgen which is also the direction of the railway. The European watershed comes between Triberg and St Georgen and the rivers, including the Gutach, which flow towards the west, the Rhine and ultimately the North Sea are now left. The first eastward-flowing stream, the Brigach, is met here. It is one of the sources of the Donau (Danube), which empties into the Black Sea.

Triberg is another place to start one of the organised walks already mentioned. This 9-day ramble follows the possible route of one of the old-time clock carriers who walked from place to place burdened with new clocks for sale. The territory covered is to the south and east of Triberg and takes in St Märgen, Titisee, Bonndorf and Villingen-Schwenningen. The going is a little easier than on some of the walks previously mentioned and this is emphasised by the distance of 187km (116 miles) covered. One does not need to undertake the whole route, however, and sections can be booked to suit the individual. In winter there is an alternative *Ski-Wandern* from Triberg to Titisee. (Details in both cases from Kurverwaltung, Triberg.)

St Georgen is another *Luftkurort* and winter sports centre. At an altitude of 800-1,000m (2,620-3,280ft), its chances of getting snow are fairly good while there are attractive walks around the town in all directions for the summer visitor. This is yet another place in which the Benedictine monks founded a monastery on the pattern of Hirsau, but in 1865 it was destroyed in a disastrous fire which also engulfed part of the town.

The present main shopping area is not particularly attractive, despite the excellent shops located there; modern architecture cannot compete with the old for charm. The beautiful town garden is worth visiting, and in the folk museum one can enjoy an educational display on the Black Forest way of life. The traditional costumes of the Forest are to be seen in many museums, but they are also still worn in many places for church-going and for special occasions such as weddings. St Georgen is one such place; here the headpiece worn by the women is the *Schäppelkrone*, an enormous decoration of glass pearls, coloured stones and tiny mirrors, the whole weighing 3kg ($6^1/_2$lbs).

It may be thought that the route to St Georgen described hardly falls within the scope of 'Valleys of the North' but it has been included here because of the continuous link from the Kinzigtal provided by the *Schwarzwaldbahn*. Other places in this area will be covered in Chapter 3.

For the purposes of this book, at least, one must retrace the route through the Gutachtal to the Kinzigtal, where the next town is **Hausach**. Its castle was destroyed during the Thirty Years' War, but the ruins remain and a good view is obtained along the valley. Once again, a history of fires means that there are no really old buildings in the town itself, but in the part known as Hausach-Dorf (village) there is an ancient church worthy of a visit. It is built on the site of a former Romanesque church which stood there in 1148. The late-Gothic choir, the tabernacle and the crucifixion scene from the twelfth century on the north outside wall all justify the visitor's attention. Hausach, together with **Haslach**, 6km (4 miles) further down the valley, attracts many visitors each year for its Shrovetide processions during which some of the participants wear historic wooden masks.

The pre-Lenten season of jollity is known in this area as *Fasnet* and its origins have something in common with *Karneval* in places like Cologne or Mainz and *Fasching* in Munich. However, the nature of the celebrations is quite different and there is less of the noisy and ostentatious revelry one associates with those places. The often grotesque masks conceal the identities of the participants in the various activities and the word *Narr*, meaning fool or jester, is used

Rathaus with colourful mural, Haslach

House in the Nordrachtal

Places of Interest In The Gutach Valley and Lower Kinzig Valley

Schwarzwaldbahn
This remarkable railway runs through the Gutach valley.

Gutach
Open Air Museum Vogtsbauernhof
Typical Black Forest farmhouses collected and reassembled with furnishings and implements.

Triberg
Highest waterfall in Germany.

Pilgrimage Church 'Maria in der Tanne' (1699-1702)
High altar incorporates the miraculous image.

Heimatmuseum
Excellent display of costumes and clocks and relief model of *Schwarzwaldbahn*.

Haslach
Heimatmuseum
Klosterstrasse 1. In former *Kapuzinerkloster* (1630)
The definitive collection of traditional Black Forest dress.

Rathaus (1733)
Paintings of traditional costumes on external walls.

Gasthaus 'Zur Sonne'
Birthplace of writer Heinrich Hansjakob (1837-1916).

Hansjakobmuseum
Hansjakobstrasse 17.
Memorabilia of the writer.

Steinach
Gasthaus 'Schwarzer Adler' (1715)
Regarded as the most beautiful half-timbered house in the Black Forest.

Zell am Harmersbach
Storchenturm (1402)
25m (82ft) high tower with basket for storks' nest.
Nearby are four Swedish cannon from Thirty Years War.

Hirschturm
Round tower, formerly part of defensive walls.

freely. Other places for seeing something of this seasonal letting down of hair include Zell am Harmersbach, Staufen, Rottweil, Villingen, Bad Dürrheim and Freiburg. Examples of the wooden masks will be found in the *Heimatmuseen* in these places.

In addition to the annual attraction of the Shrovetide processions, Haslach has several historic buildings for the traveller's delight, and the *Heimatmuseum* is in one of them, the former Kapuzinerkloster, which dates from 1630. The Zehntscheur (tithe barn) (1550), the town wall, the Sebastiansbrunnen (fountain) and the Gutleutbrücke (bridge) all contribute to a pleasant tour of inspection which should include the town church, with its Gothic west tower, a sandstone relief from the twelfth century and the tomb of Count Götz of Fürstenberg. As well as all these, there is the *Rathaus* (1733) which has unusual paintings of traditional costumes on the exterior walls.

The local writer, Heinrich Hansjakob (1837-1916), commemorates Count Götz in one of his Kinzigtal stories, *Der steinerne Mann von Hasle* (*The Stone Man of Haslach*). Hansjakob was born in the Gasthaus 'Zur Sonne'; this and another historic *Gasthaus*, the 'Zur Kanone' should not be omitted from one's exploration of this little country town.

The river, which flowed southwards from Freudenstadt then westwards from Schiltach, now completes its U-turn to flow in a northerly direction towards Offenburg. On its way, it meets several small places worthy of our attention.

There are those who contend that the Gasthaus 'Schwarzer Adler' (Black Eagle) in **Steinach** is the most beautiful timbered house in the Black Forest. Only the façade of this fine building is genuinely old, dating from 1715. The main structure of the house has been meticulously rebuilt behind, following 'clearance' of the site by the Royal Air Force during World War II. It was believed that the private railway saloon which was the headquarters of Nazi SS Chief Heinrich Himmler was being concealed in and moved between the various tunnels of the *Schwarzwaldbahn*; it was during attempts to sever the line by bombing, that the 'Adler' came to grief. Its restored *Flösserstube* (raft room) is like a little museum. A meal here could well be something to remember, as could one in another old *Gasthaus*, the 'Alte Bauernschänke' (literally translated: old public house for farmers), where the original interior has been preserved.

In the village of **Biberach** (population 3,000) there is a small *Heimatmuseum* and there is a *Waldparkplatz* about 1km ($^1/_2$ mile) east of the station adjacent to the attractive heated *Freibad* called the Terrassenbad, which has a big, curved chute. Numerous short round walks are indicated on the sign at the parking place together with a woodland nature trail to Zell am Harmersbach. The nature trail (*Waldlehrpfad*) makes for a pleasant 7km ($4^1/_2$ miles) ramble through the woods into the Harmersbach valley. The sign to follow is 'WL'; some signs also show Rebeck which is a point where paths meet.

Leave the car park past the swimming pool entrance and follow a broad, steadily rising track almost to the ridge, where care must be taken not to miss the narrow footpath going back sharply to the right. Climb a little more on this path until emerging on to wider tracks at Rebeck. Go straight forward down the one opposite and watch out for a diversion into another footpath going to the right and dropping steadily down towards Zell. Turn right on arriving at another broad track and, with the buildings of the town now clearly visible through the trees, go down a path which soon appears to the left and reach the first houses of Zell a few minutes later. Just before emerging from the woods, notice the entrances to two old mining galleries. ✳

A path back to Biberach about 4km (2¹/₂ miles) along the slopes of the hill will be seen before reaching the town itself. Allow about 1¹/₂ hours each for the outward and return legs. There are also trains and buses from Zell to Biberach. Even if the ramble described has not been undertaken, most visitors will wish to leave the Kinzigtal at Biberach for an excursion into the Harmersbachtal and this is certainly to be recommended.

The former 'free' town of **Zell** is today a *Luftkurort* lying in a splendid holiday valley which, like the town itself, formed part of a 'free' farmers' republic until 1803. Prominent in Zell is the Storchen- turm of 1402, which is 25m (82ft) high and still bears the basket intended to encourage storks to nest here although the birds have not made an appearance for many years. There is a small museum in the tower and four Swedish cannon are a relic of the Thirty Years War. They have survived more significant dangers since then, even the scouring of the land for scrap metal during World War II. Nearby is the smaller, round Hirschturm, a former strong point at a corner of the town wall, now standing in a peaceful little garden.

From Zell, a small road branches off to the north through the tiny Nordrachtal and an excursion through here is a pleasure no visitor to the area should miss. If the little river Harmersbach is followed up the main valley, note the fine old farmhouses along the way and several *Bildstöcke* (wayside shrines or memorials).

Yet another *Luftkurort*, **Oberharmersbach**, is reached in about 10km (6¹/₄ miles); this is a place for peaceful relaxation but it also has good facilities for visitors and ample access to the countryside. The Harmersbach comes down from Löcherbergwasen, the wooded upland between Oberharmersbach and the Renchtal. There is a *W-Parkplatz* up there with circular walks of 2-8km (1-5 miles) in length.

The visitor reliant upon public transport can readily explore the valley by using the little private railway, the *Harmersbachtalbahn*.

There is a fairly frequent service between Biberach station and Zell (5 minutes journey) and a less regular service on to Oberharmersbach. Many of the 'trains' are actually buses which start from just outside the station at Biberach.

The river Kinzig continues in a north-westerly direction from Biberach through Gengenbach and Offenburg (described in Chapter 1) and finally loses itself in the Rhine opposite Strasbourg.

3

THE CENTRAL AREA

Had the right-hand fork of the road been taken in Triberg, the traveller would have found him- or herself climbing through a series of sharp bends to the upland and the holiday area of **Schönwald**. It is not so many years since this was an enclosed village with old farms in a picturesque landscape; the development of holiday facilities has not been to the advantage of the general environment — a case of too much and too quickly perhaps.

Nevertheless, this is a most popular *Erholungsort* situated in the splendid rambling area of the Stöcklewald 1,067m (3,500ft) and Brend 1,149m (3,771ft). The nature conservation areas around the Blindensee and the Schwarzenbachtal are readily accessible. There are some big hotels here as well as accommodation in every other category. However, this is on the way to **Furtwangen** which, lying at 870m (2,854ft) above sea level, is the highest town in the southern half of the Black Forest.

It is not a beautiful town, despite its fine surroundings. After a disastrous fire in 1857 a decision was taken to only build in stone — in more recent times the 'stone' has become concrete, of course — and the resulting buildings are practical rather than charming. This is another clock-making town and one should visit the fine clock museum, which has more than a thousand examples of clocks of every kind. There are also mechanical organs which play from time to time, and models which can be operated by the visitor. Furtwangen stands on the young river Breg as it hastens eastwards to become one of the principal tributaries of the Danube.

Six kilometres (4 miles) north-west of the town is Brend where there is car-parking space to enable one to explore this 1,149m

(3,771ft) high formation on foot. There are outstanding views in all directions over very typical Forest landscape from its 46m (151ft) look-out tower. Close to the tower there is a *Gasthaus* as well as a youth hostel. Brend is the general name for the long-stretched ridge between Furtwangen and Elzach with summits running from south to north such as Brend itself, Rosseck 1,152m (3,781ft), Obereck 1,180m (3,872ft) and Rohrhardtsberg 1,155m (3,790ft).

An attractive little road runs along the ridge just to the east of these heights before descending to Schonach near Triberg. Near Brend is the ancient Martinskapelle, thought to have been built in about the year AD700. Many visitors go down the few steps to the source of the river Breg; the mighty Danube may thus be said to begin its 2,288km (1,430 mile) journey eastwards to the Black Sea here.

The great farmhouses in this area are well protected from the severe winter weather by their enormous roofs which reach almost to ground level in exaggerated, typical Black Forest style. Those same winters however, make the area a splendid playground for winter sports enthusiasts, for whom snow ploughs keep the road clear. The lives of these upland farmers have always been hard but now, at least, they have electricity, telephones and motor vehicles. More and more of them supplement their incomes by taking in paying guests.

An excursion of 10km (6$^1/_4$ miles) to the south-west through Neukirch takes a minor road towards St Märgen to visit the famous Hexenlochmühle (mill in the witches' hole). This is a working sawmill of unique design in the Black Forest because it has two contra-rotating waterwheels which can be operated simultaneously. Traditional cuckoo clocks are finished on the premises and there is a small, well-stocked shop where these and other souvenirs can be bought.

Westwards from Furtwangen, is the picturesque Simonswälder-tal, which contains the resorts of Gütenbach and Simonswald. The altitude decreases steadily as one drops towards the Elztal and road B294, which is still on its way from Pforzheim to Freiburg. **Gütenbach** is a small *Luftkurort* only 7km (4 miles) from Furtwangen and is an ideal resort for a quiet holiday. There is a fine network of marked footpaths allowing for walks of varying grades. The waterwheel no longer turns at the little old sawmill *Sägehäusle* on the outskirts of the village in the direction of Hintertal. However, this makes an excellent spot to start a typical round walk of 4km (2$^1/_2$

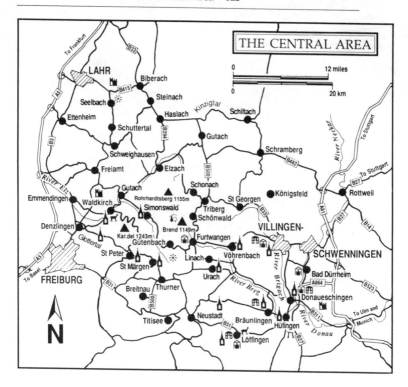

miles) which takes in the charming Hübschental.

There is parking space at the sawmill at 859m (2,814ft) which is passed on one's left as the track is taken gently uphill in an easterly direction past isolated houses. At one of these, an attractive cluster of miniature houses stands beside the track for the passer-by to admire. After going past a small fish pond, the track curves round to the right at the end of the valley, to climb fairly steeply and complete a semi-circle for the return walk, which is mostly in woods, to the sawmill. As the whole route is on unsurfaced roads, the walk is fairly easy and can be completed comfortably in 1 1/2 hours.

Although Gütenbach is quite small, the village has a fine, modern *Hallenbad*, and its other attractions include a fully automatic bowling alley (*Kegelbahn*) at the Park-Café 'Wendelbeck'. The well-known toy firm of Faller has a small factory here and music-lovers may be interested to know that the forefathers of Wilhelm Furtwängler, the

The Hexenlochmühle, near Furtwangen

famous conductor, lived and worked in Gütenbach.

The name **Simonswald** covers the hamlets of Ober-, Alt-, Haslach- and Untersimonswald, which straggle along the Simonswäldertal. An oddity here is that the valley does not take the name of its river, for the river is the Wilde Gutach. Gutach is a name which crops up many times in the Black Forest and this one has no connection with that mentioned earlier when the Gutachtal was explored. The Simonswäldertal, some 30km (19 miles) north-east of Freiburg, is within walking distance of several centres including St Peter and St Märgen. However, the less energetic will find it more comfortable to arrive in the valley by road and perhaps explore it on foot. There is no railway, but the valley is served by a bus service operating between the station at Bleibach and Furtwangen.

The church occupies a prominent position in Obersimonswald — another place to see traditional dress during Sunday churchgoing. The costumes in this valley are some of the most decorative that can still be seen in ordinary use. In the church there hangs a famous picture, *The Seven Holy Sleepers*, which tells of seven youths who were walled up alive in Ephesus and awoke when discovered 175 years later. The Gasthof 'Engel', closed in November and on Tuesdays, is a rural inn with stables and its own chapel. The walled church in Altsimonswald, a place of farms and sawmills, stands on a small hill and contains two artistic wooden sculptures from the sixteenth century. At Untersimonswald, a small side valley, the Haslachtal, accommodates the community of Haslachsimonswald. At the valley entrance there is a *Märchenwald* — a fairytale wood.

The scattered community of Simonswald constitutes yet another *Luftkurort* which has an altitude range of 300-1,200m (984-3,940ft). It offers all that the visitor seeking a peaceful holiday could wish for, including a heated swimming pool. The river Wilde Gutach is not usually particularly wild where it passes through the resort. However, to the south it parts company with the main road and enters a sombre valley which has many legends of witches, goblins and the like, eventually leading to the *Hexenloch* (witches' hole) and the famous mill mentioned earlier.

Continuing down the valley, road B294 is joined at Bleibach and a right turn here leads through the small *Luftkurort* of Elzach back to Haslach in the Kinzigtal. **Bleibach** has an old charnel house chapel with a Dance-of-Death frieze from 1733. The parish church dates from the sixteenth century. The visitor should spend a little time in **Elzach** (population 6,400), an old-world place with a pretty townscape. Do not miss the old *Apotheke* (apothecary's shop) from 1523 nor the St Nikolausbrunnen (fountain) from 1610. The parish church of St Nikolaus has a late-Gothic choir, a seventeenth-century nave and stained glass from 1524.

This charming little health resort with its modest but more than adequate range of accommodation makes an ideal base for those who prefer to be away from the main tourist centres yet to have easy access to a very attractive countryside. A popular short ramble is that to the pilgrimage chapel of the Neun Linden (nine lime trees). Beyond Elzach, the river Elz may be followed north-eastwards into the steep, twisty but very pretty Prechtal.

In the village of Oberprechtal, about 8km (5 miles) from Elzach, the road divides and the river makes a sharp turn southwards. The left fork descends steeply to reach the Gutachtal between Gutach and Hornberg in about 8km (5 miles). The right fork (signposted Triberg) follows the river and climbs steadily for some 14km (8$^3/_4$ miles) to **Schonach** (population 4,600), a *Luftkurort* only 4km (2$^1/_2$ miles) from Triberg.

This is a summer holiday town and a winter sports centre with 100km (62 miles) of ski touring routes marked out. There is a baroque parish church but also an unfortunate tendency to follow the bad example of nearby Schönwald, with new building construction marring the hitherto unspoiled countryside. There is still a fine view from the Wilhelmshöhe but even this is not as beautiful as it used to be. Triberg was visited in Chapter 2 so steps must now be retraced to Bleibach. Turning left here on leaving the Simonswäldertal, one is almost immediately in yet another Gutach, a pretty little village lying mostly a little aside from the main road which arrives at Waldkirch in another 3km (2 miles).

Waldkirch (population 19,000) is a *Kneippkurort* which developed from a Benedictine nunnery founded in AD916 and received its town charter in 1300. The suburb of Kollnau just to the north is even older, having originally been an Alemannic settlement. Waldkirch now includes many outlying areas so the town itself is not as big as the population figure might suggest. It is served by a branch railway line from Freiburg.

There is too much high-rise development and industrial intrusion for this to be an immediately attractive town, despite its *Kur* status, but it has a fine position at the foot of the 1,243m (4,077ft) high Kandel. There are a number of interesting buildings, not the least of these being the town church (1732-4). This is a masterpiece of baroque architecture from the hand of Peter Thumb, of whom more will be said later. One of the original bells, cast in Strasbourg in 1763, is displayed outside the church. The rococo banqueting hall of the priory and the beautiful *Marktplatz* are both worth seeing.

The prosperity of the town was founded on the preparation of semi-precious stones and the construction of musical instruments; the name Waldkirch can still be seen on some splendid fairground organs. There is an important clinic above the town on the lower slopes of the Kandel where people with heart and circulatory conditions are treated. In the town itself there is a small but interesting zoo, while a stiffish climb takes one up to the inevitable ruined castle, the Kastelburg, for fine views over the town and valley.

The ruins were purchased by the town in 1971 and are now cared for by the fire brigade which organises cheerful folk events up there from time to time. It is a feature of Black Forest life — indeed of Germany in general — that the voluntary fire brigades play an active part in the social and cultural life of the community. Though the outlook from the Kastelburg is not what one normally regards as typical Black Forest scenery, it is one of the many joys of the Black Forest that a few kilometres can make all the difference to the surroundings. That is certainly the case in Waldkirch; the beautiful Simonswäldertal lies only a short distance to the north, but it is to the magnificent Kandel east of the town that the Waldkirchers mostly look for their recreation. Twelve kilometres ($7^1/_2$ miles) of steep, winding road climb the 1,000m (3,280ft) from the town to the summit, but it is only necessary to go a short part of this distance to be among the pinewoods and have access to the numerous footpaths which criss-cross the slopes. At every bend the motorist may catch a tantalizing view back over the valley, but the driver will find little opportunity to relax as he or she negotiates the numerous Z-bends and will need frequent stops if not to feel utterly frustrated.

The long-distance footpath *Kandelhöhenweg*, which started away in the north at Oberkirch, passes close to Waldkirch before making the steep ascent to the summit. It is possible to join the path for this section, thereafter returning to Waldkirch by bus. A less strenuous alternative, of course, would be to do this in the reverse direction. Once the path is located it can be readily followed along the *Schwarzwaldverein* trail, marked by a white letter 'K' in a red diamond, and no detailed description of the route is necessary here.

A pretty but little-known, pear-shaped area lies north of Waldkirch, bounded on the south-east by the Elztal and B294 and on the west by the *Badische Weinstrasse* (B3) which converge at the south end near Denzlingen. The north end is enclosed by the Kinzig valley road B33 and its branch from Biberach down into Lahr, the B415. The area measures some 25km (16 miles) from north to south and almost as much from east to west; at the centre is **Schweighausen**, mentioned briefly in Chapter 1 in the course of an excursion from Ettenheim. The five roads which converge at Schweighausen all have to climb to reach the village which stands close to the 726m (1,732ft) Schillingerberg. The area can conveniently be explored by taking each of these roads in turn.

From Lahr, the B415 follows the Schuttertal past Kuhbach, which has already been mentioned, and at Reichenbach the main road is left to follow the valley south to **Seelbach**, a *Luftkurort* of 4,500 inhabitants reached in 7km (4 miles) from Lahr. The B415 is picturesque as it continues eastwards towards Biberach, climbing first to the Schönberg pass at 370m (1,215ft) before dropping gently down into

Places of Interest In and Around Furtwangen, Simonswald and The Elz Valley

Furtwangen
Deutsches Uhrenmuseum
In town centre
Comprehensive collection of
timepieces and mechanical
instruments. Film shows.

Brend
1,149m (3,770ft) summit, 6km
(4 miles) north-west of town.
Observation tower and outstanding
views. Martinskapelle and source
of river Breg.

Hexenlochmühle
10km (6¼ miles) south-west
through Neukirch.
Unique mill with two waterwheels.
Shop for clocks and other gifts.

Urach
Village Church
Prominent 'onion' tower and
beautiful interior.

Vöhrenbach
Parish Church (Thirteenth-century)
Notable Gothic Madonna.

Zur-Sieben-Frauen-Kapelle
Gruesome reminders of witch
hunts.

Simonswald
Obersimonswald Church
Contains a famous painting,
The Seven Holy Sleepers.

Altsimonswald Church
Artistic sixteenth-century wooden
sculptures.

Märchenwald
Fairytale wood at
Untersimonswald.

Elzach
Apotheke (1523)
Apothecary's shop

Nikolausbrunnen (1610)
Fountain

St Nikolaus' Church
Late-Gothic choir, seventeenth-
century nave, stained glass from
1524.

Bleibach
Old Charnel House Chapel
'Dance of Death' frieze (1733)

Parish Church (sixteenth-century)

Waldkirch
Kastelburg
Castle ruin with fine views.

Baroque Church (1732-4)
In town centre
A masterpiece by the architect
Peter Thumb.

Zoo
Close to town centre
Small but interesting collection well
laid out.

Kandel
1,243m (4,077ft) summit, 12km
(7½ miles) south-east on road to
St Peter
Splendid views.
Hang gliding.

Mosaic of St Christopher, Glottertal church

the Kinzig valley. Near the summit is the ruined Burg Hohenger-oldseck built in the twelfth century to protect the pass. It is well-worth the climb up to the castle for the splendid view. Needless to say, there is a hostelry at the pass; the Löwen (lion) which is one of several claiming to be the oldest *Gasthaus* in Germany.

Near Seelbach, in the side valley called Litschental, is a real rarity among Black Forest craft workshops — the Geroldsecker Waffen-schmiede or armourer's workshop. The smithy has been in the possession of the Fehrenbach family for many centuries and the present smith works in the same traditional way as his predecessors of 700 years ago. The smithy was always in the service of the Counts of Geroldseck (hence the name) and provided them with their swords and halberds.

After the Burg Hohengeroldseck fortress was overthrown by the French in 1689, the Fehrenbachs took a vow never to manufacture weapons of war again. The business continued with the making and repair of domestic and agricultural implements but twentieth-century economics made the livelihood ever more precarious. Some years ago, Ludwig Fehrenbach, master smith, decided to break the vow of his forefathers and resume manufacture of weapons by the same methods and to the same patterns as 300 years earlier. Although quite usable weapons, today they are not produced for warlike purposes but for ceremonial occasions, museums and private collectors.

The products of this little workshop, each bearing the family's symbol of a clover leaf, are now to be found all over Germany and Switzerland. Indeed, so great is the demand, that a younger Fehrenbach has already been installed in the smithy to carry on the great tradition. Visitors are welcomed on Saturday and Sunday afternoons when the three waterwheels which provide the power are set in motion. At 6.5m (21ft), the main wheel is the second largest in Germany.

Before leaving the Seelbach area, it is worth visiting the ruins of Burg Dautenstein, often destroyed and rebuilt, with its three fine corner towers. Southwards from Seelbach, the observant traveller will notice that many of the farmhouses are built of a reddish sandstone, a material widely available in this area, as can be seen from the ruins of Burg Hohengeroldseck.

Continuing up the Schuttertal, the *Luftkurort* of that name (population 3,400) is reached in another 5km (3 miles) and it seems quite appropriate in this idyllic valley that the modest mountain to the east is called the Himmelsberg (Heavenly Mountain). Then go on to Dörlinbach, an outlying part of Schuttertal, and follow the road as it climbs up out of the valley to Schweighausen. The several resorts in the Schuttertal are by no means prime tourist centres but they each have *Gasthöfe* and a certain amount of other accommodation for the visitor.

The second road to be followed is that which leaves Steinach in the Kinzigtal, with its famous hostelry, and passes through Welschensteinach to reach Mühlsbach on the eastern flank of the Himmelsberg in about 7km (4 miles). The road is picturesque throughout and it becomes quite twisty after Mühlsbach as it climbs towards Schweighausen. The Welschensteinach area is particularly lovely in spring, when the many fruit trees blossom. The valley is also notable for its many well-preserved, traditional houses.

Just south of Elzach, a little road climbs north-westwards out of the Elztal, passing in turn through the villages of Unterbiederbach, Biederbach and Oberbiederbach, past which there is a camp site. The previously mentioned road is joined just 4km ($2^1/_2$ miles) before Schweighausen. The road in the opposite direction, from Ettenheim on the *Weinstrasse*, has already been referred to in Chapter 1. Herbolzheim and Kenzingen, also on the *Weinstrasse*, are starting points for tourists making their way into the area through the quiet Bleiche valley. There are numerous parking places in the valley, enabling nature-lovers to leave their vehicles and ramble in the pleasant countryside.

From Emmendingen and Denzlingen on the *Weinstrasse*, and from Bleibach in the Elz valley, three roads straggle gradually northwards, to merge and run together into the scattered holiday resort of **Freiamt** (population 3,900). It is only another 8km (5 miles) from here to Schweighausen. Freiamt is a good centre for the visitor seeking a peaceful holiday in pleasant surroundings with, perhaps, an emphasis on outdoor pursuits. The village occupies a sunny position on the south-west slopes of the Hünersedel which, at 746m (2,447ft), is the highest mountain in this area. It is readily ascended on foot or by car and from the heights there are good views into the Elz valley to the east and the Rhine plain and valley to the west.

There is a good network of footpaths all round and these can be used for getting to a number of places of interest in the vicinity. Two kilometres ($1^1/_4$ miles) west of Freiamt, **Ottoschwanden** has a church

Places of Interest In and Around Schweighausen, Glottertal, St Peter and St Märgen

Seelbach

Burg Hohengeroldseck
(Twelfth-century)
Impressive castle ruin 4km
(2½ miles) north-west near B415.
Panoramic views. Ancient
Gasthaus 'Löwen'.

Geroldsecker Waffenschmiede
Old armourer's workshop in
Litschental near Seelbach.
Huge waterwheel.

Burg Dautenstein
Above Seelbach
Another castle ruin.

Ettenheimmünster

Impressive former *Kloster* church.

Ottoschwanden

Church with Romanesque and
Gothic elements.

Tennenbach

Chapel of former Cistercian *Kloster*
and graves from 1812-5 wars of
liberation.

Glottertal

Village Church
Huge mosaic picture of St
Christopher outside and a fine
carved triptych within.

Schwarzwaldklinik
Location of the television series of
the same name.

St Peter

Baroque Church (1717-19)
Another imposing edifice by
architect Peter Thumb.
Organ concerts in summer.

Former Kloster
Magnificant rococo library also by
Peter Thumb.
Conducted tours of whole
complex.

Lindenberg
2km (1¼ miles) from village
Charming pilgrimage church.

Zweribach Waterfalls
7km (4½ miles) north-east of St
Peter via Schmittenbachstrasse
Nature conservation area.
(Also accessible on foot from St
Märgen)

Sägendobel
4km (2½ miles) north on road to
Kandel
Roadside display of models
operated by water power.
Chapel with wood carvings by local
artist.

St Märgen

Rankmühle
1km (½ mile) from village on field
road
Picturesque old water mill.

Klosterkirche (1723)
Baroque pilgrimage church.

House with fruit trees near Welschensteinach

with a sacral choir and there are Romanesque and Gothic elements in the building itself. It is not a long walk to the Bleichtal, through which the road climbs from Kenzingen, and here there is another historic smithy.

In the village of **Tennenbach** — still part of Freiamt — the chapel of a former Cistercian *Kloster* may be inspected together with soldiers' graves from the 1812-5 wars of liberation. Back in the centre, the *Kurhaus* provides for the unsophisticated entertainment of the guest. There is a sauna at the *Hallenbad* and massage facilities are available.

A modern dual carriageway runs from Waldkirch to Freiburg and 7km (4 miles) from Waldkirch is the entrance to the Glottertal. This name not only refers to the valley but also the twin villages of Unter-und Oberglottertal. First though, at the mouth of the valley, is the little town of **Denzlingen**, through which the river Glotterbach flows on its way to the nearby Rhine. The town, with a population of some 9,000, lies in the 'V' formed by the convergence of roads B3 and B294 coming in from the north and is thus spared the worst of the heavy traffic. It does, however, lie on the route of the long-distance path Rhein-Kaiserstuhl-Schwarzwald which starts at Breisach and runs some 114km (70 miles) eastwards to Donaueschingen.

There is an early Gothic church in the town and the waymarks of the named path (red diamond on yellow background) could be followed northwards up to the little wood called Mauracher Hölzle where there is a good view up into the Glottertal. The route then turns east to the Mauracher Hof, a rural inn, and from here the ruins of St Severius (or Severin) Chapel may be visited for an extensive view over the Rhine valley and towards the steeply rising Black Forest hills to the east. The town's indoor and outdoor swimming pools will be found near here. Return to the town centre by any of the quite pleasant streets running downhill.

The Glottertal has no railway but a somewhat infrequent bus service operates from Freiburg. There is significant fruit and wine production here and the sunny, south-facing slopes of the valley are clothed with vineyards. The vines even grow at an altitude of 500m (1,640ft) — higher than anywhere else in Germany and evidence of the sheltered situation on this flank of the Kandel.

There is a splendid timber house in **Unterglottertal** which is the hotel and restaurant 'Engel' (Angel), venison dishes are a speciality on the menu here. In fact, this is only one of several very fine hostelries encountered along this road, most of them in historic buildings.

In **Oberglottertal** there is a heated swimming pool with the usual large and well-kept grassed area around it for sunbathing and games. There is also a new *Hallenbad* at the sports centre, which is available during the months when the *Freibad* is closed, usually about mid-September to mid-May. The exterior of the village church has a large and colourful mosaic depicting St Christopher, the patron saint of travellers, and inside is a fine carved triptych (a carving on three panels with sides able to fold over the centre). Traditional dress is still worn by some of the villagers for going to church on Sundays. Oberglottertal's scattered farmhouses can be seen all around on the slopes of the Kandel and other mountains. As one leaves the village, there are large sawmills serving the forests which crowd into this end of the valley.

Because of its favourable climate, the Glottertal was one of the first areas settled by the Alemannians and it has long been the haunt of the discerning holidaymaker. **Glottertal** is a health resort and it is recorded that as early as 1500, intrepid travellers were coming here to enjoy the healing properties of the Glotterbad. By 1880, about a hundred visitors were coming annually; the local information office now records around 200,000 bed-nights each year. This is the location of the *Schwarzwaldklinik* (Black Forest Clinic) made known to the world through the German television soap opera of that name.

The visiting angler may fish in the river Glotter from April to September. Day tickets are obtainable from the tourist office which also has bicycles for hire. Here, as in most other resorts, the visitor, upon paying the *Kurtaxe*, is provided with a card which entitles him or her to free use of certain amenities in the area, as well as reduced admission charge to swimming pools, museums and so on. Fortunately, the growth of tourism in recent years has not been allowed to spoil this lovely place.

After leaving Glottertal, the road climbs quite steeply to the resort of **St Peter**, which is dominated by the twin towers of the fine baroque church designed, once again, by Peter Thumb. Thumb, who lived from 1681 to 1766, was the most significant member of a family of German master-builders and architects from the Vorarlberg. The church in St Peter must surely be one of the loveliest in the whole Black Forest and, having received a thorough renovation, the interior makes a bright and colourful impression. It is attached to the former *Kloster*, now used as a school for those entering the priesthood.

The *Kloster* was moved to this site in 1091 by Duke Bertold II of Zähringen and was granted many privileges by the rulers. At that time, this area was in the Austrian border region and the *Kloster* suffered a great deal from the various border incidents, with fire and looting being responsible for the loss of many medieval art treasures. The church was the funerary church of the Zähringen dynasty, eight members of which are buried here. The very fine organ is one of those used regularly for the Black Forest cycle of organ recitals which takes place each year.

A guided tour of the church and *Kloster* complex includes a visit to the remarkable rococo-style library which cannot otherwise be seen. It is noted for an interesting ceiling painting by B. Gambs (1751). There is no charge and no gratuities are accepted, but one is invited to make a contribution to charity.

It is the custom in suitable weather, for the congregation to linger before and after Mass, in the square in front of the church where they exchange news and gossip with their friends and relatives. This sometimes provides an opportunity to see the wearing of *Tracht*, the traditional dress; many girls wear the colourful festal costumes to their first communion and on the occasions of other special church services such as those for the ordination of the new priests from the seminary. The outstanding feature of the St Peter *Tracht* is the *Schäppel* or head-dress, with its many coloured glass pearls and silver ornaments which glitter in the sunshine. Many hours of toilsome handwork are required for the construction of these 'crowns' which then become a valued possession. In many places, especially where the blight of

Baroque interior of church in St Peter

St Peter with the twin towers of its church

St Märgen church

The Rankmühle, an old water mill near St Märgen

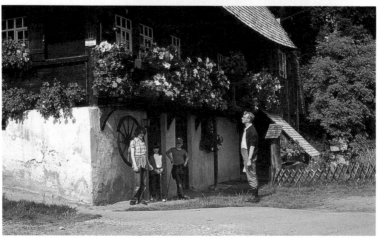

modern tourism is most marked, the wearing of *Tracht*, particularly the head-dress, has virtually died out but this is by no means the case here.

The farmhouses belonging to St Peter are scattered widely over the surrounding slopes and many of them have self-catering flats to let. There are ample facilities in the village including a *Freibad* and a modern *Hallenbad*. Regular folk evenings, slide shows and other entertainments are provided during the summer months. There is also winter activity here, for the surrounding hills are sufficiently high to ensure that there is usually suitable snow for skiing. As well as the open slopes, there are marked paths through the woods for skiers.

Like St Peter, St Märgen depends on the bus service from Freiburg for its public transport. St Märgen is a mere 8km (5 miles) from St Peter and the road continues to climb through a series of bends with wide views over the countryside to the south. There are lay-bys at the most suitable points for viewing or photography. As the twin towers of St Peter disappear behind, those of the former *Klosterkirche* of St Märgen come into view ahead. There are some fine old farmhouses to be seen, the finest being, perhaps, the Luxhof with its own small chapel and a pond constructed to provide a supply of water for fire-fighting. Both of these features are typical of the farms in this area and the little chapels are nearly always beautifully kept and worth a peep inside.

St Märgen is a health resort on a smallish scale and, like all the other resorts in this area, has a wealth of holiday accommodation, largely in private houses or in self-catering flats. As with St Peter, there are no ugly modern developments to offend the eye. The church has been undergoing renovation both inside and out during recent years but is still something of a disappointment after the splendours of St Peter. There is skiing here in winter with a ski shop in the village. Although St Märgen is one of the better-known holiday locations, the newcomer can easily find the peace and beauty which he or she is seeking. An open-air pool and an ingenious children's play area contribute to the popularity of the resort for family holidays.

St Märgen is one of the places in which traditional Black Forest dress may be seen on the days of certain religious celebrations. The *St Märgener Rosstag* or '*Tag des Schwarzwälder Pferde*' (Day of the Black Forest Horse) takes place every third year on the 10 September and

is associated with *Maria Geburt*, the church festival which tradition-
ally celebrates the birth of the Virgin Mary. The ceremonial blessing
of the horses takes place in the morning and in the afternoon, horses,
riders and carriages assemble for a colourful procession with, of
course, musical accompaniment provided by local bands.

St Peter and St Märgen, each with a population of about 2,000, lie
at altitudes of 720m (2,362ft) and 887m (2,910ft) respectively, although the surrounding hills are much higher. There is a lot of dairy-
farming in this area and, in addition to the pinewoods, there are
pleasant upland pastures to vary the scenery. Both places are excellent walking centres. A walk up from St Peter to the peaceful
pilgrimage church on the Lindenberg gives one a salutary reminder
of the horrors of the Nazi regime. Here, on a plaque in the church, one
finds the names of some of the many priests who died in Hitler's
concentration camps or within a few days of their 'release'.

The field path to the Lindenberg passes wayside 'Stations of the
Cross'. Such series of monuments are widespread in one form or
another and the Black Forest is also rich in individual wayside
shrines. These vary from a simple cross erected in memory of a
beloved member of the family to a small chapel with a miniature altar
and perhaps one or two bench seats.

An interesting marked 13km (8 mile) walk (black spot on yellow
ground) leads from St Märgen to the Zweribach waterfalls. Signs to
the Rankmühle are followed from the village and lead to a picturesque old water mill, no longer in use, in less than 1km ($\frac{1}{2}$ mile).
After this, the path climbs steadily through the Rankwald to the
highest point of the walk, where, at a height of 1,029m (3,375ft), there
is the tiny but beautiful Kapfenkapelle, which has an interesting
story. A certain Josef Hummel loved to walk up and enjoy the view
from the Kapfenberg but in 1848 he suffered a stroke and thereafter
could only walk with difficulty, using a stick or a crutch. He vowed
that if God restored him sufficiently for him to go once again to the
mountain unaided, he would have a chapel built there in gratitude.
He was able to do this in 1850 and his chapel stood until 1973, when
it was burned down. Two years later, a local resident had it rebuilt
and this is the lovely wooden building seen today. Josef Hummel's
view is still there as one looks down the valley from the front of the
chapel.

Continuing through the woods, one soon crosses a tiny stream,
the Hirschbach, and turns right to the Geschwanderdobelhütte and

the start of the nature conservation area known as Zweribach. (The hut is occasionally open for refreshments.) Almost hidden in the trees near a small spring is a memorial to freedom fighters of the 1930s. The path follows the edge of the reserve in a north-westerly direction for about 1.5km ($^3/_4$ mile) and then plunges abruptly down into the heart of the reserve towards the waterfalls.

The Zweribach reserve is known as a *Bannwald,* an area which is left entirely to nature without the aid of man to clear fallen trees, maintain paths and so on, the aim being to discover how the landscape will develop without human intervention. For this reason, the paths here are not of the normal standard and great care is needed to negotiate the steep slopes; stout footwear is essential. The main waterfall can be quite spectacular but the visitor is warned against following the example of one local who stepped back to admire it and plunged to his death on the rocks below. The nature-lover will find much of interest in this small area, which is eventually left to follow an alternative route back to St Märgen.

Four kilometres (2$^1/_2$ miles) up the Schmittenbachstrasse north-east of St Peter, there is a parking place known as Potsdamer Platz which makes a good base for a day's ramble, which covers 18km (11 miles) including the summit of the Kandel. Since the starting point is already at about 1,000m (3,280ft), the climb is not too strenuous. About 1km ($^1/_2$ mile) along the surfaced road from the car park, one reaches a farm called Gschwinghof. Here a left fork leads to a field track marked 'Kandel' and identified by the blue diamond on white ground of a *Schwarzwaldverein* connecting route. The track climbs gently, first northerly and then westerly until, about 4km (2$^1/_2$ miles) from Gschwinghof, the main St Peter to Waldkirch road is crossed at a bus stop and small car park called Linie. The woodland path is now parallel to the road and after passing a hut called Schwärhütte at 1,064m (3,490ft), the remaining distance of 2km (1 mile) involves a stiffish climb to the summit viewing platform at 1,243m (4,077ft).

Part of the summit is marked off to protect the rare sub-alpine plants and this area should not be entered. Late summer visitors should look for the remarkable low-growing silver thistle in pasture-land and on sunny banks. The flower is of the everlasting type and is not often found below the 1,000m (3,280ft) line. In any case, it soon disappears, as the local women collect it for winter floral arrangements. In summer the Kandel is ideal for rambling at quite high level through the woods round the summit, and in winter it is a paradise

Woodcarving of preacher in St Märgen

for skiers. Not only are there good walks and good views in every direction, but there is good food here too. As the rest days of the two hotels, the Berghotel Kandel and the Kandelhof, do not coincide, one need never go hungry.

For the return to the starting point, the *Kandelhöhenweg* (white 'K' on red diamond) can be followed from the summit to descend fairly steeply for 5km (3 miles) to the sleepy little village of Sägendobel 760m, (2,493ft) lying just off the main road. The bubbling Glotterbach runs down through the valley to power the small sawmills, and there are two inns. It is worth going into the little chapel, constructed in the basement of the old school house, to admire the beautiful wood carvings made by a local craftsman. After crossing the main road to continue the walk, one ought to stop for a few moments, especially if accompanied by children, to see the little water-driven models which are found on the side of the road further from the village. The clever builder has included a roundabout, men sawing and chopping wood, and even a woman tolling the church bell.

Unless one wishes to follow the 'K' route back into St Peter itself, turn left from the models and walk beside the road towards the Kandel for a short distance. Turn right into a small road marked, somewhat inadequately, by blue and red arrows and a sign to Eckjörghof, a farm which is soon passed on the right. After about 1.5km (³/₄ mile) of fairly stiff climb, one should see a red triangle sign indicating the path back to Potsdamer Platz. Always proceed in a generally easterly direction; a tendency to follow more obvious tracks going north must be resisted as these lead down into the upper part of the Glotterbachtal and would add some 4km (2¹/₂ miles) as well as an unnecessary climb.

Apart from the longish walks described, there is ample opportunity for shorter excursions in an area which has countless small car parks beside the roads or at the edge of the woods. The list of walks exhibited in St Märgen includes this as yet another place from which to ramble to the Hexenlochmühle.

South of St Märgen, the road runs through fairly sparsely populated but beautiful country and soon joins the B500, the so-called *Panoramastrasse*, to Breitnau, a scattered resort in a wide valley beneath the 1,125m (3,692ft) high Rossberg. At several places, laybys allow the motorist to pull off the road to admire the view. With so many variations, it is difficult to say just what constitutes 'typical' Black Forest scenery but this area, with its many traditional farmhouses, lush meadows and forested slopes, must surely approach it.

The farms in the vicinity are noted for their length of ownership by the same family. There is a simple explanation for this; instead of the eldest son inheriting the property, here it is the youngest son who does so and accepts the responsibility of caring for his other brothers and sisters as well as for aged parents. The arrangement is often difficult in practice but it ensures that the properties remain undivided and explains the widely spaced scattering of the farm houses over the landscape.

Each farm has a name, often derived from a name in Christian history. Thus Thomalihof, Barthleshof and Simonshof have fairly obvious origins. Nazihof is not so immediately evident. Needless to say, it has nothing to do with Hitler's ill-famed political party but means, in fact, the farm of Ignatius. There are several farms having this name; one of them is close to the main road at Breitnau while a mile or so further north there is a Nazishäusle (the little house of Ignatius). These great old farmhouses are ideal for farm holidays (*Ferien auf dem Bauernhof*) and many of them have holiday flats or rooms to let.

There are several *Gasthäuser* on the main road, although the village centre of **Breitnau** (population 1,900) lies just to the west of it. One of those south of the village is called 'Zur Ravennaschlucht' and it not only makes a good stop for a drink or a meal but is a place from which to commence a walk to the famous Ravennaschlucht (gorge) itself. There are other hostelries in the village and there is a *W-Parkplatz* right in the centre, a starting place for a number of round walks.

A typical one of 6km (3³/₄ miles) starts in a south-westerly direction (waymark; blue spot) towards the rim of the Höllental (Hell valley). After about 2km (1¹/₄ miles) this track crosses the east-west long-distance path, from Freiburg to Lake Constance, which is marked by a red/white diamond on a yellow ground. Turn east along this latter route for a good 2km (1¹/₄ miles) until it crosses the little river Ravenna, about to plunge down into the lower *Schlucht* (gorge). One can also add about 4km (2¹/₂ miles) for the worthwhile side excursion (waymark; green spot) down into the gorge and back (more about this in Chapter 4). On returning to the original route, continue into the upper gorge, stick with the green spot route going northwards back to the starting point in Breitnau, reached in another 2km (1¹/₄ miles).

The visitor will find many old water mills in this area — several are encountered in the course of the walk just described — but unfortunately most of them are more or less derelict and they are steadily disappearing altogether. In the past, every big farm had its own mill but the internal combustion engine has changed all that. However, funds are available for the restoration of a few mills that are already over 150 years old. Some of these were real works of art and the mill builder was just as important as the miller himself. Water power in the mills was principally used for grinding corn and sawing timber. The message for the visitor is clear; if a water mill is found which is in presentable condition, take the opportunity of examining and photographing it — it may be gone by the next time one passes this way. Breitnau is much concerned with winter activities and has an extensive network of ski-touring routes. Breitnau is under the administration of Hinterzarten, a few kilometres further south, described in the next chapter.

Walking on the Kandel

Return northwards along the B500, and one will come to **Thurner**. Here the road from St Märgen comes in and there is the principal *Langlauf* (cross-country skiing) centre in the area. The Thurnerwirtshaus, at 1,036m (3,398ft), has fifty-five beds, an indoor pool and a sauna but it is closed from 15 November to 15 December. Although this comfortable hotel is eminently suitable for the winter visitor, it is fine at all other seasons too and specially welcomes family holiday-makers in the summer months. There is also a certain amount of more simple accommodation here including some self-catering.

The B500 now continues north-eastwards in the direction of Furtwangen and, in a few kilometres, bypasses the village of Waldau where the valleys Jostal and Langenordnachtal come in from the direction of Neustadt. In another 4km (2¹/₂ miles), take a right turning signed 'Donaueschingen' leading down into the Urachtal and, after a few minutes, notice the remarkably large church in the village of **Urach**. Its red onion tower is a prominent feature on the skyline and there is an unusual barrel vault roof inside, with every panel painted most beautifully. The pulpit is also a splendid creation and the visitor should certainly take the opportunity of stopping to

*Interior of church
with painted, barrel
vault roof, Urach*

inspect this fine church with its surrounding fortified wall.

Continue down the valley to Hammereisenbach where several roads come together. Turn north here to follow the river Breg — a tributary of the Danube — upstream in the direction of Vöhrenbach. The minor road leading into the Linachtal goes off to the left after about 2km (1¹/₄ miles). This is another place for those who want to relax in rural surroundings of great charm and there is a large *Stausee* (man-made lake) with recreational facilities.

Vöhrenbach is an *Erholungsort* of about 3,900 inhabitants. It was founded in 1244 and is now an important centre for the production of Black Forest clocks. There is a Gothic Madonna in the thirteenth-century church which should be seen. One of the more gruesome tales of medieval witch-hunting is commemorated in the 'Zur-Sieben-Frauen-Kapelle' where there is a picture showing the burning of seven young women. They had protested their innocence but, as witches, they were sentenced to death on a funeral pyre. All seven uttered curses which were later fulfilled. The youngest threw a bunch of seven keys to the ground and prophesied that as a sign of her innocence a spring would burst forth at the spot. This did, in fact, happen and even today many people visit the spring with its reputedly healing water.

A road runs westwards from Vöhrenbach to Furtwangen (visited earlier in this chapter) but the route to be followed now turns towards the north-west and reaches the *Luftkurort* and winter sports centre of **Unterkirnach** after about 8km (5 miles). For a small place, there is a lot of accommodation and there is the *Gartenhallenbad*, an all-weather pool with solarium. Unterkirnach is the mid-point on a walk from Villingen to be described a little later. However, do not turn towards that city at this stage but continue for another 8-10km (5-6 miles) in the same direction to **Königsfeld**, a health resort of 5,400 inhabitants.

The famous doctor and organist Albert Schweitzer had a house in Königsfeld from 1923 until 1957. In a letter written from Lambarene, in March 1965, he declared 'I think back to Königsfeld so often. There I could walk in the woods, had friends and those friends still think of me.' Not surprisingly, a huge medical complex here is known as the Albert-Schweitzer-Klinik. This, like other public buildings such as the new high school and the *Haus des Kurgastes* (the social centre for visitors) has been designed to blend harmoniously with the countryside.

The town is comparatively new; it only started in 1806 as a settlement for the Brüdergemeine Herrnhut, a religious fraternity from Saxony. Permission had earlier been obtained from the lord of the land, one Friedrich based in Stuttgart, with the proviso that the place should be named Friedrichsfeld. However, through the political manipulations of Napoleon, Friedrich was made a king (*König*) soon afterwards and the order went out that the name was to be changed to Königsfeld. The brothers were at first rather put out that the new king should play fast and loose with the name of their community but soon came up with the solution that the name should be interpreted as meaning *'our* King's field' — in other words, named after their heavenly king.

They quickly built essential accommodation for their life in this new area and this was followed by the ecclesiastical buildings. The first house outside the religious community was built in 1807 as an inn for those visiting the brothers and is now an hotel called Herrn-huter Haus. Many years were to pass before it was realised that the gentle surrounding countryside would be ideal for people able to take only modest exercise for health reasons and thus a very pleasant health resort came into being. Now there is a good range of hotel and pension accommodation and a modest selection of visitor facilities although it appears that most of the guests are those coming for health reasons.

The Baar

Where the spectacular hills and valleys of the central Black Forest give way to a more gentle upland, is the area known as *die Baar*, a land of broad horizons lying at an altitude of between 700 and 800m (2,300 and 2,625ft). This has been regarded as fine arable land for centuries and the grain grown here found ready markets in Switzerland and Italy. Evidence of this international trade is to be found in Löffingen where the Mailänder Tor (the Milan gate) still stands. The Baar has no geographical boundaries laid down but Löffingen, Donaueschin-gen, Villingen-Schwenningen and Geisingen, for example, are all within it.

The landscape does not make the same immediate impact on the senses as do the mountains and valleys of most of the Black Forest. Nevertheless, the visitor is soon likely to consider it an area of considerable charm and there is certainly no lack of accommodation and facilities in general for his or her benefit. The bigger centres already mentioned and many of the smaller towns and villages are of considerable interest; they are all the more pleasant for being a little aside from the more popular tourist routes.

Villingen is 13km (8 miles) due south of Königsfeld and is the more historic twin town which united with Schwenningen in 1972 to form a city with a combined population of about 80,000. Villingen was one of the towns founded by Duke Bertold III of Zähringen (see Chapter 4). Much of the original encircling wall and most of the gate towers are still in existence. The old town centre is one of the best preserved in Germany, thanks largely to the stoutness of the wall which withstood attacks during the peasant revolt in 1525 and, 100 years later, the onslaughts of the Swedes allied with the forces of Württemberg. Bombardments by the French under Marshalls Villars and Tallard in 1703-4 also failed to breach the defences.

Riettor, Villingen

The present Liebfrauenmünster was built to replace the earlier building which was destroyed by fire in 1721. Some parts of the old are incorporated and some of the original furnishings survived, notably the stone pulpit (around 1500-10) with its fine sculptured decoration and the fourteenth-century Nägelein crucifix on the altar of the Cross. The Romanesque double portal on the south side should not be overlooked. The late-Gothic *altes Rathaus*, with its Renaissance extension, houses a museum with exhibits on early and prehistory, applied arts, sculpture and painting.

 The Franziskaner-Museum has collections on folklore and finds from the Celtic period with a special section on the dating of archaeological finds. The *Heimatmuseum* concentrates on the development of clock- and watch-making over the past 400 years and has a collection of some 1,500 timepieces. The former Franciscan monastery, founded in 1268, is worth seeing with its church, cloisters and

Romanesque minster portal, Villingen

chapel — there are concerts in the cloisters during the summer months. Villingen is famed for its *Fasnet* celebrations and large crowds assemble to see the parades of the 'fools' in their historic costumes and grotesque wooden masks, some of which may be seen at other times in the museums.

Schwenningen was previously a farming community but has now developed into a modern industrial town in which clock-making is an important activity. Indeed, the Kienzle factory is one of the biggest clock-making centres in Germany and the firm's museum has a valuable collection of timepieces. The former Benedictine monastery, which has an eighteenth-century church and buildings, is worth inspecting.

The prospective visitor should not fear the industrial aspect of these twin towns. There is ample open space and about half the total area is taken up by parks, gardens and woods. There are indoor and outdoor swimming pools and a golf course. Plenty of accommodation is available in and around the towns and the area is a good one for farm holidays. There is also a youth hostel and many restaurants which are noted for the variety of local dishes on offer. At the nearby Schwenninger Moos, a favourite goal for ramblers, is the source of the river Neckar which flows northwards out of the forest on its way to Heidelberg and the Rhine. Other modest excursions are to the Lorettokapelle (1705) and to the Magdalenenbergle, a little hill where graves from the Hallstatt period have been found.

The valley of the Brigach may be followed for a splendid walk to St Georgen, about 16km (10 miles) upstream. Another valley walk is westwards through the Kirnachtal. The route follows the road towards Furtwangen at first but when this turns south-east at Unterkirnach, go straight ahead following the river and a minor road to Oberkirnach. It is worth making the modest ascent of the Kesselberg 1,000m (3,280ft) for a lovely view back down the valley. The distance from Villingen to Oberkirnach is about 11km (7 miles).

An easy walk of 16km (10 miles) in the other direction takes one to Bad Dürrheim. The *Ostweg*, Pforzheim to Schaffhausen (black/red diamond on white ground) passes through Villingen and east of the town centre it crosses the railway and the B33. Identify and follow this long-distance path. East of the railway, turn south and for a short distance share the route with the Baden-Württemberg cycleway. The cycle route continues eastwards and the walker turns to the left to go roughly north through woodland for about 450m (492yd), passing near the *Aussichtsturm* (look out tower) at the Wannenhohe.

Turn east here through open country and, after less than 2km (1 mile), enter woods on the outskirts of Schwenningen. Notice the especially fine trees in the open country and in the woods where there is a *Waldlehrpfad* and a *Wildgehege*. Follow the waymarks as the route turns south and as it curves in an anti-clockwise direction round he town and across the railway into the *Naturschutzgebiet* (nature conservation area) of the Schwenninger Moos. Here the source of the river Neckar may be visited. The path then crosses the B27 after which, in about 250m (270yd), fork right into a path leading directly to the centre of Bad Dürrheim.

For the return, pick up a walking route near the church in the main street and follow it westwards, at first through little streets, until it passes over the B27 (a dual carriageway here) and turns right to cross the B33. Then turn left, roughly parallel with the main road and, after 1.5km (1 mile), cross the railway and enter a small wood. On emerging from the wood, cross the Zollhäusleweg—which is the cycleway — and walk due north and dead straight for exactly 1km

($^1/_2$ mile). Then make a right-angle turn to the left (west) and after another 1km ($^1/_2$ mile) rejoin the outward route for return to Villingen station or town. The motorist can, of course, travel direct between the two places along the B33.

All the usual amenities of a holiday and health resort are at hand in **Bad Dürrheim** which suffers the cumbersome designation *Sole-Heilbad und Heilklimatischer Kurort*, reflecting its possession of the only saline baths in the Black Forest with a salt content of up to 6%. The visitor should visit the 'Narrenschopf' museum which is housed in an old mushroom-shaped salt store. All the different forms of Alemannic and Swabian carnival lore are displayed here.

The B27 between Bad Dürrheim and Donaueschingen is a fast dual carriageway so this is a journey of no more than a few minutes. **Donaueschingen** is a pleasant town of around 18,000 inhabitants, lying on the *Grüne Strasse* (green road) which runs from Breisach on the Rhine to Lake Constance. This is where the rivers Breg and Brigach unite to form the Donau (Danube). The twin-towered parish church of John the Baptist and St John was built between 1724-47 and has an imposing façade as well as a richly decorated interior. The style is Bohemian baroque; the only surviving example of this in the whole of Germany. The most significant relic here is a Madonna dating from around 1525.

The straightforward baroque layout of the *Schloss*, built about 1723, was drastically altered by rebuilding at the end of the nineteenth century and lost most of its architectural significance because of this. In the courtyard one finds the so-called *Donauquelle* (Danube spring) with an allegorical group of figures in marble by A. Weinbrenner. However, it is in the interior of the *Schloss* and the nearby Karlsbau that one finds a splendid collection of works of art from the Renaissance and baroque periods. The gallery of paintings has many old German masters, including works by Holbein the Elder and Matthias Grünewald. The court library, where the poet Joseph Victor von Scheffel was librarian from 1857 to 1859, houses a fine collection of valuable books.

The Romans came to this area as early as 15BC when the Emperor Tiberius set up a fortress at nearby Hüfingen where he thought he had discovered the source of the Danube. Three centuries later, the Alemannic tribes started to drive the Romans out, but it was not until AD889 that the settlement in the middle of the Baar is recorded with a name — *Esginga* — the forerunner of Donaueschingen.

Places of Interest In The Baar

Villingen
Towers and walls
Well-preserved medieval fortifications.

Liebfrauenmünster
(eighteenth-century)
Gracious church replacing former building destroyed in 1721.
Fourteenth-century crucifix.

Altes Rathaus
Late-Gothic and Renaissance building now housing museum.

Franziskaner Museum
Folklore and finds from Celtic period.

Heimatmuseum
Clock- and watch-making history.

Schwenningen
Former Benedictine Monastery
Interesting complex includes eighteenth-century church.

Schwenninger Moos
2.5km (1½ miles) to the south
Source of river Neckar.

Bad Dürrheim
Sole-Heilbad
Only saline baths in Black Forest.

Narrenschopf Museum
Display of Alemannic and Swabian carnival artefacts.

Donaueschingen
Church of John the Baptist and St John (1724-47)
Richly decorated church in Bohemian baroque.

Schloss (1723)
Baroque with later rebuilding. Situated in splendid parkland.

Donauquelle
At the Schloss
Traditional source of the Danube.

Karlsbau
Art gallery with large Renaissance and baroque collection.

Entenburg (1471)
At Pforen, 5km (3 miles) to the south-east. Moated castle with four round corner towers.

Hüfingen
Well-preserved medieval town centre with fourteenth-century fortified tower.

Roman bath

Parish Church
Enlarged in 1553, restored in 1910.

St Leonhard's Kapelle (1476)

Stadtwald
Fine woodland noted for orchids.

Bräunlingen
Mühlentor
One of the original Gothic town gates.

St Remigius-Kapelle
Known as the mother church of the Baar.

Löffingen
Mailänder Tor
Attractive old town gate.

Rathaus
The former Kornhaus
(corn exchange).

Heimatmuseum
Includes finds from Alemannic burial place.

Witterschneekreuz
1km (½ mile) north-west
Pilgrimage church (1894-7) with wooden chapel (1846-7).

Wildpark
2km (1 mile) north-west
Spacious family leisure centre.

Former Benedictine Nunnery
(founded in 1125)
At Friedenweiler, 8km (5 miles) to the north-west
Incorporates splendid church (1725-31) by Peter Thumb.

Donaueschingen Schloss

*Traditional source
of the Danube,
Donaueschingen*

155

It has long been a town which supported culture and the arts, mainly due to the earlier influence of the princes of Fürstenberg for whom the *Schloss* was built. Mozart, Liszt and Kreutzer were among the notable musicians called upon to appear at the court. Today, the autumn music festival called the Donaueschinger Musiktage attracts lovers and performers of contemporary music from all over the world.

Every September another great international event brings visitors in their thousands for a feast of riding, coach-driving, dressage and so on. Seven hundred or more horses from all over Europe congregate in the Schlosspark which provides a splendid setting for the various events. Five kilometres (3 miles) south-east of the town, at **Pfohren**, stands the moated, cube-shaped castle of Entenburg with four massive round corner towers. It was built by the Counts of Fürstenberg in 1471.

The little town of **Hüfingen** (population 6,000) lies about 3km (2 miles) to the south and has a well-preserved medieval centre. Historically, it was a place of residence of the Fürstenberg and Schellenberg dynasties. There is quite a lot to see here, including the old Roman bath and a fortified tower from the fourteenth century. The parish church was enlarged in 1553 and thoroughly restored in 1910. St Leonhard's Kapelle (1476) is also worth a little of the visitor's time. The *Stadtwald* (town forest) is of particular interest and is sometimes called the orchid paradise because of the number and variety of the plants which grow there.

Another floral event is on Fronleichnamstag (Corpus Christi), the Thursday after Trinity Sunday, when the main street of the town is covered with a carpet of flowers. The citizens also collect millions of wild flowers and use them to create clever ornamental designs and religious motifs in front of their houses to adorn the route of the traditional procession. The custom originated about 150 years ago when a local sculptor, Franz Xaver Reich, brought the idea back from a journey he made to Italy.

Bräunlingen, just 3km (2 miles) to the west, is another historic little town. Like Hüfingen, its history goes back to a Roman settlement on the site. However, it shares with Villingen — and several other towns in the area — a more 'modern' history which is associated with the activities of the Dukes of Zähringen in the twelfth century. One of the original Gothic town gates, the Mühlentor, still stands as a reminder of that period. There are a number of carefully restored medieval houses in the old town centre.

St Remigius-Kapelle is the parish church and is known as the mother church of the Baar. It is well-worth seeing and has a fine late-Gothic carved altar. Bräunlingen is a good centre for less strenuous walking and there is a pleasant excursion westwards along the stream called Brändbach to the Kirnbergsee, about 6km (4 miles) from the town. The stream has been dammed to create this charming little lake with its camp site and bathing place. (There is a car parking charge.)

The *Grüne Strasse* (B31) runs westwards from Hüfingen and, after 5km (3 miles), passes through Döggingen where there is a *W-Parkplatz* which is a good starting place for the descent into the Wutachschlucht. This is a remarkable gorge but something for a later chapter. **Löffingen** is reached in 12km (7$^1/_2$ miles) and is one of the Baar towns the visitor should certainly endeavour to visit. It is an old market town and in earlier years was much involved in the grain trade. Indeed, the old *Kornhaus* is now the *Rathaus* and is a building well-worth seeing. The *Heimatmuseum* has a varied collection which includes finds from an old Alemannic burial place.

If one follows the signs 'Wildpark' from the town centre, the unusual pilgrimage church known as Witterschneekreuz soon comes into view. The story begins in the winter of 1740. A traveller reached the hill then known as Witarsne in a snowstorm and did not know which way to turn. He prayed for Divine guidance, soon heard the church bells of Löffingen and a wood-cutter came by and took him into the town. As a sign of gratitude, he had a cross erected at the spot where he heard the bells and, as the story spread, the local people made it a place of pilgrimage.

A little chapel was erected in 1792 and in 1846-7 this was replaced by the present 'old' wooden chapel. The years from 1894-7 saw the construction of the present pilgrimage church in neo-Romanesque style under the direction of the town priest, Stephan Wehrle. The old chapel has been kept and renovated to contain the many votive tablets and pictures which have accumulated over the years. The 'new' church has numerous items of beauty and interest.

The heated *Freibad* is passed a little further on, before one reaches the extensive *Wildpark* with its enclosures for bears, wolves, wild boar, deer and other creatures. This is a good place for families, with many amusements for the children and a summer *bob-bahn*. There is a wide range of accommodation in Löffingen and its satellite villages

*Witterschneekreuz
pilgrimage church
with its
painted ceiling,
Löffingen*

Friedenweiler

as well as every facility for activity holidays including tennis courts, riding stables, a *Hallenbad* and heated *Freibäder*. There is also ample scope for skiing in the winter. A road running north-west from Löffingen leads, in about 8km (5 miles), to Friedenweiler. Mid-way between the two is the attractive village of **Rötenbach**, another access point to the Wutachschlucht.

Friedenweiler is a Kneippkurort where, once again, the *Kur* treatments are in accordance with the principles of Sebastian Kneipp. The small, heated *Freibad* adjoins a lake with boats for hire and one may swim there too, if desired. Here, in the pretty Kloster-bachtal, provision is also made for winter sports. The former Bene-dictine nunnery founded in 1125 is worth seeing, together with its church which was built between 1725 and 1731 by the renowned Peter Thumb. Friedenweiler is a quiet and dignified resort yet it is within very easy reach of more sophisticated centres such as Titisee or Donaueschingen. The western part of the B31 in the direction of Freiburg will be explored in the next chapter.

4

FREIBURG AND THE HELL VALLEY

Freiburg, the Black Forest capital, is a busy city today with some 180,000 inhabitants but it does not have a particularly long history. Duke Bertold III of Zähringen had been held prisoner in Cologne; he got to know that old Roman city well and was much impressed by its prosperity, which was based largely on international trade. He realised that his own part of Europe was backward in terms of commerce and, after his release in 1118, he called for the establishment of a brand new trading city to take advantage of the growing cross-border traffic. He invited businessmen and workers from Cologne to assist him in the project. The Bertolds had come west from Swabia in the tenth century and established a family seat in a castle above the village of Zähringen, now a northern suburb of Freiburg, whose name they adopted as the family title. They were ambitious and despite the fact that they were by no means big landowners, they became one of the most powerful families in this part of Europe before the line died out in 1218.

Bertold III chose a level, 'green fields' area between the Black Forest mountains and the Rhine where he started the building of his new market town from scratch, complete with its imposing minster. It was walled, of course, and the streets were laid out with geometrical precision. The settlement was christened Freiburg, the word *frei* (free) having subtle political connotations. Each new settler was given exactly the same start; a plot of land measuring 50ft by 100ft (16.2 x 32.4m) to build his house and establish his business on. Most of the plots filled the distance between two of the narrow streets and the living quarters were built at the sunny end with the workshops, etc at the shady end.

The minster was built diagonally across its square in order to maintain the tradition of having the high altar at the east end. Only two years after Bertold's first call for support, the town had become a reality and was granted all the appropriate rights to regularise its existence. With the successful founding of his completely new town, Bertold then looked for similar opportunities elsewhere and, in the Black Forest area, he was responsible for Offenburg, across the Rhine from Strasbourg, and for Villingen and Rottweil on the eastern side. Another Freiburg (Fribourg) was established in Switzerland and he was also the founder of Bern, now the Swiss capital.

Freiburg is the cultural and economic centre of the southern part of the Forest and, like other German towns, it always seems to have much more importance as a transport and business centre than a town of similar size in England would. It is a calling point for inter-city trains on the main route to Basel, and also an interchange station for a number of branch lines, in particular that running to the east, serving many important towns and eventually reaching Munich.

The city of Freiburg has a considerable tramway network and is the terminus for a number of bus routes which serve outlying areas not reached by the railway. Some of the main shopping streets are pedestrian zones, although in several cases the tramcars still pass through them. The attractive open channels which carry streams through some of the streets are the remnants of a sewage system from the thirteenth century but now, needless to say, the water is sparkling and clean. One cannot claim to be a genuine Freiburger unless one has at some time inadvertently stepped into one of these channels! There are many cafés and other eating places, some with tables on the pavement, and a number of attractive high-class stores, especially in the Kaiser-Josef-Strasse, with its cool arcades.

Freiburg is dominated by the 116m (381ft) high tower of the minster. The filigree-like spire which surmounts the more solid tower is an architectural marvel and one can only wonder at the skill of the artisans who created this masterpiece in the year 1330. The Freiburg minster is the only German cathedral which achieved its final form in the Middle Ages, the year of completion being recorded as 1513. As in many old cathedrals, there is nearly always work going on, with scaffolding erected and sections closed off. There will be some excitement when all the work of restoration and cleaning is finished and the whole building is revealed in all its glory. As it is, there is much to be seen and wondered at, whether it be the sun or

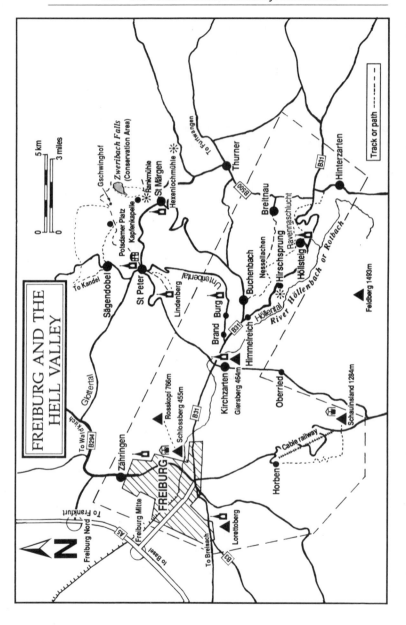

FREIBURG AND THE HELL VALLEY

moon shining through the lacy stonework of the tower, the view from the tower watchman's room or that from the belfry itself. Be warned, however, that Germany's oldest bell, the 5-ton 'Hosanna', cast in 1258, has been sounding loud and clear over the countryside for more than 700 years and its thunderous peal will not be halted because tourists are present.

There are some rather fine medieval towers and several other old buildings, all of which have been lovingly restored since the grievous bombing inflicted on the city in 1944, when the greater part of the old town was destroyed. Thanks to the existence of detailed plans and photographs, the restoration work here, as in many other German towns, has made it possible to reproduce the architecture of earlier centuries in every minute detail. The university, founded in 1457, is one of the oldest in Germany, and has 18,000 students. Other educational establishments include the State High School for Music. Two principal museums, a fine theatre and numerous churches ensure that there is plenty for the visitor to see and do in the city.

The Augustinermuseum contains not only the town collection of paintings, tapestries and folk art but also the Diocesan Museum of objects of sacred art. There is a separate ethnological department in the Adelshauser Kloster. The study of nature in its several forms is the speciality of the Museum für Naturkunde. The Protestant Ludwigskirche is a good example of modern church architecture and was built on a new site to replace the older church of the same name destroyed in World War II. The modern synagogue stands in the city centre and was built a few years ago to replace the former Jewish place of worship which was destroyed during the Nazi regime.

The forested hills extend into the city limits, which also enclose a considerable acreage of vineyards. In an easy half-hour walk from the city streets, one can reach the excellent vantage point of the Schlossberg 455m (1,492ft) for wonderful views over the city and countryside and then wander on to the Rosskopf which, at 766m (2,513ft), is the highest point in the immediate vicinity. The Friedrichsturm there is a 100-year-old observation tower which provides extensive vistas in every direction. The Schlossberg can also be reached without effort in a few minutes by means of the *Gondelbahn*, the small cabin cable cars which carry one up swiftly from the town.

The Schauinsland 1,284m (4,215ft) is the mountain which the Freiburgers regard as their own. The summit area can be reached readily by road or by cable car from the lower terminus of the *Schauinslandbahn* at 490m (1,608ft) near Horben in the Günterstal, Horben being served by tram from the city. Literally translated, Schauinsland means 'look into the countryside' and one can certainly do that admirably from the top. However, the name is comparatively new; earlier the mountain was called Erzkasten, Erz meaning ore and Kasten meaning coffer. It was rightly regarded as Freiburg's treasure chest in the days when silver was mined there, an industry which was at its peak in the fourteenth and fifteenth centuries. The remains of entrances to the underground workings are still to be found here and there. There is a window in the Freiburg minster depicting scenes of the mining activity which was of considerable financial advantage to the minster itself.

The Schauinsland can be included in a day's ramble from the city, in the course of which one should also see the Lorettokapelle, which dates from 1657. It actually consists of three small chapels under one roof; the centre one was erected to commemorate the freeing of the city from the armies of France following a fierce battle in 1644 in which the Bavarian Field Marshal, Mercy, used the strategically important Lorettoberg to the disadvantage of the French. There was much interest at the time in the pilgrimage chapel Loreto at Ancona in Italy and it was resolved to make the new chapel in Freiburg an exact replica of this. It is the centre chapel seen today, the two smaller side chapels were added at a later date. It was presumably only after construction of the chapel that the hill became known as the Lorettoberg, from which, incidentally, the sandstone for building the minster was quarried.

In winter there are excellent skiing facilities on the Schauinsland and some of the numerous ski-lifts are floodlit. There are countless rambling opportunities in summer and even if one has not walked all the way up from Freiburg, an enjoyable stroll can be made round the summit area, starting either from the upper cable car station at 1,200m (3,940ft) or from one of the many car parks. The cable railway has been in continuous operation since it was built in 1930. There is an observation tower at the summit which raises the vantage point to 1,302m (4,267ft) — this is included in the route of many of the marked walks.

One of these, covering $9^1/_2$km (6 miles), starts from the upper cable car station and climbs to the summit, returning by a parallel path to the saddle near the station, this section will take about 1 hour.

The path leads along the edge of and then through the woods before heading west to the *Gasthof* at Giesshübel at 1,071m (3,513ft). Turning north with several good viewpoints on the left, there then follows a steep zig-zag descent through Kaltwasser to the Lehhof and on to a junction of several paths and a good all-round vantage point at Eduardshöhe. Here there is a choice of routes, but the shortest goes almost directly north, passes the inn at Buckhof in about 1.5km (1 mile) and in about the same distance again, about 200m (220yd) before the church, reaches a turning to the right. This leads back to the lower cable car station, the descent from the upper station having taken about 2$^1/_2$ hours.

There is a registered health resort known as Schauinsland, officially an outlying suburb of Oberried in the Bruggatal. This includes the summit of the mountain and there are quite a number of hotels scattered about the area as well as a ski-school and the usual supporting facilities.

At around 1,000m (3,280ft) on the south-east slopes of the Schauinsland, at Hofsgrund, is an old farmhouse called Schniederlihof, which was occupied by Walfried Lorenz until his death in 1966. Five years later, the nearly 400-year old building was acquired by the local authority with the object of preserving this rare example of a typical house of the period. The building was set in order and fitted out to form a small museum showing the rural life of the area, including the mining activity already mentioned. A brief visit will certainly open the visitor's eyes to the interesting history of the Schauinsland area.

Leaving Freiburg in an easterly direction along the B31 road — the so-called *Grüne Strasse* (green road) — the suburbs are soon left behind and one is heading for the Höllental (Hell valley). This is a busy road and it is infinitely more pleasurable to make the journey by train, stopping off here and there for exploration. **Kirchzarten**, aside from the main road, is a bustling little town, a useful and reasonable shopping centre for the self-caterer. There is a good choice of inns and restaurants and the information centre will gladly provide details of a wide range of attractions and activities in the vicinity.

The parish church is a late-Gothic building (1508-10) with some Romanesque influence; it is dedicated to St Gallus and has Renaissance and baroque furnishings, etc. It has, among other things, a rather fine coloured triptych. Of interest in the town are the Talvogtei

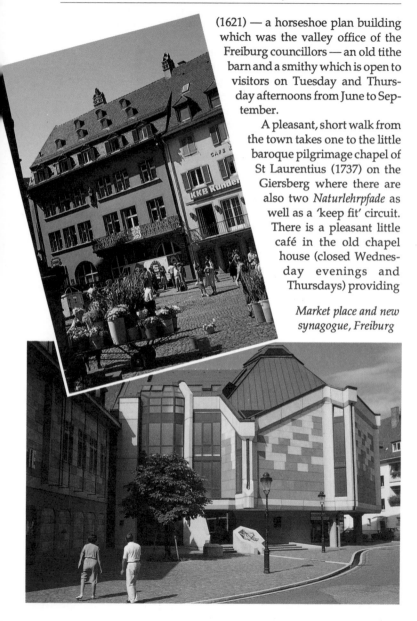

(1621) — a horseshoe plan building which was the valley office of the Freiburg councillors — an old tithe barn and a smithy which is open to visitors on Tuesday and Thursday afternoons from June to September.

A pleasant, short walk from the town takes one to the little baroque pilgrimage chapel of St Laurentius (1737) on the Giersberg where there are also two *Naturlehrpfade* as well as a 'keep fit' circuit. There is a pleasant little café in the old chapel house (closed Wednesday evenings and Thursdays) providing

Market place and new synagogue, Freiburg

Cable car on the Schauinsland

an opportunity for rest and refreshment.

Kirchzarten's heated, open-air pool is called the *Schwimmbad* and is, in fact, a complex of four separate pools catering for every taste and degree of proficiency. There is the usual extensive sunbathing area, children's play park and so on. The adjoining well-appointed camp site has 500 pitches for caravans or tents. It is one of those used by the Eurocamp organisation and is popular with British and Dutch campers. Kirchzarten is a useful base for the traveller by train who does not wish to stay in Freiburg but wishes to have easy access to both the city and the countryside to the east. It is also a good base for the motorist wishing to explore the Feldberg and other mountains lying to the south-east of Freiburg.

Back on the main road beyond Kirchzarten, one comes almost immediately to a left turning signposted to Burg and Unteribental. About 2km (1¹/₄ miles) along this road is the beautiful, modern *Vaterunserkapelle* (Lord's Prayer Chapel) in which the Lord's Prayer is written as a frieze right round the inside of the circular building. Items of interest in this little church include a handmade copy of an ancient book of music in plainsong with text in Latin.

About 1km ($^1/_2$ mile) further on, at the village of Unteribental, a woodland nature trail passes close to the *Rathaus* where information is available. Incidentally, *Lehrpfad or Naturlehrpfad* is a nature trail and *Waldlehrpfad*, as in this case, is one which is concerned with trees in particular. Another type of trail which is found in many places and especially near holiday centres is the *Trimm Dich* (keep fit) path. This is laid out in the woods with a series of sixteen or twenty stations, at each of which there is simple equipment and a pictorial sign indicating the exercises which should be undertaken there. The signs are then followed to the next station, walking or jogging as instructed.

Returning to road B31, one soon passes a *Gasthaus* called Himmelreich (Kingdom of Heaven). Behind this is the railway station of the same name, a name which is surprising, since one is now on the threshold of Hell valley — the Höllental. The origin of the name Höllental is not clear, but it is probably related to the history of disasters which befell travellers passing this way in earlier times. If they managed to survive sudden rock falls and unexpected flash floods of the little river Rotbach, also called Höllenbach, they were likely to be attacked by brigands lurking in the crags above the road.

Only in 1770 was a passable track made through the narrow ravine which was the route of the little river. The 'road' was provided to facilitate the journey of Marie-Antoinette from her Austrian homeland to Paris for her marriage to Louis XVI. Today's motorist may have his own ideas about the name of the valley after he has negotiated it. In fact, no surfaced road was built through the valley until 1857 and the railway did not follow until 30 years later.

Robert Gerwig, who had built the *Schwarzwaldbahn* described in Chapter 2, was also the engineer responsible for the *Höllentalbahn*, the first section of which, between Freiburg and Neustadt, was opened in 1887. The line was extended to Donaueschingen in 1901. In avoiding the huge curves of the *Schwarzwaldbahn*, it was necessary to accept a maximum gradient of 55% between Höllsteig and Hinterzarten necessitating, until 1938, expensive cog-wheel operation. The costs were defrayed by imposing on passengers a special *Bergzuschlag* (mountain supplement). The line between Freiburg and Neustadt was electrified in 1939 using single phase AC current at 50Hz, 20,000 volts — the first railway use of the so-called industrial frequency in Germany. However, in 1960 the supply was converted to 16,000 volts DC to conform with the rest of the West German railway network.

After Himmelreich, the valley quickly narrows until there is barely space for the river and road, while the railway is squeezed up on to the northern slope and has to dive in and out of short tunnels to pass the steep cliffs. Above are the ruins of the Falkenstein, hideout of the robber knights in earlier times, while one of the many summit crosses to be found throughout the Black Forest can also be seen here.

The busy, winding road must be negotiated with care but in one place the near-vertical walls have left sufficient space for a small car park on the roadside where one must park diagonally. It is worth getting out for a few moments to view the bronze stag which stands proudly on a rock high above the road. This is the Hirschsprung (Stag's Leap) and the story tells of a fine stag pursued by huntsmen, which made a spectacular leap from one side of the valley to the other in order to escape. There is a footpath from the car park through a tunnel and then along the river, partly on wooden walkways, until a wider part of the valley is reached near Hirschsprung station, some 600m (657yd) further on. Unfortunately, it is impossible to reach the actual position of the bronze stag easily from either direction and the climbing of the steep cliffs is prohibited.

Despite the widening of the valley, the railway continues to twist and turn, sometimes in a tunnel or on a viaduct, in order to climb 450m (1,476ft) before reaching Hinterzarten, less than 30km (18¹/₂ miles) from Freiburg. The longest viaduct is that over the Ravennaschlucht (Ravenna gorge); 40m (131ft) high and 224m (735ft) long, it was built in its present form with south Black Forest granite in 1926. The railway traveller has no more than a fleeting glimpse of the gorge but the motorist can turn aside at Höllsteig on to the old road.

Near the junction is the St Oswalds-Kapelle, a little chapel built in 1148; there are frescos inside dating from the fourteenth to sixteenth centuries. To view the interior, obtain a key from the Hofgut (Gasthaus) Sternen. Park on the old road and enjoy a pleasant walk through this picturesque ravine. The path makes its steep way up beside the little river, sometimes on walkways or over bridges until, after climbing a steep wooden stairway, the great Ravenna waterfall is reached. One can go further on to the small waterfall and to the Grossjockenmühle (1883), an old Black Forest water mill which, although disused, is still in good order.

Incidentally, the Gasthaus 'Sternen' is an old coaching inn — as was Gasthaus Himmelreich — which provided for the frequent changes of horses necessary to negotiate this steepest part of the

Kirchzarten

*St Laurentius'
chapel,
Kirchzarten*

An early music book in the Lord's Prayer chapel, Unteribental

House and wayside shrine, Unteribental

valley in the days before motorised transport. Marie Antoinette is said to have stopped at the 'Sternen' on her fateful journey in 1770 and Goethe was certainly a guest here in 1779. The present modern 'Sternen' building was only completed in the mid-1980s and is at least the third hostelry of the same name. The previous one, built in 1859, still stands and provides additional accommodation.

In order to continue up the valley, one returns to the modernised main road, but before doing so, a visit to the nearby glass-blowing works and shop may provide an interesting gift or souvenir. It was a marvellous engineering achievement to lift the B31 road out of the Höllental to the comparatively level upland where Hinterzarten lies. While low gears will be much in use, the modern motorist is unlikely to endure the agonies of earlier travellers faced with the gradients and twists of the old road, which may be appreciated by going to the end of that road past the 'Sternen'.

With an indigenous population of only 2,200, **Hinterzarten** caters for many times this number in the course of a year. It is not only a health resort but also a winter sports centre which has developed in a quite pleasing way over the years, with several first-class hotels and a great variety of more modest accommodation. Hinterzarten is justifiably proud of its gastronomy and two of the hotels are often recommended in this respect. The 'Park-Hotel Adler' has been in the ownership of the same family since 1446 while the 'Weisse Rössle' is referred to in records as far back as 1347. There is a *Hallenbad* in the 'Adler' which, upon payment, is available to non-residents. The Kur-Zentrum makes provision for the visitor with pleasant reading rooms, a television room, games rooms, restaurant and a cinema/concert hall.

The modern Catholic church has been skilfully grafted on to the onion-domed tower of an earlier building. There is a Pietà from the school of Tilman Riemenschneider (1440-1531), the master-carver of the Middle Ages. This is an unusual find in this area for most of Riemenschneider's work is to be found far away in Würzburg and the Tauber valley. In its turn, the Protestant congregation has also built a modern church of unusual design. There is a signboard in the centre of the village giving directions for a vast selection of walks. Few resorts can have more walks available and it is, therefore, particularly well-suited to the visitor who has arrived by train.

The fit walker can obtain what is almost a bird's eye view of the Höllental by walking along the ridge on the north side. The 14km (9 mile) walk starts at Himmelreich station, where there is space for parking. Leaving the station, one goes north for about 250m (280yd) to the road eastwards to Buchenbach. The path, whose sign is a red and white diamond on a yellow ground, runs beside the road for 1.5km (1 mile), and then leads into the Pfaffendobelweg just opposite the church in Buchenbach which, incidentally, is worth a brief visit. The little road is followed until after the last of the houses. Soon after passing an attractive *Waldspielplatz* (playground), leave the road and take a footpath on the right to climb fairly steeply to the Pfaffeneck 748m (2,454ft), where several paths meet, already 300m (984ft) above the starting point in Himmelreich. Pauses for breath during this climb allow one to admire the view back towards Buchenbach in the valley below.

At Pfaffeneck, the route-marking is joined for a while by the blue diamond on white ground of one of the long-distance connecting paths. Continue to climb until, at about 1,000m (3,280ft) the viewpoint of Nessellachen with its nearby *Gasthof* 'Sonne' (closed on Fridays) is reached. A path (red spot on white) to the right leads down towards the valley and is an alternative route back to Himmelreich. Nessellachen is a good spot for a break and perhaps some refreshment; this is the half-way point of the tour, reached after about 2 hours' walking. Continuing in an easterly direction, the red and white diamond soon takes leave of the blue diamond as the path swings to the right to head directly for Hinterzarten.

The altitude remains around the 900-1,000m (2,950-3,280ft) mark and there is a continually changing panorama as the path gradually edges closer to the Höllental with its road, river and railway far below. Several distinctive rocky outcrops clinging to the steep valley walls are passed, and 6-7km (4-5 miles) from Nessellachen, the Ravenna river is crossed. From here one can take a side excursion into the Ravennaschlucht. After this, the route turns southwards towards the main road, which is crossed on the outskirts of Hinterzarten. Carry on through the resort to the station for a train back to Himmelreich or Freiburg. A further 3 hours should be allowed for the walk from Nessellachen.

Climbing by railway or road into Hinterzarten, the Höllental is left behind and the landscape assumes quite different characteristics, with rivers no longer flowing westwards but south and east into the area which will be described in Chapter 6.

Places of Interest
In and Around Freiburg

Freiburg
The Minster
116m (380ft) high spire can be climbed for a bird's eye view of the old town.
5-tonne 'Hosanna' bell.
Numerous important relics.

Augustinermuseum
In town centre.
Paintings, tapestries, folk and sacred art.

Museum für Naturkunde
In town centre
Natural history.

(Several other smaller museums on various topics in the city).

Ludwigskirche
In town centre.
Highly commended modern church architecture.

Synagogue
In town centre
Modern centre of Jewish worship.

Schlossberg
456m (1,495ft) hill on eastern edge of city
Views of the minster and old town.

Rosskopf
East of city, 3km (2 miles) from Schlossberg
766m (2,512ft) high with observation tower.

Lorettoberg
Just south of city
A modest hill with interesting Lorettokapelle.

Schauinsland
12km (7$\frac{1}{2}$ miles) south of city.
7km (4$\frac{1}{2}$ miles) to lower cable car station in Gunterstal.
Freiburg's own mountain. 1,284m

(4,215ft) high with observation tower.

Kirchzarten
Parish church (1508-10) with painted triptych

Talvogtei (1621)
Former valley office of Freiburg councillors.

Kienzle-Schmiede
Old smithy with two waterwheels.

St Laurentius' Kapelle (1737)
On the Giersberg, 1.5km (1 mile) to the south-east
Baroque pilgrimage chapel.

Unteribental
Vaterunserkapelle
Modern church with theme of the Lord's Prayer.

Höllental
Hirschsprung
Bronze stag on rocky outcrop commemorates legendary leap by hunted animal.

Ravennaschlucht
Deep gorge spanned by 224m (245yds) long railway viaduct.

Waterfalls and water mill
The Grossjockenmühle is an old water mill which is disused but worth seeing.

Glass-blowing workshop and gift shop
Interesting gifts and souvenirs

Gasthaus 'Sternen'
Visited by Marie-Antoinette in 1770 and by Goethe in 1779.

St Oswalds-Kapelle (1148)
Chapel with frescos from fourteenth to sixteenth centuries.

Grossjockenmühle,
Ravennaschlucht

Street-side café in Hinterzarten

5
MOUNTAINS OF THE SOUTH-WEST

This area contains nearly all the highest mountains of the southern Black Forest and lies between the *Badische Weinstrasse* and the Wiesental, through which road B317 runs in a north-easterly direction from Basel to Neustadt. Almost every road is green-edged on the map, meaning, according to the legend, 'Stretches with particularly beautiful landscapes'. It is impossible, in the space available, to give a comprehensive survey of every place of beauty or interest, but those mentioned are typical of very many more in this concentration of natural splendours. There are no large towns, but almost every town and village is dedicated to the needs of the holidaymaker, in this, the most popular part of the Forest.

Here, in a compact group, we find mountains such as the Feldberg 1,493m (4,895ft), the Seebuck 1,450m (4,754ft), the Stübenwasen 1,388m (4,549ft), the Belchen 1,414m (4,636ft) and the Blauen 1,165m (3,823ft). Just to the north is the Schauinsland, mentioned in the previous chapter, and a little to the east, are the Hochkopf 1,263m (4,147ft) and the Hochgescheid 1,205m (3,956ft). These are some of the giants which serious walkers feel they must conquer, but there are many, many more, less known and less visited summits which offer an equal challenge and pleasure.

There is little access to this area by train because, with the exception of the Feldberg/Seebuck group, the nearest stations are too distant to be of value without road transport. However, the Feldberg/Seebuck area can, given some determination, be reached on foot from Bärental station on the Schluchsee branch line. Steep hills, deep valleys, serpentine curves and many small villages are the significant features here. So, instead of towns, it is more appropriate to describe a few of the mountains and valleys, and to mention, in passing, some of the little resorts encountered on the way.

Its superior height is almost the only attraction of the climb to the summit of the Feldberg, for it is the most unlovely of all the Black Forest mountains. If one can ignore the clutter of functional buildings associated with the television/radio transmitter, the weather station and various military installations, there are magnificent panoramic views in all directions, perhaps the most spectacular being that over the Feldsee towards the Bärental. In the middle of the last century, the intrepid tourist determined to reach the summit of the Feldberg had to obtain the services of a guide in Freiburg.

Today the picture is very different; in summer and winter alike, thousands of visitors make their way to the top without supervision or guidance. As there is also road access for most of the way, the treeless summit plateau is almost always busy during favourable weather. Germany's first ski-club was founded here in 1892, the polar explorer Nansen being one of its original members. The Feldberg, the most popular winter sports centre in the Black Forest, is especially busy during winter weekends. A large number of designated walks, both local and of longer distance, include the climb to the summit of the Feldberg in their itinerary.

In common with other Black Forest summits, the Feldberg area is especially popular in late autumn and early winter when there is the best chance of a clear and pure atmosphere. These are the seasons beloved by the photographer, who will often be able to obtain clear pictures of the surrounding mountains and, perhaps, southwards to the Alps. Sunrise and sunset can produce quite splendid effects on the heights while the valleys below may well be shrouded in mist and not get a glimpse of the sun all day. This can have the unusual effect of making it several degrees warmer on the mountains above the mist than it is in the valleys.

Once the snow comes, the winter walker must beware of the *Schneewächten*, the overhanging walls of snow driven by the wind, which can sometimes break free unexpectedly and bury anyone unfortunate enough to be below. This hazard is said to be particularly noticeable in the Zastler area.

The 'Feldbergerhof', a first-class hotel with 145 beds, is at an altitude of 1,279m (4,199ft), making it one of the highest hotels in the

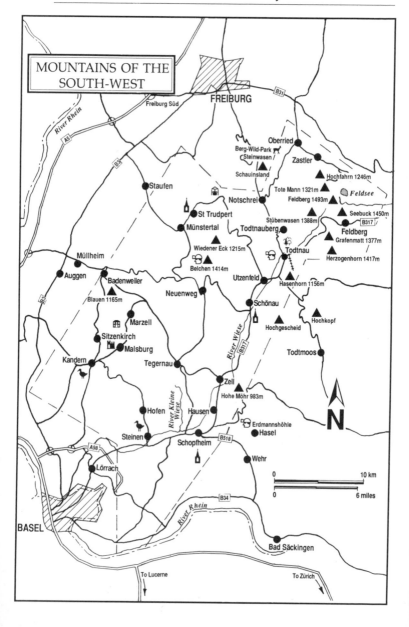

MOUNTAINS OF THE
SOUTH-WEST

Black Forest. It is nearer the Seebuck than the Feldberg and is reached by the principal access road into the area off the B317 Basel to Neustadt main road on the south side of the group.

The little town of **Todtnau**, to the south-west of the Feldberg massif, is an ideal centre for exploring the surrounding mountains and valleys. Again there is a history of disastrous fires; hence there are no very old buildings, but the town is quite attractive and a recognised health resort. For the walker it would be difficult to find a place with more possibilities for expeditions on foot — *Wander-möglichkeiten* as the Germans would say.

About 4km (2¹/₂ miles) north of Todtnau is the separate part of the resort called **Todtnauberg**; between the two is a spectacular

The summit of the Feldberg and one of the mountain's panoramic views

100m (328ft) high waterfall. There are swimming pools in both places and Todtnauberg has several hotel *Hallenbäder* as well, some of these being available to the general public. Pleasantly free of through traffic, this is one of the most popular Black Forest resorts. Near the main street in Todtnau is the lower station of a chair lift for an effortless journey to the Hasenhorn 1,156m (3,794ft) behind the town, while within easy distance of Todtnauberg there are seven ski-lifts for the winter visitor, several of them flood-lit.

Many consider the Belchen to be the most beautiful of all the Black Forest mountains. The views in every direction from the summit are as grand as those from the Feldberg. A good road goes right to the top, but there is ample parking space and the unfortunate clutter of the Feldberg is absent — even the inevitable hotel is not intrusive. The walker may make the ascent by a variety of routes, each of which has its own attractions and devotees. Several pleasant *Gasthäuser* and cafés along the way provide sustenance for the quite energetic climb.

One, perhaps less obvious, route to the summit of the Belchen is from Neuenweg which lies directly to the south of the mountain. Start at the Taubenbrunnen (fountain) in the middle of the village. Leave the filling station on the left and after 100m (110yd) turn sharp left in a westerly direction. A steep, curving path soon brings one to the last houses of the village and, in 15 minutes, to the open ridge. Before reaching a main road, go to the right (north) between two telegraph poles and continue on a broad forest track which climbs gently.

In rather less than 1 hour from the start, one reaches a five-way junction of paths and from here the red diamond of the *Westweg* is followed towards the summit. Look back after 15 minutes or so for a splendid view down the valley. Now the way becomes steep as it goes through the rocky corries of the Hohe Kelch. There are some viewpoints which provide opportunities to interrupt the romantic climb. Near a seat there is a sign to the Felsenkranz, the ridge viewpoint which should on no account be missed.

Now the red diamond is followed along a shady woodland path and a sign to the right, 'Belchenhaus', will soon be seen. However, continue forward on the path which now becomes smaller, reaching the summit at 1,414m (4,636ft) in half an hour for an unforgettable panoramic view all round. It is splendid at any season but the best time of all is in October when the autumn colours are at their best and the air is clear enough for a view of the Alps.

From the summit, walk down to the Belchenhaus (hotel) and then, at the turning place for the car park, look for a sign reading 'Neuenweg, Wanderheim 3.5km'. A blue diamond leads down the steep path with rocky outcrops and fine views, back to the starting point. Stout walking footwear is necessary for this ramble which involves a distance of 13km (8 miles) and includes a total climb of some 700m (2,300ft).

As with the Feldberg, many walking tours include the Belchen climb, while for those who make the ascent by car, there is a well-marked path round the summit which can be encircled in about 1 hour. The Belchen is a favourite spot with hang gliding enthusiasts, who take to the air from just below the summit car park.

Todtnau and the little holiday town of **Schönau** are popular starting points for routes to the Belchen. The church at Schönau, although only built in 1890, is worth a visit, on account of the late-Gothic carved altar. The church is known as the minster of the Wiesental. The popularity of Schönau is reflected in the fact that despite the 600 beds available for visitors, accommodation there always seems to be that bit more difficult to obtain than at most other resorts in the Forest.

At the northern end of this area, only 3 or 4km (2-2$^{1}/_{2}$ miles) from Kirchzarten, the little resort of **Oberried** is an excellent centre for exploring not only the Schauinsland, but several other mountains, notably the Hochfahrn 1,264m (4,150ft) and the Tote Mann (Dead Man) 1,321m (4,329ft), which form part of the Feldberg group. Most of the 900m (2,950ft) ascent from Oberried to the Tote Mann can easily be made by the motorist.

Leaving the village through the hamlet of Zastler, the sharp right turn into the Stollenbachstrasse is reached in about 5km (3 miles). This road climbs steeply with many Z-bends for about 4km (2$^{1}/_{2}$ miles) and ends at the Stollenbacher Hütte, a traditional *Gasthof* at about 1,100m (3,610ft). The extensive parking area here is virtually deserted in summer but thronged with crowds during the winter sports season. The nursery slopes with a short ski-lift lie just behind the *Gasthof* and twin ski-lifts climb in the opposite direction almost to the summit of the Tote Mann.

There is a most enjoyable 5km (3 mile) summer walk which starts from the car park and includes the summit. A small, surfaced road leads to some cattle sheds, about 400m (437yd) away and then it

Waterfall,
Todtnau

Stations of the Cross,
Schönau

Hang gliding on the Belchen

becomes a farm track swinging round to the left, eastwards, to cross under the ski-lift cables and past some pastures, continuing through woods until a fine viewpoint is reached about 1.5km (1 mile) from the start. The waymarking from the *Hütte*, a red cross on yellow ground, is followed along a right-hand fork at the view point, curving steadily right, through plantations of young fir trees, until the way divides at the foot of a fenced meadow. The red cross now takes the left fork south-eastwards towards the Feldberg, but the summit of the Tote Mann lies due south from here and one must go into the meadow through the fence openings provided and climb steeply up the grassy slope to reach the top in about 600m (650yd). The Feldberg and its buildings are clearly visible about 3km (2 miles) away, and many other summits are identifiable.

For a short time the path is in a *Naturschutzgebiet* (nature reserve), but this is soon left as either of two paths, with red spot on white marking, is followed westwards, gradually curving round to the north to reach a junction of six or seven paths in 1.5km (1 mile). The red spot marking goes away to the left but the Stollenbacher Hütte is now clearly visible some 800m (875yd) away on the right, down a well-trodden path.

Back in Oberried, the rather strange church occupies a prominent position. The *Bauernhaus* (farmhouse) museum of Schniederlihof has already been mentioned but if the weather is good the visitor may prefer to visit the Berg-Wild-Park (mountain wildlife park) which is also on the slopes of the Schauinsland at Steinwasen, 5km (3 miles) south of Oberried. A selection of creatures can be found in their natural habitats in an area of 40 hectares (99 acres) of forests, rocky cliffs and a lake. Deer, ibex, chamois, marmots and wild pigs are among the species to be seen from the well-kept paths which surmount the steep slopes. The young of many of these have been brought together in a *'Kindergarten'* as they can rarely be seen otherwise. This is, of course, a special attraction for children, and there are also two 750m (820yd) long summer 'toboggan' runs to round off the visit.

It is, perhaps, unfair to single out a few mountains for particular mention, as they represent only a very small proportion of the many delightful summits in a small area. There is always an attraction in the highest peaks — if, indeed, Black Forest mountains can be said to have 'peaks' — but many of the lesser ones can be just as rewarding, perhaps even more so because they are less visited. Nearly all of them can be climbed without much difficulty if suitable footwear is worn. The acquisition of good maps, such as the 'Atlasco' Schwarzwald Wanderkarte series, which come complete with a large selection of suggested walks and details of the signs to be followed, is strongly recommended.

The mountains mentioned, together with numerous other summits, are included in a rather strenuous 11-day ramble which is organised, on the same lines as those previously described, by the Kurverwaltung Titisee-Neustadt under the title *Rund um den Feldberg* (Round about the Feldberg). Again, if the whole tour is too much, separate sections can be booked to suit individual wishes.

Before leaving this area the visitor should explore at least two of the main valleys. The lovely Münstertal takes its name from a small town which was destroyed in 1346 and never rebuilt. It must have been an attractive place with its walls and towers, but today every trace has disappeared. The valley leads from the comparatively flat lands of the Rhine in the west, right into the heart of the mountains described earlier, with the Belchen prominent ahead as one travels eastwards. The main town, Staufen, is where the valley really starts and here again are the vineyards which line the *Badische Weinstrasse*.

Going up the valley beside the tiny river Neumagen, one soon enters the health resort called **Münstertal** which has a good selection of accommodation. Opposite the Untermünstertal station there is another 'Löwen', a beautiful old *Gasthof*. This valley of the Untermünstertal now swings south to run along the west flank of the Belchen. A left turn leads into the Obermünstertal, which is dominated by the buildings of the Kloster St Trudpert.

Around AD600, the Irish missionary Trudpert ventured over the Rhine into this valley in order to convert the inhabitants to Christianity. He was murdered by fanatical heathens and the natives pursued their pagan way of life until the Benedictine monks founded their monastery about AD800 and named it after Trudpert. The present baroque buildings are obviously not the original ones; the settlement has been destroyed by fire no fewer than three times in its 1,000 years' history.

The present church was another brainchild of Peter Thumb, who was able to incorporate parts of the former Gothic church in his plans. Today, organ and orchestral concerts are held in the church and it is a popular place for wedding ceremonies. The *Kloster* itself, now the mother-house of the Sisters of the Holy Joseph, is not open to the public. The St Trudpert chapel behind the church is worth a visit. The oldest *Gasthof* in the whole Münstertal, the 'Spielweg', is to be found in this part of the valley at the end of the resort. It has an interesting history and a reputation for good food, but is closed on Mondays and until 3pm on Tuesdays.

The Untermünstertal has a former silver mine which has been turned into the museum 'Teufelsgrund'; there are tours underground and its relics date from the eleventh century. One of the side galleries in the mine has been set aside as an *Asthmatherapiestation* for it has been found that the air in the mine is beneficial to sufferers of that complaint. There is another specialised museum in Obermünstertal, the Bienenkundemuseum which deals with every aspect of bees and bee-keeping. There is a total of 200km (124 miles) of well-marked paths at various altitudes round the resort. In addition, there are three *W-Parkplätze* on the main road through the Obermünstertal, including one at St Trudpert, with a total of eight suggested walks.

The river Wiese enters Switzerland briefly before joining the Rhine at Basel. The first town on the German side of the border is Lörrach, which has been mentioned earlier. Only 4km (2$\frac{1}{2}$ miles)

Protestant church, Geschwend

Gasthaus Linde, Münstertal

Some Places of Interest In The South-West

Todtnau
Todtnauer Wasserfall
1.5km (1 mile) north of town
Spectacular waterfall 100m (328ft) high.

Schönau
Parish Church (1890)
Known as the minster of the Wiesental. Late-Gothic carved altar.

Oberried
Bauernhausmuseum 'Schniederli-hof'
At Hofsgrund, Schauinsland, 7km (4½ miles) south-west
Small but interesting collection of local relics in a traditional farm-house.

Berg-Wild-Park Steinwasen
5km (3 miles) south
Mountain wildlife park with deer, chamois, wild pigs, etc. Summer 'toboggan' runs.

Münstertal
Kloster St Trudpert
Benedictine monastery founded about AD800. Church by Peter Thumb, with St Trudpert chapel behind the church.

Gasthof 'Spielweg'
Oldest hostelry in the valley with an interesting history.

Besuchsbergwerk 'Teufelsgrund'
Former silver mine now a museum. Tours underground.

Bienenkundemuseum
Located in street called Spielweg. Specialist museum about bees and bee-keeping.

Kandern
Station
Terminus for historic steam train from Basel.

Stork Sanctuary
In Holzen, 3km (2 miles) to the south-west

Sausenburg
4km (2½ miles) to the north-east
Castle ruin with fine views.

Schloss Bürgeln (1762)
5km (3 miles) to the north
Beautiful palace known as the Pearl of the Markgräflerland.

Blauen
1165m (3,823ft) mountain with outstanding panorama reached from Marzell, 8km (5 miles) north-east of Kandern.

Steinen-Hofen
Vogelpark Wiesental
4km (2½ miles) north of Steinen
More than 300 species of native and foreign birds in natural surroundings.
Tropical house.

Schopfheim
'Hans Sachs' Gasthof
Historic inn located in the castle.

St Michael's Church (1492)
Well-preserved frescos.

Erdmannshöhle
Hasel, 6km (4 miles) to the east
Spectacular subterranean caverns.

Hausen
Memorial to poet Johann Peter Hebel, in front of church.

Feldberg
Feldsee
Lake with cliffs of geological interest.

Bismarck memorial tower
Located on the Seebuck 1,450m (4,754ft).
Fine viewpoint.

from the *Autobahn* near Lörrach, there is the group of villages which make up the resort of **Steinen**, the focal point being the pleasant little town of Steinen itself (population 4,000). It is little more than a stone's throw from France in the west and Switzerland in the south and it is hardly surprising, therefore, to find that the local dialect is shared with the residents of the nearby corners of those countries.

Various parts of the resort lie between 335m (1,100ft) and 1,000m (3,280ft) in altitude and between them contain most of the ingredients for a successful family holiday. There is a large, heated swimming pool, indoor and outdoor tennis courts and a sports centre. One hundred kilometres (62 miles) of well-kept footpaths provide for the walker and the long-distance path from Pforzheim passes through on its way to its destination in Basel. The Wiesental Bird Park (*Vogelpark*) at **Hofen**, a few kilometres north of Steinen, is attracting international attention as a superb example of wildlife conservation. The exotic plants and birds in the tropical house are particularly worth seeing.

A pretty but rather twisty road runs north-westwards from Hofen to the important town of **Kandern**. This is a holiday centre with about 6,500 inhabitants, lying on the route of the long-distance *Westweg* from Pforzheim to Basel with the ruins of Sausenburg castle (1230) nearby. Kandern is known as the *Brezel- und Töpferstadt*, reflecting the fame of its *Brezeln* (pretzels) and its pottery and ceramic ware. By 1813, the crisp *Brezeln* were famous all over Germany and it is recorded that thirteen bakers were employed in their production. Pottery goes back to 1564 when the suitability of a local clay for this purpose was discovered. The modest shopping centre provides adequately for those occupying the abundant self-catering accommodation in the area.

The poet Johann Peter Hebel made the name of Kandern known when he related the story of a ghost on the Kandern road. It seems the apparition was liable to appear to all those who had sat too long over the wine in the *Gasthaus*. Today's motorist probably has better grounds for moderation in his enjoyment of the local wine. Johann August Sutter, the pioneer and so-called emperor of California, was a famous son of Kandern. Each September, a local festival called the Kanderner Pferdemarkt (horse market) is now the occasion for a variety of riding and associated events.

The town is surrounded by a network of well-marked paths which make it easy to organise rambles to various places of interest in the vicinity. The terrain is fairly easy so that stout walking shoes will suffice rather than the boots usually desirable in more mountainous areas. Footpath No 2 can be followed for about 1.5km (1 mile) southwards from the town to the bizarre Wolfsschlucht (wolf ravine) which is in a small *Naturschutzgebiet*. The path then continues in the same direction for a further 2km (1$^1/_4$ miles) to the photogenic village of **Holzen**, which has a stork sanctuary on its outskirts; there is also a stork's nest on the church roof.

Northwards from Kandern, local path No 1 (it is also the *Westweg* — red diamond on white ground) may be followed to the Sausenburg ruins, a distance of about 4km or 2$^1/_2$ miles. This is a long, steady climb for one has to overcome an altitude difference of more than 300m (985ft) in this fairly short distance. However, the splendid view on reaching the Sausenburg at 665m (2,185ft), high above the village of Sitzenkirch, makes it well worthwhile. The Sausenburg once belonged to the Zähringen dynasty and later to the Margraves of Hachberg-Sausenberg, but it was unoccupied by the time it was reduced to ruins by French artillery in 1678.

Shortly after the Sausenburg, the *Westweg* and path 1 separate; follow the latter westwards to Schloss Bürgeln, about another 3km (2 miles). Where the paths divide, there is a car park reached via Sitzenkirch, from which the Sausenburg may be reached in about 1km ($^1/_2$ mile), nearly all on level ground. The fine palace of Bürgeln is known as the Pearl of the Markgräflerland and it occupies a lovely vantage point looking south from this spur of the Blauen, the summit of which at 1,165m (3,823ft) lies about 4km (2$^1/_2$ miles) to the north above Badenweiler.

Schloss Bürgeln was built by J.K. Bagnato in 1762 and until Secularisation in 1803, it was the residence of the prior of St Blasien monastery. There are guided tours of the palace and there is a *Gaststätte* here so this would make a good place for a break and refreshment before resuming the circular walk along path 1 back to Kandern, a distance of some 5km (3 miles) through fields and woods. The whole walk covers 12km (7$^1/_2$ miles). It should be noted that it is impossible to see even the exterior of the *Schloss* unless one pays for and participates in the guided tours.

Kandern has an excellent heated *Freibad* with an extensive *Liegewiese* (grassy area for sunbathing) and a small restaurant. Table tennis is available and there is also a small bowling alley. In the summer months, a museum railway, the *Kandertalbahn*, operates

St Trudpert church, Münstertal

Picturesque café, Schopfheim

steam passenger trains between Kandern and Basel.

About 4 to 8km (2-5 miles) north-east of Kandern there is another holiday area known as **Malsburg-Marzell**, made up of these two places and several smaller ones strung out along the valley of the river Kander. Marzell, at the northern end, is the starting point for two routes to the summit of the Blauen involving a round distance of 9-12km ($5^1/_2$-$7^1/_2$ miles) with a climb of about 460m (1,500ft) and a descent of the same order to get back to the starting place. Those desiring to do so can, however, get close to the summit by car and ample parking space is available.

For the visitor seeking a holiday amidst beautiful scenery but without too many of the trappings of modern tourism, this valley would appear to be ideal. Both Kandern and Malsburg-Marzell are on the Atlasco Wanderkarte, sheet No 257, which not only has the large-scale map (1:30,000) but also numerous easily followed suggestions for walks in the area.

The beautiful Eggenertal (Eggen valley) runs northwards from Sitzenkirch for about 12km ($7^1/_2$ miles) to Müllheim in the Rhine valley, with lesser roads running off westwards towards Auggen and Schliengen. The routes include the villages of Obereggenen, Niedereggenen and Feldberg — a different place from that associated with the Black Forest's highest mountain, of course. The valley is famous for its fruit trees which consist principally of the various varieties of cherry. A drive through here in May, when thousands of trees are in blossom, provides a sight to remember. By August the harvest is in full swing and the heavily laden branches droop down to the roads and footpaths, tempting the rambler to refreshment along the way.

About 1.5km (1 mile) from Sitzenkirch, the road ascends to a miniature pass at St Johannis Breitehof at 482m (1,582ft) before the descent into the valley proper. At this highest point there is a car park which gives access to the circular walk already described, taking in Schloss Bürgeln and Kandern. The name comes from that of a tiny chapel which once stood here, dedicated to St Johannis, the patron saint of Bürgeln. The Breitehof farmhouse was built in 1826 by the forbears of the present owners.

Going on up the Wiesental from Steinen, one comes, in about 7km (4 miles), to **Schopfheim**, where a certain amount of the old has been rescued from the scourge of modernisation. Places of interest here include the historic inn, the 'Hans Sachs', which is to be found in the castle, and St Michael's Gothic church which dates from 1492. There are well-preserved frescos inside which date from about the time the church was built.

A gallery of paintings can be found in the *Rathaus* (1820), a building in pure Classical style, and in the so-called *Hirtenhaus* (shepherd's house) there is a historical museum. Three *W-Parkplätze* are to be found in or near the town, each with one marked walk. A diversion can be made from Schopfheim into the idyllic Kleine (small) Wiesental with its fine farmhouses and country inns. The Kleine Wiese is a tributary of the main stream and there are splendid views if it is followed to its source near the Höhen-Restaurant Haldenhof.

The various hostelries in the Kleine Wiesental pride themselves on their cuisine and offer many local specialities prepared in accordance with time-honoured recipes. They have published a *Gastron-omieführer* (gastronomic guide) to the valley which may be obtained from the *Verkehrsamt* in Steinen. Another worthwhile excursion from Schopfheim takes one 6km (4 miles) eastwards to Hasel for a visit to the spectacular subterranean caverns known as the Erdmannshöhle.

The main road bypasses Hausen, the home of the dialect poet Johann Peter Hebel (1760-1826), to whom there is a memorial in front of the church. Ten kilometres ($6^1/_4$ miles) from Schopfheim, the little town of **Zell** (another!), though busy with weaving and spinning industry, lies in typical Black Forest countryside and is a good starting point for walks in the locality. By travelling a few more kilometres up the valley to Mambach, all traces of industry are left behind, and one is in completely beautiful surroundings again.

After Wembach, which is a village a little aside from the main road but with a number of spacious and comfortable Black Forest farmhouses, is Schönau, at the foot of the Belchen. Further up the valley is Geschwend, from where a twisty road runs eastwards towards Bernau and the Albtal. Continuing in this direction, the traveller arrives once again in Todtnau, attractive both as a centre for exploring the highest mountains and for many more modest excursions.

Past Todtnau, road B317 is still accompanied for a while by the river Wiese. There is a path for the walker called the Feldbergpfad which runs parallel to the road and river, all three being hemmed into the steep-sided valley by the mountains on either side. These are dominated to the north by the Stübenwasen and the Feldberg itself.

There are several parking places giving access to the paths in the valley bottom, but it is not until about 6km (4 miles) from Todtnau that there is an opportunity to take to the hills. Then suddenly, at the foot of the Seebuck, one is in the resort called **Feldberg** and among a veritable network of ski-lifts going up to the slopes of the Ahorn-bühl and Grafenmatt to the south and to the Seebuck north of the road.

A hotel and several *Gasthöfe* close to some of the ski-lifts provide for the traveller, and a little further on is the main access road to the Feldberg mountain. (One of the many youth hostels in the area is here.) The summer walker will find countless opportunities for exploring the heights or going round the lake, the Feldsee, with its near vertical rocky cliffs on three sides. Close to the summit of the Seebuck is the Bismarck memorial tower which has a fine viewpoint. Here one is in the large *Naturschutzgebiet* which protects the whole of the Feldberg area.

Bärental and its railway station are reached in another 6km (4 miles) while road B317 combines with B500 to continue north-eastwards to Titisee and the area to be described in the next chapter.

6
THE SOUTH-EASTERN CORNER

The Hinterland

Like all the other parts of the Black Forest, this is an area of great natural beauty, but here most of the big mountains are left behind and the rivers are insignificant, even compared with the modest ones further north. The rivers here flow southwards and, while they still join the Rhine, they do so in that stretch which forms the border with Switzerland.

Again, it is an area of villages and small towns, apart from a few larger centres, mostly close to the Rhine, such as Bad Säckingen and Waldshut. In general, the area is less well-known than those already described, but it does contain, at its northern extremity, the very popular holiday centres around the Titisee and the Schluchsee.

The village of **Titisee** has only a small resident population of about 2,000. On a summer weekend one could be forgiven for thinking that it might be nearer 20,000, for the lake, beaches and streets will be crowded with sun- and water-lovers. Titisee is, without doubt, the modern tourist mecca of the Forest and if one is on a coach tour which includes an overnight stop in the Forest, it is likely to be here. There is a great deal of first-class accommodation and large camping and caravan sites, as well as a youth hostel at the south end of the lake.

In an area not very well endowed with lakes, it is understandable that the 2km ($1^1/_4$ miles) stretch of water from which the village takes its name is a huge attraction and it is not surprising that water

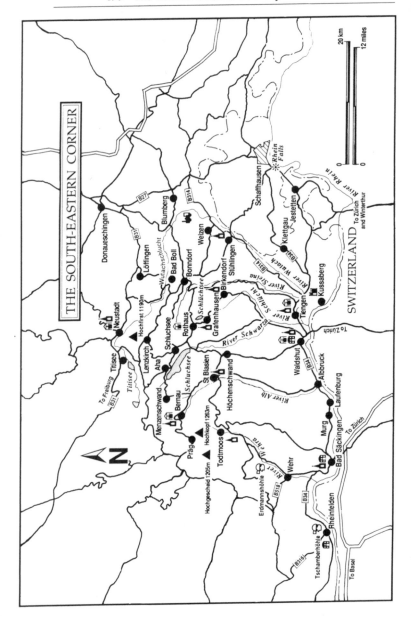

activities of every kind occupy the major part of the day for many holidaymakers. The village has souvenir shops, boutiques and cafés and is very much a tourist centre. Leaving aside the commercial aspects, it is a good walking centre and is crossed by several long-distance paths, including those from Pforzheim to Basel and from Freiburg to Bodensee.

An excellent and not too strenuous walk of 13km (8 miles) starts in Titisee and takes in the summit of the Hochfirst. Leave the busy resort near the Hotel Seehof — a fine traditional building — and follow the red diamond waymarks along the south-eastern shore of the lake. A short distance past a camp site at the end of the lake, turn back sharply to the left and follow the path steeply uphill and under the railway to the busy main road which must be crossed with care. Go a few paces to the left to pick up the path on the other side of the road (sign 'Saig-Hochfirst') and continue uphill to a road junction and car park at Rotes Kreuz, about 1 hour from the start of the walk. (This would be an alternative starting point if it has not been possible to find parking space in Titisee.)

Follow the waymarks (blue beetle) along the edge of and just inside the wood to the Saiger Höhe and the hotel of the same name, passing the Café Alpenblick a little later on the right and skirting the village of Saig itself. Before reaching the Waldhotel at the foot of the Hochfirst, notice the red/white diamond on yellow ground way-mark coming in on the left from Titisee. This should now be followed for the best route to the summit at 1,190m (3,908ft) where there are wonderful panoramic views if one has the energy to climb the observation tower.

For the descent, follow the woodland path (blue bird waymark) and rejoin the outward route near the Waldhotel. Now follow the red/white waymark past the hotel and into the path already mentioned which is marked 'Titisee 2km'. Continue downhill on a broad track and pass under the road and the railway to get back to the starting point. Rest and refreshment can be found at Hotel Saiger Höhe, Café Alpenblick, on the Hochfirst (*Ruhetag* Friday) and at the Waldhotel. Ordinary stout walking shoes will be adequate for this walk which is almost entirely on well-kept paths or tracks.

Titisee is one of the constituents of the combined resort of **Titisee-Neustadt**, the latter being the much larger place with a population of some 8,500 and having the status of *Kreisstadt* (administrative centre of a district). The resort is listed as a *Heilklimatische Kurort* and

Neustadt has the additional designation of *Kneippkurort*, reflecting its adoption of the medical treatment pioneered by Sebastian Kneipp. **Neustadt** has considerable possibilities as a centre for touring by road or rail and the town itself is a pleasant place to return to after a day of exploration. The mighty neo-Gothic church has a number of features of interest and there is a small folk museum which contains items of local significance, including a clock-maker's workshop. The area offers good skiing facilities in winter although there is only one short ski-lift in the immediate vicinity of the town.

As the main road B31 now bypasses the town, one is not unduly disturbed by heavy traffic. However, parking can be quite a problem in this important centre, despite the four car parks provided. There is a surrounding network of footpaths, many of them linking with the neighbouring resorts of Titisee, Hinterzarten, Saig and Lenzkirch. Some 3km (2 miles) south-west of the town is the Hoch-first 1,190m (3,595ft) with a *Gasthof* and a *W-Parkplatz*. A short marked walk includes several good viewing points, but this could be a base for walks of any desired length. As already described, some of the path markings in this area are in pictorial form — birds, animals, butterflies, etc, instead of the more usual geometrical designs.

An interesting excursion from Neustadt is that north-westwards into the sparsely populated, rural Jostal through which the little river Josbach runs. This is another area in which there were once many water mills, some of which can still be seen. Another feature of the Jostal and the several little side valleys leading from it is the considerable number of wayside shrines, often in the form of a crucifix and sometimes with a tiny chapel nearby. These *Bildstöcke*, as they are called, were erected for various reasons. Sometimes it was in thanks to the Almighty for deliverance from illness or the saving of a threatened harvest, sometimes in memory of a deceased member of a family and quite often as a place of worship to be resorted to when the winter snows made travel to the church impracticable.

About 2km (1¼ miles) from the point at which the valley road leaves the main road at Hölzlebruck, between Neustadt and Titisee, is the first westward running side valley, signposted to Schild-wende. The *W-Parkplatz* 'Jostal' is at the junction. The tiny Klaus-Kapelle will be seen nearby; this is a chapel looked after by the residents of the two nearest farms.

Outside the chapel, there is a fine example of a cross which was erected in memory of a 37-year-old soldier who was killed in Alsace in World War I. The details are inscribed in the stone from which the cross is made. The figure of Christ is made of wood and has a gilded loin-cloth. The car may be left here for a 12km (7½ mile) walk in which a number of *Bildstöcke* may be seen, as well as some fine farmhouses.

Take the little road towards Schildwende. Beyond the first farm (Griesbacherhof), two *Bildstöcke* will be passed before a track goes off to the left to the Pfrenzleshof, just a few minutes away, where there are the remains of a mill. Continue along the main route past Joseppenhof (*Bildstock*) and

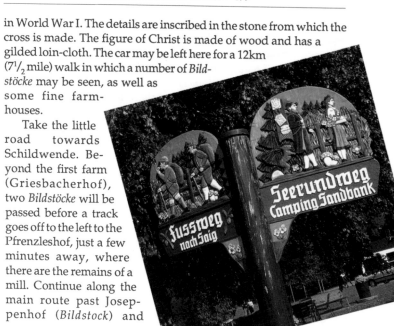

Wooden signpost at Titisee

Boating on the Titisee

Knöpfleshof (mill) and then climb steadily to Fürsatzhöhe at 1,071m (3,513ft). Here, 3.5km (2$\frac{1}{4}$ miles) from the starting point, there is a junction of several little roads and footpaths. The long-distance *Westweg* crosses here, as does a cross-country ski route from Thurner on the *Panoramastrasse*; there is also a *Gasthaus* nearby.

Turn northwards following the *Westweg* and, after about 300m (330yd), note a short path going right to a viewpoint. Shortly after this, the *Westweg* is joined by another path (red spot) coming in from the left and the two run together along the ridge for about 1km ($\frac{1}{2}$ mile) when the *Westweg* goes off to the left (west) while the red spot continues to mark the path being followed.

Four kilometres (2$\frac{1}{2}$ miles) from Fürsatzhöhe, this comes down to a little road at Danielenhof where there is a mill and a *Bildstock*. Turn right and continue for about 500m (545yd) to the group of buildings around the Rainhof and the Josenhof where the main Jostal valley road is regained. Here there are three *Bildstöcke* as well as a *Gasthaus*. Turn right and follow the valley road south-eastwards back to the starting point which is reached in 4km (2$\frac{1}{2}$ miles) from the Josenhof. Walk along the field edges to avoid walking on the road. There is yet another *Gasthaus* at about the midway point.

An alternative walk of about the same length from the W-*Parkplatz* is the 'Jostal Rundwanderweg' which is illustrated on the sign there. However, the route does not always follow footpaths shown on the *Wanderkarte* for the area and the quite adequate signs have to be relied upon.

At many of the farms a smaller dwelling house will be seen. This is the *Liebgedinghaus*, a little home for the old people and an indication of the youngest son caring for the other family members, as was mentioned earlier. Another very pleasant valley, the Langenord-nachtal, runs northwards from Hölzlebruck for about 7km (4 miles) to a *Gasthaus* called Schneehof near which there are two ski-lifts. There are several other *Gasthäuser* on the way but, unfortunately, there is no very obvious footpath along the valley bottom, although the road is bisected by numerous paths running between the ridges on either side. The skier can, however, follow the *Langlauf* track parallel with the road.

The train traveller has to change at Titisee to reach the Schluchsee, the biggest lake in the Forest, which is more than 7km (4 miles) long, and has three holiday resorts, namely Aha, Schluchsee and See-brugg. There is a station at each of these; Seebrugg, at the south end of the lake is also the end of the branch line. The so-called *Dreiseen-bahn* (Three Lakes Railway) from Titisee to Schluchsee was only opened in 1934. The three lakes are the Titisee, the idyllic Windgfäll-weiher and the Schluchsee. Although comparatively short (21km, 13 miles) and without the major engineering features of the *Höllental-bahn*, this little line has the distinction of serving the highest station on West Germany's public railway network at Bärental, 937m (3,074ft) above sea level.

The lake occupies a splendid position among woods and meadows and is popular for its excellent bathing. Steamers ply between the resorts and many sailing events contribute to the general interest. Windsurfing is probably the activity most practised on the Schluchsee today. Keen fishermen retire to the more peaceful west bank, where, it is said, a good catch can be assured.

The new **Schluchsee** *Kurhaus* is open from 8am until 10pm and the complex includes a restaurant and a concert hall, the latter also being used for ballroom dancing and tea dances. There are also TV rooms and bowling alleys. Schluchsee is one of the resorts which organises a baby-sitting service. There are several camp sites around the lake and there is a modern *Feriendorf* (holiday village) but, in general, it seems to have escaped the excessive commercialism which tends to spoil Titisee.

The Schluchsee seen today is a man-made lake and its principal purpose is to provide a head of water for the hydro-electric power stations at Schwarzabruck and Waldshut. There are considerable variations in the water level of the lake because, at periods of peak demand, the power stations use more water than can be replaced quickly by natural means. As a result, old roads and bridges long since lost beneath the waves sometimes come into view, particularly opposite the Auerhahn *Gasthof*. At night, when electricity in the Federal network is cheap, water is pumped back from the Rhine to restore the proper level in the lake.

A mere 7km (4 miles) south of Seebrugg along the B500, is the *Luftkurort* of **Häusern** on a saddle between the valleys of the rivers Alb and Schwarza. In addition to a *Naturfreundehaus* with twenty-eight beds, there are nearly a thousand beds available here in all other categories. The usual resort facilities are at hand including a heated *Freibad* and a *Hallenbad*. Good food is a byword and gourmets are liable to make for the Schwarzwaldhotel 'Adler', with its many local specialities.

'Village in the sky' is the title sometimes given to **Höchen-schwand** which is just a couple of kilometres away. It is Germany's highest *Kurort*, lying on a plateau at over 1,000m (3,300ft) and has the reputation of often having a clear sky when the valleys below are filled with cloud or autumn mist. The 'spa' season lasts all year and summer and winter visitors are equally well-catered for. Facilities for the latter include a ski-school — at this altitude snow can almost be guaranteed. Much of the accommodation is in hotels, several of which have their own indoor pools. Road B500 continues south to Waldshut on the banks of the Rhine, 17km (11 miles) away.

The Schlüchttal is the first of two important valleys running northwards from near Waldshut. The river Schlücht joins the Rhine just east of the town, immediately after its confluence with the Wutach. The Schlücht has its birth a mere 19km (12 miles) away in the Schlüchtsee and it is a typical, but rather reticent, small Black Forest watercourse, often hidden by rocks or undergrowth. In the Middle Ages, the valley road was an important trade route from the south, and there are various ruined hideouts that were used by robbers who preyed upon the travellers.

Another river, the Schwarza, has its source in the Schluchsee, some 15km (9¹/₂ miles) to the north-west, and flows through a pretty valley to join the Schlücht just north of Witznau. The Schlüchttal itself becomes even more narrow and enclosed, with steep rocky walls and three picturesque old water-mills on its way north towards Grafenhausen. Here the road leaves the river, which is now worming its way along the boggy valley floor. The wise motorist will leave his or her vehicle for a while and follow the nature trail round the tiny Schlüchtsee and to Rothaus where the little museum 'Hüsli', in an original Black Forest house, is a gem.

The history of 'Hüsli' (little house) is quite interesting. It was built by Frau Helene Siegfried who, in earlier times, had been an extremely attractive and popular concert singer in Berlin. She used to come to the Black Forest to recuperate between concert engagements and finally decided to build a retirement home for herself here. The house, with its great shingled roof, reflects her own tastes and requirements. She was a great collector of all sorts of objects from the old Black Forest farmhouses and in 1958 she decided to make over the house and its contents to be used as a museum after her death. She died in her hundredth year on 28 June 1966 and her wishes were honoured, the house being opened as a museum in 1968.

Working sawmill waterwheel in Jostal

The old-fashioned bathing place on the little Schlüchtsee is particularly attractive. **Grafenhausen** and **Rothaus** make a combined resort which caters for family holidays, with accommodation in well-equipped houses, and there is a fine baroque church dating from 1624. In 1985, the resort was the state winner in a competition *Ferien für die Familie* which highlighted places noted for their friendly and realistic approach to family holidays. There is much good upland walking at around 1,000m (3,280ft) in the district and as this is also the altitude of the resort, no serious climbing is involved. No fewer than six *W-Parkplätze* offer a selection of fourteen round walks, having pictorial waymarkings in this area.

One should explore the Schlücht's companion river before leaving the area. In contrast with the short Schlücht, the Wutach is one of the longest rivers which can be followed, as it half-encircles a huge area of the south-east corner of the Forest. It actually originates in the Feldsee at the foot of the Feldberg and flows eastwards into the Titisee, 5 or 6km (3 or 4 miles) away. Over this short distance, the river is known as the Seebach, but it emerges at the other end of the Titisee as the Gutach, which should not be confused with either of the Gutachs further north. This continues in an easterly direction, flows through Neustadt and then, 10km ($6^1/_4$ miles) further on, is joined by the Haslach and now assumes its third and final name, the Wutach.

Having already visited the areas crossed by the westernmost sections of the stream, it is from this point that the journey downriver is started. It continues to meander eastwards for a while, flowing through a sparsely populated landscape, twisting and turning as it is ever more hemmed in by the valley. There may be a glimpse of the ruins of Burg Stallegg far above and, a little later, those of Boll close to the valley edge near the small resort of Bad Boll.

This is one of the starting points for an excursion which no Black Forest visitor should miss. The **Wutachschlucht** (gorge) is one of the most spectacular natural features, not only of the Black Forest, but of all central Europe and has been compared with some of the grand gorges in the Alps. Steep walls, primitive forest and water foaming over the rocky river bottom make this a memorable experience. The flora and fauna of the Schlucht are exceptional, particularly the orchids and the butterflies, many hundreds of varieties of the latter having been identified in the area. However, the path through the Wutachschlucht is not for the timid, especially in bad weather. In places the walkway projects from the overhanging cliffs and although handrails are provided for safety, there can well be cause for apprehension, particularly as one will probably have to return by the same route.

At Rümmelesteg, part of the river disappears abruptly from view under a rocky cliff and reappears a kilometre later. The similar Gauchachschlucht then empties its waters into the Wutach and one reaches the old Wutachmühle 15 minutes later. There are parking places at Bad Boll and at Wutachmühle but there is no public transport between them.

If one goes into the **Gauchachschlucht**, there is a further series of natural beauties and it is, perhaps, worthwhile wandering up this valley to the Burgmühle (about 30 minutes away) and past the remains of the Birnmühle and the Lochmühle. These old water mills were continually affected by violent flooding of the river and were finally destroyed by it in 1895. Just above the Lochmühle there is a little chapel in memory of that catastrophe, and a plaque tells the story.

The section described is the most popular part of this remarkable area — it has been a *Naturschutzgebiet* (conservation area) since 1939 and has been named the Ludwig-Neumann-Weg after a president of the *Schwarzwaldverein*. A more extensive tour may be started at Rötenbach off the B31 between Neustadt and Löffingen, where a quarry provides a suitable parking place at the beginning of the Rötenbachklamm or -schlucht (ravine). One climbs down through the ravine to reach the Wutach and this is a good appetiser for the spectacular scenery to come.

The route, which includes that already described, is some 40km (25 miles) in total so requires more than a single day's walk for most people. However, there are opportunities for overnight stops here and there or the really well-organised might return to their own base and complete the expedition another time. This longer route would finish at Döggingen back on the B31. The visitor should obtain a large-scale map of the area and, if he or she can read German, the excellent guide *Wanderführer durch die Wutach und Gauchachschlucht* by Fritz Hockenjos. Needless to say, maps and guides are readily available in the area.

For those unable to arrange a linear walk through the gorges, a circular route which embraces much of the best scenery covers 13km (8 miles) and takes about 3 hours. Park at the Wutachmühle *W-Parkplatz* and follow the road uphill in the direction of Mundelfingen for about 300m (330yd) and then go left following the signs through a field path to the nearby wood. Reach the Wutach river bank, go upstream and one will arrive, after about 15 minutes, at the point where the Gauchach joins. The Wutach is spanned here by the roofed Canada/Deutschland footbridge. Now follow signs (blue diamond) beside the Gauchach up to the Burgmühle, which can be reached in 15 minutes or so. Beyond the mill, the ravine is certainly very lovely but the subsequent detour via Unadingen is not recommended. It is better to be satisfied with a further 5 minutes' walk up the valley, over a wooden bridge and then past overhanging cliffs where great care is needed. From here, one can return to the *Naturfreundehaus* at Burgmühle and make the short, sharp climb westwards to open country.

After a good 20 minutes, the big farm Neuenburg is reached with its Café Burgstüble. Turn left (south) here, leaving the surfaced access road and go straight ahead to the wood; follow the blue diamond signs to go westwards to the cemetery at the approach to the village of Bachheim and go on into the village if desired. (Time from the Burgmühle, about 45 minutes). From the cemetery, turn back south-eastwards at the sign 'Zur Wutachschlucht'. Pass a *W-Parkplatz* and follow the unmistakable route until reaching a choice of direction near a spring. If time permits (allow half an hour), a short side excursion to the right (west) takes one to Rümmelesteg where part of the Wutach goes underground. Return to the junction and now follow the red/white signs downstream.

After about 15 minutes, take the right fork at another junction and soon cross to the right bank of the Wutach over a little bridge. Now follow the rocky path through the ravine, noting the point at which the hidden stream rejoins the main river and leave the valley near the confluence with the Gauchach by crossing the Canada bridge and climbing back to the starting point which is reached in about $1\frac{1}{2}$ hours from Bachheim. Refreshments can be found at the Wutachmühle, the Naturfreundehaus Burgmühle, the Café Burgstüble and in Bachheim. Footwear with a good grip is necessary for this walk.

Visitors wishing to spend some time exploring these various river valleys should consider the little town of **Bonndorf** with its satellite villages as a convenient base. It is centrally situated and only about 3km (2 miles) from the Wutachschlucht at Boll. Bonndorf is a *Luftkurort* offering 760 beds in a variety of accommodation including

Windsurfing on the Schluchsee

A quiet corner of the Schluchsee

a youth hostel. There is a heated *Freibad* and a *Hallenbad*, together with all the usual amenities associated with a popular holiday resort. The sixteenth-century *Schloss* houses the *Kreismuseum* and also a *Narrenstuben*, for Bonndorf is another place in which *Fasnet* is celebrated. The *Schloss* is also the venue for popular concerts during the summer months. The parish church is worth seeing as an example of nineteenth-century architecture.

Back at the Wutachmühle, the river now crosses agricultural country and, before it reaches Blumberg, turns to the south for its destination in the Rhine. We are told, however, that many thousands of years ago it continued eastwards to join the Danube. The Swiss border is approached in another 7 or 8km (4 or 5 miles) but the Wutach remains German. The natural obstacles are now left behind, and ahead, in the distance, is Schloss Hohenlupfen near the little border town of **Stühlingen**. The *Klosterkirche* here is all that remains of the former Kapuzinerkloster of 1738. It has a baroque choir screen and the painting, *Madonna of Loretto*. The parish church in the lower town has a fine high altar from 1787. In the picturesque upper town there is a fine *Marktplatz* and chapel buildings from the seventeenth and eighteenth centuries.

Between Blumberg and Weizen, 4km (2$^1/_2$ miles) to the north of Stühlingen, there is a great attraction for railway enthusiasts in the steam-operated 'museum' railway which runs between these places. Motive power is provided by a former Deutsche Bundesbahn class 93 tank locomotive (originally Austrian and built at Linz in 1931) and a type T3 built by Borsig in Berlin in 1901. However, the line is important as much for its civil engineering interest as for the traction.

Built in the years 1887-90 as a strategic line for the state of Baden, with the possibility of access to the Gotthard, it was soon overshadowed in economic importance by the line through the Rhine valley to Basel but was nevertheless maintained for military reasons, regardless of cost. This aspect ceased to be of significance after 1945 and the line, by now part of Deutsche Bundesbahn, was taken out of use in 1955. At the behest of NATO, it was restored during the years 1962-4 and finally closed, as far as Deutsche Bundesbahn was concerned, on May Day in 1976. An agreement between the town of Blumberg and the Federal Railway enabled it to be reopened the following year as a museum.

The section of preserved line is almost 26km (16 miles) long, although the straight line distance between the termini is no more than 9.6km (6 miles). The line has to climb 231m (757ft) in this short distance; it has numerous horseshoe curves and the only spiral tunnel in Germany, 1,700m (1,860yd) long and rising 15.5m (50ft). Because of these features the line is nicknamed 'Sauschwänzlesbahn' (the pig's tail railway). There are four other tunnels on the line as well as three major viaducts and a bridge over the Wutach. A variety of historic passenger vehicles provides up to 500 seats on each train, as well as a buffet car. The station at Blumberg is at Zollhaus on road B27 from Donaueschingen. Passenger services operate between mid-May and mid-October, but not daily, and intending visitors are well-advised to write to Blumberg in advance for the current timetable.

Another pretty road leads south-east from Grafenhausen to **Birkendorf**, which is 5km (3 miles) away, lying at 786m (2,579ft) between the Steina and Schlücht valleys. This pleasant climatic health resort has won many new friends in recent years — people who enjoy the upland climate, the broad views of the countryside and, above all, the friendly village outlook and good lodgings. There is plenty of fine walking with easy gradients and from time to time there are conducted rambles. There is a *Freibad* in the woods, heated to 24°C (75°F), with a nearby nature trail, and an indoor pool at the hotel 'Sonnenhof .

North-east of Birkendorf in the Steinatal are the noted Roggen-bach-Schlösser which are two neighbouring ruins, visible from the road and easily reached. First, on a steep slope, comes the single-towered Burg Steinegg which was owned in the twelfth century by the Herren von Steinegg, the lords of the manor. Nearby, Burg Roggenbach — sometimes known as Weissenburg — has two mighty square towers. Its twelfth-century owners were the Herren von Roggenbach who were in the service of the dukes of Zähringen. In the fifteenth century, the abbot of St Blasien had the castle destroyed as a result of a quarrel about ownership. It was success-fully rebuilt only to suffer, with its neighbour, irreparable damage in the Peasants' Revolt of 1524-5.

Continuing southwards from Birkendorf, the road drops down towards Uhlingen which is reached in about 4km (2$\frac{1}{2}$ miles). Ten kilometres (6$\frac{1}{4}$ miles) further at Witznau, the road joins one which has come south through the Schwarzatal. Ruined castles come thick and fast in this part of the world; two or three kilometres before Witznau the remains of Allmut will have been passed and now, in quick succession, follow Schörringen, Isnegg and Gutenberg, Isnegg

Sixteenth-century Schloss, *Bonndorf*

Museum railway, in the Wutachtal

in particular, being worth a brief halt.

Seven kilometres (4 miles) west of Waldshut, the river Alb also adds its waters to the Rhine. It has followed a quite direct course from its several sources in the Feldberg area, making its way through the Albtal, which is interesting throughout its 35km (22 miles) length. (There is, of course, another river Alb in the north.) The sparsely populated valley through which this runs is ideal walking country. From this southern end, the first 6km (4 miles) are in a narrow, rocky gorge which has some impressive views. The road climbs up the valley on the steep flanks and a stop at the Gasthaus Hohenfels allows one to visit the nearby viewpoint. The road continues to climb through numerous curves and tunnels and it is only after Tiefenstein that the valley begins to broaden.

The landscape gradually assumes a more friendly countenance, farmhouses begin to appear on the slopes, and there are several comfortable *Gasthäuser* along the way to cater for the traveller. Before **St Blasien**, the Alb-Stausee is reached, a $1^1/_2$km (1 mile) long reservoir of particular beauty. It stretches to the outskirts of the village where the imposing dome of the *Klosterkirche* — said to be the fourth largest dome in the world — attracts immediate attention.

The history of the *Kloster* goes back at least a thousand years and includes many tales of disaster and destruction. The present building was erected between 1772 and 1783 to the design of the Frenchman, Pierre Michel d'Ixnard. The Benedictine monks here have been noted for their interest in cultural affairs and have made significant contributions to German cultural history. Secularisation after 1803 brought the life and culture of the monastery to an end and, in 1807, the monks withdrew to Austria where, in the Kloster St Paul in Lavanttal (Kärnten), they continue the traditions of St Blasien to this day.

Following the departure of the monks, the monastery buildings were used at first as a small-arms factory and later as a spinning mill. A fire in 1874 destroyed much of the former *Kloster* buildings and the choir and dome of the church. The dome was rebuilt in 1875 and the monks' choir restored and refurbished to become the parish church. Further renovations have taken place in the twentieth century and during the 1980s the interior was repainted in gleaming white to recapture the early Classical style of the building.

The visitor entering the church, which dominates the village, will be surprised and impressed by the mighty scale of the interior. The *Kloster* buildings have been used since 1933 as a seminary for members of the order of Jesuits. In charming contrast to the huge Catholic church, the Protestant place of worship is completely timber-built in traditional Black Forest style.

A glance at the map will reveal that St Blasien is another ideal centre for exploration of the surrounding countryside. There is a good selection of accommodation, mostly of a fairly modest type. At the north end of the village, there is a sports centre with a swimming pool and tennis courts. Several car parks give easy access to a variety of walks and a *Trimm Dich* path. There is also a *Wildgehege* (enclosure for deer, etc) nearby.

The river divides about 3km (2 miles) further up the valley to become the Bernauer Alb to the left, and the Menzenschwander Alb to the right. A little further on, the road also divides, to Bernau and to Menzenschwand. Just past the junction on the Bernau road, one of the three car parks is a *W-Parkplatz* with two round walks marked.

Some 8km (5 miles) from St Blasien, there is the quiet resort of **Bernau**, which lies in a sunny, alpine-like valley, and has a good range of facilities for visitors and plenty of accommodation in hotels and *Gasthöfe* with quite modest prices. The Restaurant and Pension 'Bernauer Hof' (1622) has changed little in over three hundred years and should be visited for its homely atmosphere as well as its food. There is a *Hallenbad* here and a camp site.

Bernau is the home of many wood-carvers and turners. The famous Black Forest artist, Hans Thoma, was born here in 1839 and there is an exhibition of his work with memorabilia in Bernau-Innerlehen *Rathaus*. He was responsible for two large paintings in the parish church. The modern *Kurhaus* and a *Hallenbad* are also in Innerlehen. There is a museum of rural history in the Resenhof in Bernau.

A variety of walks start from the resort but they can be quite strenuous, for Bernau lies only a few kilometres from the southern outposts of the Feldberg group, notably the 1,417m (4,646ft) high Herzogenhorn. Once out of the valley, the walker will spend much of his time at around 1,200m (4,000ft). The motorist will find no lack of parking places in the vicinity. The *W-Parkplatz* Rotes Kreuz (red cross) at 1,090m (3,575ft) about 3km (2 miles) along the Todtmoos road has two marked walks. With the aid of a map, one can readily devise numerous other longer or shorter routes.

One such walk, of $7^1/_2$km ($4^1/_2$ miles), is southwards from the car park, where there is a good view back towards Bernau, on to the tiny settlement of Rütte with its *Gasthof,* in about 1.5km (1 mile). Go right here without crossing the main road along a path (red cross on white) to the few houses at Prestenberg, with another viewpoint. Following the same sign, resume the southerly direction to cross the main road and turn north almost immediately into a path to the right (red rectangle on white) to head directly towards the summit of the Hochkopf at 1,263m (4,147ft). There is a very good all-round observation point with a tower here but one need not go right up; by turning away north-eastwards before the final ascent, it is possible to walk back to the car park in about 3km (2 miles). If one goes to the summit, a slightly longer return route is followed which makes the total distance 9km (5$^{1}/_{2}$ miles).

The main road through Bernau gradually assumes a westerly direction and arrives at a parking place by an old quarry in 2 or 3 kilometres which is close to the point where the *Westweg* long-distance path crosses the road. The path climbs southwards in a series of very steep, zig-zag curves to reach the summit of the Blössling at 1,309m (4,290ft) in a straight line distance of 1km ($^{1}/_{2}$ mile) but at least double this along the path. There is an altitude difference of 336m (1,103ft) from the road to the summit so it is a rather stiff climb, but the outlook from two viewpoints at the top makes it worthwhile.

The road now descends gently for about 4km (2$^{1}/_{2}$ miles) to **Präg**. This is without doubt one of the prettiest villages in this part of the Forest. It has been known as the *Gletscherdorf* (glacier village) because the valley in which it lies was formed in the Ice Age by the convergence of seven glaciers. Today, protected by the surrounding 650-750m (2,000-2,500ft) hills, it enjoys a mild climate and the valley is particularly attractive in autumn as the changing colours of the trees gradually spread down from the heights to the valley floor. There are splendid views from the nearby Spitzenberg 1,143m (3,751ft) and the Hochkopf 1,263m (4,147ft) — especially from the latter with its wooden viewing tower. It is little wonder that Präg has long been a favourite haunt of artists and photographers.

An extremely twisty road climbs southwards out of Präg; there are numerous parking places giving access to viewpoints with wonderful vistas back into the valley. The resort of Todtmoos is reached in about 8km (5 miles). Another pretty but less winding road leaves Präg in the direction of Todtnau, about 9km (5$^{3}/_{4}$ miles) away.

Menzenschwand lies northwards along the other branch of the

*Street scene in
St Blasien*

*St Blasien's **Klosterkirche**
and the dome's interior*

Bernau church

Alb, about 6km (4 miles) from St Blasien, the youth hostel being among the first buildings at the entrance to the village. Although having much the same characteristics and surroundings as Bernau, this resort is squeezed into a much narrower valley. To escape from the valley bottom, the walker has a fairly stiff climb in any direction. However, a short walk at the north end of the village leads to a waterfall. Trout-fishing is possible in the vicinity, there is a children's play area and over 100km (62 miles) of marked paths are available to the visitor. There are concerts or brass band performances nearly every week in the newly built *Kurhaus*, forming part of the variety of cultural and social events which take place.

Winter visitors are very well-catered for with convenient ski-lifts — of which there are seven in the area — and a terrain which is suitable for both downhill and cross-country skiing. There are courses for advanced skiers and for beginners, including one for 3-5 year-olds. The authoritative magazine *Euroski* commented that Menzenschwand is an ideal place for families who like to do some uncomplicated skiing together. There is a good choice of hotels and *Gasthäuser* in Menzenschwand but many of them close for the whole or second half of November and do not reopen until mid-December, as do those in St Blasien and Bernau.

The Wehra is another of those southward-flowing rivers which feed the Rhine, which it reaches near Bad Säckingen. **Wehr** is some 5km (3 miles) from its mouth and is the main town of the valley, with textile and paper-making industry down-river. There are some places of interest in and around the little town, including the spectacular subterranean caverns at Hasel 4km (2½ miles) to the north. However, Wehr is not a major tourist centre and the visitor is more likely to press on north-eastwards up the valley.

The walker could leave the north end of the town and follow the Wehratalweg (Wehra valley way), past the Wehrabecken, a Stausee or man-made lake created by the damming of the river, and continue through the almost uninhabited valley for the 12km (7½ miles) or so to Todtmoos-Au, where the situation changes quite dramatically. The river alters its character from a meandering meadow waterway to acquire all the features of a high Black Forest valley river. Here is the health resort of **Todtmoos** (population 2,400), a *Luftkurort* at the foot of the Hochkopf with its summit observation tower giving fine views in every direction.

Todtmoos is one of the foremost spas and a centre for holidays and winter sports with many favourable opportunities for *Langlauf*. The facilities here are well-suited to the younger generation. There are well-equipped playing areas for children and the 'Aqua-Treff' open-air swimming pool has a novel arrangement of water spouts and fountains. Excellent trout-fishing may be had in the vicinity.

Bypassed by the main road, the peaceful little town has a large range of entertainments and recreation for both the active and the less active visitor. Nobody should miss a visit to the significant baroque pilgrimage church of Maria Himmelfahrt which was built in 1627. Todtmoos has been a place of pilgrimage since the fourteenth century and the Gnadenbild (miraculous image) in the church stems from that time.

Wood-carving and hand-weaving workshops can be found in the numerous outlying settlements and it is possible to purchase their products. There are many hotels, pensions and *Gasthäuser*, most of them of a fairly modest size but there are, nevertheless more than four thousand beds available. Apart from the two weeks before and after Christmas, the late/early season runs from the beginning of October until the end of May; those who take their holidays during this time can take advantage of the lower rates. (Here again, closure for several weeks prior to mid-December is fairly usual.)

The Rhine, Schaffhausen to Basel

In the travels made so far, the numerous pleasant towns and villages strung out along the southern fringe of the Black Forest and facing Switzerland across the Rhine have been rather neglected. It is some 80km (50 miles) from the border near Schaffhausen to Basel and the planned *Autobahn* 98 will bring merciful relief to a number of towns through which the present main road (B34) passes.

Jestetten is the most easterly of the places along this fringe — a large village of 4,300 inhabitants in pretty surroundings and a mere stone's throw from the Swiss border. Indeed, it lies in an enclave and is almost completely surrounded by Switzerland, the narrow neck at the west end being the only direct connection with the rest of Germany. The village is only about 8km (5 miles) from Schaffhausen itself and even closer to the famous Rhine falls which provide an essential excursion for visitors to this area.

To visit the falls, one can go across country on quiet paths or tracks — about 5km (3 miles); or leave Jestetten by car in the direction of Schaffhausen, cross the border and signs to the falls (Rheinfälle)

Places of Interest In The South-Eastern Hinterland

Neustadt
Heimatstuben
Folk museum with worthwhile collection reflecting Black Forest life-style.
Clock-maker's workshop.

Parish Church
Mighty neo-Gothic building with features of interest.

Schlüchtsee
Small lake encircled by attractive nature trail.

Rothaus
Heimatmuseum 'Hüsli'
Folk art of the Black Forest.

Grafenhausen
Baroque Church (1624)

Wutachschlucht
Spectacular gorge noted for its flora and fauna.
Must be explored on foot.

Gauchachschlucht
Similar to above but additional interest with old water mills.
Include in Wutachschlucht excursion or start from Wutachmühle.

Stühlingen
Klosterkirche (1738)
Baroque choir screen and interesting painting.

Blumberg-Weizen
Museumsbahn Wutachtal
Steam-operated railway with many outstanding engineering features.
Length of line 26km (16 miles).

St Blasien
Klosterkirche (1783)
The immense dome of the church is said to be the fourth largest in the world.

Bernau
Restaurant and Pension 'Bernauer Hof'
Built in 1622 and little-changed since then. Homely atmosphere and good food.

Rathaus
Memorabilia and exhibition of the work of artist Hans Thoma.

Parish Church
Two large paintings by Hans Thoma.

Wehr
Erdmannshöhle
4km (2¹/₂ miles) to the north
Spectacular subterranean caverns.

Todtmoos
Aqua-Treff
Modern open-air leisure pool with water spouts and fountains.

Church of Maria Himmelfahrt
(1627). Baroque pilgrimage church.

will soon be seen. An enormous amount of car parking space is available and at busy times one may be faced with a walk of 20 minutes or so back to the falls. This is no disadvantage since the route is beside the river, with its ever increasing turbulence and noise, until the actual falls are reached. No simple waterfall this, with a sheer drop but rather a large area of 'rapids' over which the whole volume of the Rhine pours continually westwards in an awe-inspiring spectacle.

This may be observed in comfort from the promenade on the north side but to experience the real impact of this impressive natural phenomenon, the visitor should make the short boat trip out to a steep rock which stands as an island in the middle of the torrent. After disembarking at the foot of the rock, a narrow stairway is climbed to the top for a magnificent view of the turbulent waters.

Going west and emerging from the 'neck' of the Jestetten enclave, one soon reaches **Klettgau**, a place with just under 6,000 inhabitants, lying at an altitude of 400-700m (1,300-2,300ft) and much involved in the wine industry. As at Jestetten, there is not much tourist development but information about accommodation can be provided by the *Gemeindeverwaltung*. **Küssaberg** lies off the main road towards the river so through traffic is not a problem here. Seven small communities go to make up this resort of 4,600 inhabitants. Between them there is a considerable amount of accommodation in *Gasthöfe*, pensions, private houses and holiday flats. Indoor and outdoor tennis courts are available and there are opportunities for fishing. A bridge across the Rhine leads one to the modern Swiss resort of Zurzach with its thermal springs. There are promenades on both banks of the river with a total length of 16km (10 miles). The remains of three bridges, the earliest of which dates from Roman times, can be seen at **Rheinheim**, one of the constituent communities of Küssaberg. Important finds in this area indicate that this was the site of the earliest Roman settlement on the north bank of the Rhine. The ruined castle of Küssaburg stands nearby on high ground which provides good views over the Rhine towards the Swiss Alps. The rail traveller reaches Küssaberg by bus from the station at Waldshut-Tiengen.

Tiengen and Waldshut, already mentioned briefly, are 8km (5 miles) apart but are administered as one place with a joint population of 22,000. Both parts have interesting medieval town centres and a wide range of facilities for the holidaymaker. Two open-air pools and a *Hallenbad* are to be found, together with tennis, riding, bowling, fishing and other recreational activities. The remains of **Tiengen's** old town wall and one of the towers are of interest; the Storchenturm (stork tower) is the emblem of the town and there are examples of *Sgraffito-Häuser* where the decoration is provided by scratching in the outer layers of plaster, which often reveals other colours beneath. The baroque church of 1751 is yet another of the great works of Peter Thumb. It contains a number of interesting relics and, having recently been thoroughly restored and redecorated inside and out, it will now be seen for some years as the architect intended.

The pre-Lenten *Fasnet* celebrations here have a very long history, having first been authorised in 1503. On the first Sunday in July there is a great Trachtenfest — a festival of traditional costumes and customs — known as the Schwyzertag, which is a merry celebration of amity between the peoples on either side of the Rhine. The visitor can identify all the buildings, etc of interest in Tiengen's Altstadt from the neat plaques which have been provided by a thoughtful town council. The town has a fine *Naturkundemuseum* (natural history museum) with an excellent review of the nature of the landscape and examples of the semi-precious stones to be found in the Wutach and Gauchach valleys.

Waldshut's strategic position beside the Rhine has meant a history of frequent upheaval and changes of sovereignty but all this is long past and today the ancient walls enclose a haven of peace. The visitor is presented with a colourful and photogenic picture of tranquillity. A visit to the Friedhofskapelle may be of interest for it has a high altar which is based on the holy sepulchre in Jerusalem.

The parish church will be found in the north-east of the old town. The Gothic choir was incorporated when it was rebuilt in 1804. The interior is mainly neo-Classical and the decoration is nearly all in marble with altars by J.F. Vollmer. In the Hauptstrasse there are numerous examples of the house architecture of the sixteenth to eighteenth centuries as well as late-Gothic town towers.

The *Rathaus* in Kaiserstrasse is a baroque building completed about 1770 and the *Heimatmuseum* in the same street is housed in a sixteenth-century building and includes prehistoric exhibits. Within a kilometre ($^1/_2$ mile) or so of the town on the north side, there are no less than four strategically located parking places, one of which provides for easy access to the viewing tower on the Haitzenhöhe at 456m (1,496ft).

On the third Sunday in August, Waldshut celebrates the end of its siege by the Swiss in 1468, in a festival known as the Kilbi or Chilbi. Nowadays, the Swiss enjoy the merry-making to the full and come, not with their armies but with their traditional flag-throwers and yodellers to join in the fun. Along the river bank there is a 3km (2 mile) promenade which can provide a pleasant stroll, perhaps for those who have indulged a little too much in one of the many excellent eating places in the town. Either Waldshut or Tiengen, both with a wealth of accommodation in all categories, would provide good bases for the exploration of the river valleys mentioned earlier in this chapter as well as for rambles close to the river Rhine.

Continuing westwards, one soon reaches **Albbruck**, where the ✳ river Alb enters the Rhine. This lovely old place has been a winner in the 'Most beautiful old town in West Germany' competition which is sufficient recommendation in itself. Like many other resorts, it is made up of a number of small settlements, some of them as much as 8km (5 miles) from the centre of the old town which is also quite small itself. Here again there is a good choice of accommodation although there is only one hotel which is in Albbruck proper. The *Gasthöfe*, farms, private houses and self-catering flats supply adequate alternatives. There is a railway station in Albbruck and bus connections to the outlying villages. The 48km (30 mile) long *Hochrhein-Querweg* (Upper Rhine Way) ends here while a footbridge across the Rhine has its further end in Switzerland, making it easy for the walker to extend his explorations into that country.

Next comes **Laufenburg**; this little town has its counterpart of the same name across the river in Switzerland, the two being connected by a road bridge. In fact, it is worth crossing the river to visit the Altstadt in the Swiss town.

The medieval town north of the river has many of the characteristics of Waldshut and Albbruck, with nooks and crannies, twisty lanes, steps and fountains. Facilities for visitors include a heated open-air pool and there is an hotel and a range of more modest accommodation. Bus connections are provided from the station to the outlying parts of the resort. The barriers which separate the Swiss and German communities are officially removed once each year to allow the people on both sides of the river to celebrate their Fasnacht together. This they have done for hundreds of years, for prior to 1803 they were one community, undivided by today's political boundary. This is another place where the fools in their masks reign supreme in

*The Rhine Falls,
near Schaffhausen*

the pre-Lenten events. The fantastic masks of the participants in the fool's procession are matched only by the equally fantastic life-size cardboard figures depicting the *Salmenfischer* of yesteryear.

Unfortunately, the salmon once found in large numbers in this stretch of the Rhine have long since disappeared, along with other river-life which once provided a livelihood for many riverside dwellers. During the carnival period, the narrow streets of the town are decorated with flags and garlands and there is no musical instrument, however large or small, which does not make its contribution to the general cacophony in the streets.

Yet another pleasant little town is to be found 3km (2 miles) further on. This is **Murg** (population 6,300) and it has its own tiny river of the same name running into the Rhine through a romantic little valley with waterfalls and a ruined castle. This Murg is usually known as Murg/Baden to distinguish it from its more northerly

Sgraffitohaus
in Tiengen

Pavement cafés in Tiengen

namesake. It has a heated swimming pool and a modest selection of amenities including riding, fishing and bowling. However, the amount of accommodation for guests is somewhat limited.

Bad Säckingen is on one of the main routes to and from Switzerland. With a population of 14,800, it is of greater importance than the other little towns lying to the east. Being a spa, the accommodation of visitors is organised on a large scale and facilities for the treatment of those here for medical reasons are of a high standard in the several *Kur* establishments. Those visiting Bad Säckingen for pleasure are not overlooked and there are many amenities including a heated outdoor pool, a *Hallenbad* in one of the hotels and, rather unusually, a nine-hole golf course.

In the romantic old part of the town, one finds the baroque Fridolinsmünster which is worth seeing. It has lavish rococo decoration which was added by J. M. Feuchtmayer after a fire in 1751. Despite later additions, the church is essentially Gothic from the fourteenth century with a fifteenth-century nave and sixteenth-century towers. The fire of 1751 was not the only one to afflict the building and it has quite a long history of renovation and alteration.

A church on this site was first started in connection with a mission founded by the Alemannic apostle Fridolin on a Rhine island in AD522. Notable features of the interior furnishings in the present building are the high altar by J. P. Pfeiffer (1721), the choir stalls of 1682 and the church treasure which includes the shrine of St Fridolin (1764) in Augsburg silver. Remains of the old nunnery building can be seen around the church square.

Literary fame came to Bad Säckingen as a result of Victor von Scheffel's verse epic *The Trumpeter of Säckingen*. This tells of a romance played out in Schloss Schonau when a young trumpeter, Franz Werner Kirchhofer, came down from the forest to woo Margareta, the daughter of the Schlossherr — the lord of the manor. It was in 1853 in Capri that von Scheffel completed his great poem but it might well have been forgotten had not an opera composer, Victor Nessler, chanced upon it and written a splendid melody for the trumpeter's farewell. Since then, the little palace of Schonau has been more commonly known as the Trompeterschloss and this background has resulted in Bad Säckingen becoming known as the *Trompeterhauptstadt* (trumpet capital), with an active musical life based upon this instrument. Details of festivals planned should be obtained from the Verkehrsamt, am Bahnhof, 79713 Bad Säckingen.

The little palace dates from 1500 and is built on the site of an earlier Romanesque building. It now houses the *Heimatmuseum*, known as the Hochrheinmuseum (Upper Rhine Museum). This specialises in early and prehistory but also has an interesting collection of watches and trumpets, together with memorabilia of Victor von Scheffel, whose house may be seen in the town. Near the minster, a historic wooden bridge — the longest of its kind in Europe — provides a picturesque means for the pedestrian to cross the Rhine into Switzerland. Boat trips on the Upper Rhine can also be started here. Bad Säckingen is only 33km (20½ miles) from Basel and, like the other places mentioned, is served by the railway line running from that city to Schaffhausen.

Past Oflingen, where the Wehra joins the Rhine, is **Schwörstadt**, an old settlement beside the river on a former Roman road. The palace of the former barons of Schonau is on the river bank but the most significant sight hereabouts is the 3,000-year-old so-called Heidenstein (heathen's stone), part of a megalithic grave.

Mid-way between Bad Säckingen and Basel, is **Rheinfelden** which is another town with a Swiss namesake across the river. Rheinfelden is a *Kreisstadt* and, with 29,000 inhabitants, some of whom live in the outlying villages, it is by far the biggest town along this east-west route. There is also a great deal of very obvious industrial activity. The palace-like main building of Schloss Beuggen, once a headquarters of the Knights of St John (1246), was refurbished by J. K. Bagnato between 1752 and 1757. The ceiling painting in the church depicts the life of St Elisabeth. The bizarre 500m (546yd) long Tschamberhöhle (caves) nearby are worth a visit.

Although not primarily a tourist centre, there is plenty of accommodation in hotels and *Gasthöfe*. There are many facilities for recreational pursuits, including swimming (heated outdoor pool and *Hallenbad*), tennis, riding, fishing and gliding. If all this is not enough, a walk over to the Swiss spa town on the south bank will provide yet more diversions of various kinds.

It will be seen that this area bordering the Rhine is more populous than most of the other parts described but this should not be allowed to deter the prospective visitor. The environment is quite different from that found anywhere else in this corner of Germany and there is plenty to see and do, even if one cannot catalogue a series of outstanding ancient monuments for inspection. The warm, south-facing slopes have a number of vineyards but fruit-growing is also

Places of Interest Along The Rhine From Schaffhausen to Basel

Jestetten
Rhein Falls
Near Schaffhausen
Dramatic waterfall and rapids.

Küssaberg
Küssaburg
Ruined castle with extensive views towards Alps.

Remains of Bridges
At Rheinheim
Remains of three Rhine bridges including one from the Roman period.

Tiengen
Baroque Church (1751)
Another church by the architect Peter Thumb. Painted interior well-worth seeing.

Naturkundemuseum
Natural history museum with special reference to the Wutachtal.

Waldshut
Parish Church
Neo-Classical interior with marble decoration.

Rathaus (1770)
In Kaiserstrasse. Baroque building.

Heimatmuseum
Housed in sixteenth-century building
Collection includes prehistoric exhibits.

Albbruck
One-time winner of the 'Most

beautiful old town in Germany' competition.

Laufenburg
Picturesque riverside town with namesake across bridge in Switzerland.
Altstadt in Swiss town is worth seeing.

Bad Säckingen
Fridolinsmünster
Huge baroque church with rococo decoration added in 1751. Notable interior furnishings.

Schloss Schonau
Known as the Trompeterschloss due to Viktor von Scheffel's verse epic *The Trumpeter of Säckingen*. Now houses the Hochrhein-museum (Upper Rhine Museum).

Historic Covered Wooden Bridge
Crosses the Rhine to Switzerland. Longest such bridge in Europe.

Schwörstadt
Heidenstein
Part of megalithic grave.
Three thousand years old.

Rheinfelden
Schloss Beuggen (1246)
Once a headquarters of the Knights of St John.
Refurbished in rococo style 1752-7.

Tschamberhöhle
500m (1,640ft) long caves

Rhine bridge at Laufenburg

Schloss Schonau (Trompeterschloss), Bad Säckingen

important here and walking up through the orchards can be very pleasant, particularly during blossom time. The sights of Lörrach and Inzlingen, in the area closer to Basel, have already been referred to in Chapter 1.

This south-eastern corner of the Black Forest contains the greatest variety of scenery and the greatest scope for varied activities. The surface has barely been scratched and every visitor will uncover some new delight to add to what has been written. That is the joy of any holiday in a new environment, but if this and the preceding chapters have aroused some interest and given an indication of what may be found, the purpose of this book will have been achieved.

USEFUL INFORMATION FOR VISITORS

Note: The postcode for German addresses appears immediately before the name of the town, eg 79098 Freiburg. To telephone to the Black Forest area from Great Britain, dial 010-49- then omit the first '0' of the telephone number.

ACCOMMODATION

Accommodation is available in the Black Forest in hotels, inns, pensions, private houses, farmhouses, holiday flats or houses, youth hostels and camp sites.

Accommodation lists for the principal resorts can be obtained from the German National Tourist Offices (GNTO) overseas, but these often exclude private houses, farms, holiday flats and camp sites. More detailed lists may be obtained from the local tourist information office (*Verkehrsamt*). The following glossary lists the terms most frequently encountered when seeking or booking accommodation:

Aufenthaltsraum — Lounge; sitting-room
Bad — Bath
Bankkontonummer — Bank account number
Bauernhof — Farm
Doppelzimmer (Dz) — Double room
Dusche — Shower
Einzelhof — Isolated farm, ie not in a village
Einzelzimmer (Ez) — Single room
Endreinigung — Cleaning after departure of visitor from self-catering accommodation
Feriendorf — Holiday village, usually with specially built bungalows
Ferienhaus — Holiday house
Ferienwohnung — Holiday flat
Fernseher — Television
Frühstück — Breakfast
Gasthaus — Restaurant, inn or tavern
Gasthof — Hotel or inn
Halbpension (HP) — Half board
Hotel-garni — Hotel which does not serve meals (except breakfast)
Kinderermässigung — Reductions for children

Mehrbettzimmer (Mz) — Family room
Nebenkosten — Extras
Pension — Boarding house; board and lodging
Postleitzahl — Postcode
Ruhige Lage — Peaceful situation
Strom — Electricity
Übernachtung mit Frühstück (ÜmF) — Bed and breakfast
Vollpension (VP) — Full board
Vor- und Nachsaison (VN) — Outside the main holiday season
Wasser — Water
Wirtshaus — Inn or public house
Zentralheizung — Central Heating
Zimmer — Room/s
Zimmer frei/besetzt — Vacancies/No vacancies
Zimmer zu Vermieten — Room/s to let

Holiday Villages
In addition to self-catering accommodation (lists from local tourist information offices), there are many holiday villages, some of these being run by religious or other charitable bodies. Brief details of some of these villages are given below.

Bad Liebenzell
Schwarzwald-Ferienpark-Verwaltungs GmbH
Postfach 1164
75378 Bad Liebenzell
☎ 07052-875

Bernau
Kurverwaltung
Postfach 20
79872 Bernau
☎ 07675-316
Houses for (up to) 6 persons.

Enzklösterle
Familienerholungswerk der Diözese Rottenburg-Stuttgart eV
Heusteigstrasse 86A
70180 Stuttgart
☎ 0711-603077

Feldberg
Feriendorf Neumatte
79868 Feldberg/Schwarzwald 4
☎ 07655-562

Grafenhausen-Rothaus
Familienferienhöfe eV
Postfach 1362
70736 Fellbach (Stuttgart)
☎ 0711-586771
(☎ in Grafenhausen, 07748-302)

Kappelrodeck
Verein für Familienerholung in Deutschland eV
Kurt-Schuhmacher-Strasse 23
60311 Frankfurt am Main 1
☎ 0611-2165229

Lenzkirch
Ferien Touristik im Hochschwarzwald
79853 Lenzkirch
☎ 07653-821

Lossburg-Wittendorf
Sonnenrain-Schwarzwälder-Ferienhaus GmbH
72290 Lossburg-Wittendorf
☎ 07462-2172

Neuhausen-Schellbronn
Ferienpark-Schwarzwald
75242 Neuhausen-Schellbronn
☎ 07234-8515

Sasbachwalden
Gaishöll Wohn- und Ferienpark Sasbachwalden
Gaishöllpark 7
77887 Sasbachwalden
☎ 07841-5775 or 5773

Schluchsee-Faulenfürst
Eva Woelk
79859 Schluchsee-Faulenfürst
☎ 07656-319

Schramberg-Sulgen
Address as for Enzklösterle

Todtnau
Deutsches Erholungswerk eV
Schlüterstrasse 26
20146 Hamburg 13
☎ 040-456208

Waldachtal-Oberwaldach
Feriendorf Waldachtal
72178 Waldachtal-Oberwaldach
☎ 07445-1022

Youth Hostels and Similar Accommodation
A complete list of hostels in Germany can be obtained in exchange for eight International Reply Coupons or DM6.50 sent to Deutsches Jugendherbergswerk, Weinweg 43, 76131 Karlsruhe, Germany. ☎ 0721-962100. Details can also be obtained from *Guide to Budget Accommodation Vol 1*, published by International Youth Hostels Federation, 9 Guessens Road, Welwyn Garden City, Herts AL8 6QW, England ☎ 0707 332487 or American Youth Hostels Inc, PO Box 37613, Washington, DC 20013 ☎ (202) 783 6161

Hostels in Germany can be recognised by the familiar green triangle and the letters DJH (Deutsche Jugendherberge).

The *Schwarzwaldverein* operates many *Wanderheime* (ramblers' hostels) along its waymarked routes. Information about these and also about maps and guides, can be obtained from

Schwarzwaldverein,
Hauptgeschäftsstelle,
Bismarckallee 2a, 79098 Freiburg.
☎ 0761-22794

Hostel-type accommodation is also provided by the tourist association *Die Naturfreunde* (Friends of nature) with more than forty establishments (*Naturfreunde-häuser*) in the Black Forest. Admission is not restricted to members. Information is available from Touristenverein 'Die Naturfreunde', Landesleitung Baden, Alte Weingartner Strasse 37, 76227 Karlsruhe.

BANKS AND POST OFFICES

The unit of currency in Germany is the Deutsche Mark (DM).
100 Pfennige (Pfg) = 1DM.
Typical bank (*die Bank*) and post office (*die Post* or *das Postamt*) opening hours are 9am-12noon and 2-4pm (except Saturday) but banks may close all day on Saturday. In small towns or villages, both may open part-time or may be mobile offices calling at fixed times.

All banks exchange travellers' cheques. If the cheques are in Deutschmarks, the full face value will be given but if they are in foreign currency, the bank will make a charge, usually 2 per cent.

Eurocheques, obtained from one's own bank together with a cheque card, are used exactly as ordinary domestic cheques and must be made out in the local currency. They may be used for paying bills and making purchases but filling stations make an additional charge, usually 70pfg.

Credit cards such as Access, Visa, American Express, etc are now widely accepted in Germany especially in major tourist centres and in most filling stations on main roads. Cashpoint machines will accept Visa, Mastercard and Eurocard (with your 'PIN 'number) as indicated for cash withdrawals. British Eurocheque (EC) cards cannot, however, be used in German EC cashpoints.

Bank of England notes and US dollars may be exchanged but not Scottish bank notes. Some main post offices can also undertake currency transactions.

BUILDINGS AND GARDENS OPEN TO THE PUBLIC

It is not possible to list all the many buildings open to the public. Many of the museums are housed in historic buildings and there are hundreds of ruined castles, many of which are free admission. All the spas and many other resorts have libraries, reading rooms, games rooms etc which visitors may use.

Gardens are also mainly associated with resorts and are often beautifully laid out with fairly formal areas. Many have a restaurant or café and outdoor games such as garden chess, mini-golf and table tennis. There is usually no charge for admission to such gardens (*Kurpark*).

The brochure *Burgen und Schlösser* listing more than 120 historic buildings is available from the Fremdenverkehrsverband, Freiburg. It gives history, architec-

tural style, refreshment facilities, opening times, etc, for many of the places.

CHURCHES

The brochure *Kirchen und Klöster*, listing nearly 200 churches, etc, which are of merit for one reason or another, is available from the Fremdenverkehrsverband, Freiburg. The following churches mentioned in this book are particularly worth seeing.

Alpirsbach
Klosterkirche (1125).
In town centre.

Baden-Baden
Autobahnkirche. On A5 at Baden-Baden Raststätte

Breisach
Minster. In town centre.

Donaueschingen
Catholic parish church of John the Baptist and St John (1724-47).

Ettlingen
Schlosskapelle (former palace chapel). No longer used for religious purposes. In town centre.

Freiburg
Minster. In city centre.
Ludwigskirche. In city centre.
Synagogue. In city centre.

Freudenstadt
Stadtkirche. At corner of the market square.

Friedenweiler
Baroque church. 6km (4 miles) north-west of Löffingen.

Grafenhausen
Baroque church (1624). In village.

Hirsau
St Aurelius Church (1071). In village.

Kappelwindeck
Baroque church (1765).
3km (2 miles) south-east of Bühl.

Kentheim
Ninth-century church.
3km (2 miles) south of Calw.

Löffingen
Witterschneekreuz (nineteenth-century). 1km (½ mile) north-west.

Münstertal
Klosterkirche and St Trudpert chapel. 9km (5½ miles) east of Staufen in Obermünstertal.

Nagold
Eighth-century Remigiuskapelle.
South of town near bypass (road B28).

Niederrotweil
Late-Gothic church of St Michael.
In village.

Rottweil
Heiligkreuzmünster (fifteenth-century). In town centre.
Kapellenkirche (fourteenth-century). In town centre.

St Blasien
Klosterkirche (1783). In village.

St Peter
Baroque church (1717-19).
In village.

St Ulrich
Baroque church. 4km (2½ miles) south-east of Bollschweil.

Schenkenzell
Kloster Wittichen (church of nunnery founded 1324). 8km (5 miles) north of Schenkenzell.

Schwarzach
Former Benedictine Klosterkirche (1220). 9km (5½ miles) north-west of Bühl.

Stühlingen
Klosterkirche (1738). In town.

Sulzburg
Synagogue (1823). In village.
Church of St Cyriak (1510).

Tiengen
Baroque church (1751). In town centre.

Unteribental
Vaterunserkapelle. 3km (2 miles) north-east of Kirchzarten through Burg.

Urach
Fortified village church

Waldkirch
Baroque church (1732-4). In town centre.

LOCAL EVENTS AND FESTIVALS

Every resort has a programme of activities available from the local information office. Freiburg issues a visitors' newspaper, the *Freibürger Gästeblatt*, with a wealth of information and suggestions for excursions, theatres and concerts. A free weekly news-sheet, the *Wochenbericht*, is for the city itself.

In the resorts there are *Heimatabende* (folk evenings with traditional music and dancing), open-air concerts, slide shows of the district and conducted walks.

Seasonal events include *Silvesterabend* (New Year's Eve) with bonfires and fireworks. There is also *Karneval* or *Fasnet*, festivities which precede Lent, with dances, folk evenings and processions in which many of the participants wear grotesque masks. National *Wandertage* (rambling days) usually take place on the first or second Sunday of September and local assembly points are well-publicised in the weeks beforehand. Horse shows are also likely to be held in the early autumn.

The various religious festivals are celebrated enthusiastically throughout the Black Forest and often provide the visitor with an opportunity to see traditional dress.

MINES AND CAVES

Many parts of the Black Forest are riddled with old mines; some have been opened up as tourist attractions and, with the caves listed, allow for safe, conducted underground excursions.

Erdmannshöhle
79686 Hasel
4km (2½ miles) north of Wehr, 6km (4 miles) east of Schopfheim.
Open: April to November, afternoons. Stalactite caves, 2,150m (7,050ft) accessible.

Besuchsbergwerk Teufelsgrund
Mulden, 79244 Münstertal
☎ 07636-1450, 70730 or 70740
Open: April to mid-June and mid-September to end-October,

Tuesday, Thursday, Saturday and Sunday 2-6pm; mid-June to mid-September, Tuesday-Sunday 2-6pm.

Historisches Silberbergwerk
Hella-Glückstollen,
75387 Neubulach, 8km (5 miles) south of Calw
☎ 07053-7591 (*Kurverwaltung*)
Open: April to October, Monday to Saturday 10am-5pm, Sunday 9.30am-5pm.
Old silver mine. Also mining and mineral museum open on April-November daily 10am-12noon, 2-4pm. At other times by prior arrangement.

Frischglück
Besuchsbergwerk
75305 Neuenbürg
☎ 07082-7970 (*Verkehrsamt*)
Open: April-October, Friday, Saturday and Sunday 10am-5pm. Groups by prior arrangement also on Wednesday, Thursday and Friday.

Oberwolfach
Bergbau- und Mineralien-Museum
77709 Oberwolfach
☎ 07834-9462
Open: March-October, Tuesday, Wednesday, Friday, and Saturday 2-5pm; November-February, Saturday 2-5pm.

Tschamberhöhle
79618 Rheinfelden
Visit by prior arrangement by telephoning 07623-5482
500m (1,640ft) long cave.

Landesbergbaumuseum Baden-Württemberg
Hauptstrasse 58, 79295 Sulzburg
☎ 07634-702

Open daily except Monday 2-5pm.
State mining museum.

Besuchsbergwerk Finstergrund
79695 Wieden
4km (2½ miles) west of Todtnau
☎ 07673-7002
Open: May to October, Wednesday, Saturday, Sunday and
holidays, 10am-5pm.

MOTORING

At the filling station (*Tankstelle*)
Unleaded (*bleifrei*) petrol is now the
norm in Germany. There are two
grades, 'Benzin' (normal) and
'Super' while a third grade, 'Super-
Plus', is gradually being introduced. Leaded petrol is also
available everywhere.

Vehicle Lights
Left-dipping headlights must be
adjusted to dip to the right. Cars
may not be driven on sidelights
and headlights must be used, even
during daylight hours, if visibility
is impaired by fog, snow, rain, etc.
Rear fog lights may be used if
visibility is less than 50m (160ft)
but not in built-up areas.

Documentation
There are no special requirements
for private cars. The vehicle
Registration Document should be
carried and although not obligatory, the possession of an insurance
'Green Card' may well help to
avoid complications in the event of
an accident.

On the Road
All traffice drives on the right-hand
side of the road. General speed
restrictions are 50km per hour

(31mph) in built-up areas; 100kph
(62mph) on ordinary roads outside
built-up areas; 130kph (81mph)
(recommended) on *Autobahnen*.
These speeds are not indicated by
signs but variations from them are
shown in km per hour. The
rectangular yellow sign bearing the
place name denotes the entrance to
a built-up area and the similar sign
with a diagonal stripe indicates the
exit from this. Place names on a
green sign do not constitute a
speed restriction.

Other than on minor roads in
rural areas and in residential
streets in built-up areas, priority is
indicated on signs approaching a
junction. Special care is needed in
residential areas as many previous
priority signs have been removed
and 'priority from the right'
applies. Traffic on a *Bundesstrasse*
(state main road) always has
priority. *Bundesstrassen* are
recognised by a small rectangular
yellow plate bearing the road
number. Priority is shown
elsewhere by a yellow square with
white border set on its corner while
the same sign with diagonal black
line indicates the end of priority.
Standard 'Give Way' or 'Stop' signs
will be found on converging roads.

Parking is forbidden on main
roads or those with fast moving
traffic, on or near tram lines, near
bus or tram stops, traffic lights, taxi
ranks and intersections. It is also
forbidden to park on the 'wrong'
side of the road, except in one-way
streets.

The German police are very
strict on tyre condition and a
vehicle found with less than 2mm
tread depth over the whole surface

will not be allowed to proceed until the tyres have been replaced.

Warning triangles are compulsory and must be placed 100m behind a broken down vehicle. (200m on an *Autobahn*).

The German motoring association is ADAC (*Allgemeiner Deutscher Automobil-Club*) and members of associated organisations will be given advice or assistance should the need arise. ADAC operates a road patrol service with yellow patrol vehicles recognised by the word *Strassenwacht* on the front. The organisation has branch offices in the Black Forest towns of Baden-Baden, Freiburg, Lörrach, Offenburg, Pforzheim and Villingen-Schwenningen.

Motorway telephones are clearly indicated and may be used by the motorist in distress to communicate with the police who will, if appropriate, inform the ADAC patrol. Emergency telephones are now gradually being installed on other main roads.

Traffic signs, in general, conform to international standards but the meanings of the following signs should be memorised:

Ausfahrt — Exit from motorway or dual carriageway
Bankett nicht befahrbar — Soft verges
Einbahnstrasse — Nothing to do with the railway (*Eisenbahn*) but a one-way street
Einordnen — Get in lane
Freie Fahrt — End of restrictions, usually after passing roadworks
Gegenverkehr — Oncoming traffic
Glatteisgefahr — Danger of icy road
Langsam fahren — Drive slowly
Rollsplit — Loose chippings

Umleitung (on yellow arrow) — Not the way to the next village but a traffic diversion
Links/Rechts fahren — Drive on the left/right

MUSEUMS AND ART GALLERIES

This alphabetical list by town excludes museums with very limited or irregular opening hours, and the many *Heimat* museums unless they have exhibits of particular interest to foreign visitors.

Achern

Sensen und Heimatmuseum
Berliner Strasse 31, 77855 Achern
☎ 07841-641511
Open: February-December, Sunday 2-6pm.
Groups by prior arrangement.

Bad Dürrheim

Narrenschopf
Luisenpark, 78073 Bad Dürrheim
☎ 07726-666295
Open: weekdays 2-5pm, Sunday and holidays 10am-12noon, 2-5pm.
Displays of Alemannian *Fasnet*

Baden-Baden

Römische Badruinen
Römerplatz, 76530 Baden-Baden.
☎ 07221-275920
Open: Easter to October, daily, 10am-12 noon and 1.30-4pm.

Brahms Museum
Maximilianstrasse 85,
76534 Baden-Baden
☎ 07221-71172
Open Monday, Wednesday and Friday 3-5pm; Sunday and holidays 10am-1pm.

Staatliche Kunsthalle
Lichtentaler Allee 8
76530 Baden-Baden.
☎ 07221-25390
Open: daily except Monday 10am-
6pm (8pm Wed).

Cistercian Abbey Museum
Kloster Lichtental
Hauptstrasse 40, 76534 Baden-Baden.
☎ 07221-72332
Open: Monday to Saturday 2.30-
5pm and Sunday (except first in
month) 3-5pm.

Kleines Spielzeugmuseum
Gernsbacher Strasse 48,
76530 Baden-Baden
☎ 07221-32511
Open: daily except Monday 2-6pm.
Toys

Stadtmuseum
Küferstrasse 3, 76530 Baden-Baden
☎ 07221-278488
Open: daily except Monday 10am-
12.30pm and 2-5pm.
Free museum prospectus available.

Stadtgeschichtliche Sammlungen
Schloss-strasse 22,
76530 Baden-Baden
☎ 07221-278381
Open: Easter-October, daily except
Monday 10am-12.30pm and 2.30-
6pm.
Collections relating to town history.

Bad Herrenalb
Spielzeugmuseum
Klosterstrasse 2
76332 Bad Herrenalb
☎ 07083-4144
Open: June to September, daily
except Monday, 10am-12noon and
2.30-5.30pm. In other months only
Saturday, Sunday and holiday
afternoons. Collection of toys.

Bad Krozingen
*Sammlung Historische Tasten-
instrumente*
Schloss, 79189 Bad Krozingen
☎ 07633-3700
Open: only after concerts in the
Schloss and Thursday 4-5pm.
Admission free.
Old keyboard instruments.

Bad Säckingen
Hochrheinmuseum
Schloss, 79713 Bad Säckingen
☎ 07761-51311
Open: Tuesday, Thursday and
Sunday 3-5pm.
Heimatmuseum and displays
covering pre- and early history,
timepieces; European trumpet
collection.

Baiersbronn
Galerie Root
72270 Baiersbronn-Obertal
(on main road)
☎ 07442-6706
Open: Tuesday to Friday, 9am-
12noon and 3-6pm, Saturday 9am-
12noon. At other times by prior
arrangement.

Bernau
Holzschnefler- und Bauernmuseum
Resenhof, 79872 Bernau/Oberlehen
☎ 07675-160040
Open: May to October, Tuesday to
Sunday 2-5pm, also July and
August, Tuesday to Saturday
10am-12noon, November to April,
Wednesday and Sunday 2-4pm.
Museum prospectus available.

Hans Thoma Gemälde-Museum
Im Rathaus,
79872 Bernau-Innerlehen
☎ 07675-160040
Open: Tuesday to Friday 9am-

12noon, 2-5pm; Saturday, Sunday and holidays, 10.30am-12noon, 2-5pm.
More than eighty original examples of the artist's work. Memorabilia. Prospectus available. Hans Thoma's birthplace at Oberlehen 24 may also be visited by arrangement free of charge.

Bonndorf
Kreismuseum
also *Schloss-Narrenstuben*
Schloss-strasse, 79848 Bonndorf.
☎ 07703-7978
Open: Wednesday to Sunday 10am-12noon and 2-5pm. November-April *Narrenstuben* open Wednesday 10am-12noon, Sunday 2-5pm only. Admission free.
Changing exhibition and carnival masks etc. Museum prospectus available.

Calw
Hermann-Hesse-Museum
Marktplatz 30, 75365 Calw.
☎ 07051-167260
Open: Tuesday to Saturday 2-5pm, Sunday 10am-5pm. Town Gallery is also open at these times.

Donaueschingen
Die Fürstenberg-Sammlungen
Karlplatz 7, 78166 Donaueschingen.
☎ 0771-86563
Open: Tuesday-Sunday 9.30am-12noon, 1.30-5pm.
Art Collection.
Museum prospectus available.

Elzach
Heimatkundliche Sammlungen
Hauptstrasse 39
79215 Elzach
☎ 07682-8040

Open: daily 10am-12noon.
Admission free.
Regional and folk art collection.

Ettlingen
Städtische Sammlungen
(Albgau- und Albickermuseum)
Markplatz 2, 76275 Ettlingen
☎ 07243-101273
Open: daily except Monday 10am-5pm. Admission free.
Art and local history, East Asian exhibition, mechanical musical instruments. Karl Albicker and Karl Hofer galleries.

Freiburg
Augustinermuseum
Am Augustinerplatz,
79098 Freiburg
☎ 0761-2163300
Open: Tuesday-Friday 9.30am-5pm, Saturday and Sunday 10.30am-5pm.

Museum für Naturkunde
Gerberau 32, 79098 Freiburg
☎ 0761-2163325
Open: as above. Admission free.

Museum für Ur-und Frühgeschichte
Rotteckring 50, 79098 Freiburg
☎ 0761-2163311
Open: as above. Admission free.
Pre- and early history.

Museum für Völkerkunde
Gerberau 31, 79098 Freiburg
☎ 0761-2163342
Open: as above. Admission free.
Ethnology.

Kleines Stuckmuseum
Liebigstrasse 11, 79108 Freiburg
☎ 0761-500555
Open: Monday to Friday 1-6pm, Saturday and Sunday by arrangement. Admission free.
Stucco.

Zinnfigurenklause
Im Schwabentor, 79098 Freiburg
☎ 0761-24321
Open: end-May to September,
Tuesday-Friday 2.30-5pm; Satur-
day and Sunday 12noon-2pm.
'Tin' soldiers and other figures.
Admission free.

Museum für Neue Kunst
Marienstrasse 10a, 79098 Freiburg
☎ 0761-2163671
Open: as Augustiner Museum.
Admission free.
Modern art.

Furtwangen
Deutsches Uhrenmuseum
78120 Furtwangen.
☎ 07723-656117
Open: April to November daily
9am-5pm, December to March,
enquire at Verkehrsamt.
Museum prospectus available.

Gengenbach
Narrenmuseum
Im Niggelturm, Hauptstrasse,
77723 Gengenbach
☎ 07803-5749
Open: April to October, Saturday
2.30-5.30pm; Sunday 10am-12noon,
2.30-5.30pm.
Exhibition on the *Fasnet* 'fools'.

Grafenhausen
Museumsmühle Tannenmühle
79865 Grafenhausen
☎ 07748-215
Open: daily 1.30-6pm, but closed
Tuesday November to mid-
December. Children under 9 free.
Milling history, etc.

Gutach
Schwarzwälder Freilichtmuseum
Vogtsbauernhof, 77793 Gutach
☎ 07833-218 (*Bürgermeisteramt*)

Open: April to October, daily
8.30am-6pm.
Museum prospectus available.
Children under 6 free, concessions
for school parties.

Gütenbach
Puppenmuseum
Hildegard Mutschler
Krenzstrasse 5, 78148 Gütenbach
☎ 07723-7461
Open: Monday, Tuesday, Thursday
2-5pm, or by arrangement.
Private doll collection. Children free.
(Also in Gütenbach at Uhrenhaus
Späth, Hauptstrasse 1, at 3pm
Monday, Wednesday and Friday a
free film about the traditional
cuckoo clock.)

Haslach
Schwarzwälder Trachtenmuseum
   (Heimatmuseum)
Klosterstrasse 1, 77716 Haslach
☎ 07832-8080
Open: April-October weekdays
except Monday 9am-5pm, Sunday
10am-5pm; November-March, Tues-
day-Friday 9am-12noon, 1-5pm.
Museum prospectus in English.
Ticket also admits to next below.
Concessions for school parties.

Hansjakobmuseum
Freihof, Hansjakobstrasse 17,
77716 Haslach
☎ 07832-4715
Open: Wednesday 10am-12noon
and 3-5pm, Friday 3-5pm; also
April-October Sunday 10am-5pm.

Herrischried
*Heimatmuseum Klausenhof and
   Lindauer Säge*
Grossherrischried, 79737 Herrischried
☎ 07764-6191
Open: January-April Tuesday and

Saturday; May and October
Tuesday, Saturday, Sunday and
holidays (except Easter and Whit
Mon); June-September Tuesday,
Wednesday, Saturday, Sunday and
holidays; 2-5pm on all dates.
Old Hotzenwald house reputed to
be the oldest dwelling in the Black
Forest. Sawmill.
Also exhibition of glass handwork
and glassworks, Tuesday-Friday 2-
6pm, Saturday 9am-1pm, 2-5pm.

Hirsau
Klostermuseum
Calwer Strasse 6
75365 Hirsau
☎ 07051-59015
Open: Tuesday-Sunday 2-5pm
(6pm Sunday).

Karlsruhe
There are numerous museums and
art galleries in Karlsruhe. Details
from *Verkehrsverein*,
76137 Karlsruhe. ☎ 0721-35530

Kenzingen
Oberrheinische Narrenschau
Verbande Oberrheinischer
    Narrenzünfte
Alte Schulstrasse 20
79341 Kenzingen
☎ 07644-79138 or 79140
Open: May to October Tuesday,
Thursday, Saturday, Sunday and
holidays; November, Saturday and
Sunday; January-April, Sunday
and holidays; 2-5pm on all dates.
Groups by prior arrangement.
Exhibition of fools' costumes etc.

Lenzkirch
Zunft und Heimatstube
Im Kurhaus
79853 Lenzkirch
☎ 07653-68439

Open: Monday to Friday, 8am-
12noon, 1-5pm. Admission free.
Guilds and folk museum.

Lörrach
Museum am Burghof
Basler Strasse 143, 79540 Lörrach.
☎ 07621-415613
Open: Wednesday 2.30-5.30pm and
7.30-9.30pm, Saturday 2.30-5.30pm,
Sunday 10am-12 noon and 2.30-
5.30pm. Admission free.
Museum prospectus available.

Marxzell
Fahrzeugmuseum
76359 Marxzell (near Bad Herrenalb)
☎ 07248-6262
Open: daily 2-5pm.
Transport including early rail
vehicles.

Müllheim
Markgräfler Wein- und Heimatmuseum
Wilhelmstrasse, 79379 Müllheim.
☎ 07631-801132 or 15446
Open: all year Sunday 2-5pm; also
April-October Tuesday and
Thursday 3-6pm. Groups on other
days by prior arrangement.
Museum prospectus available.

Münstertal
Bienenkundemuseum
Spielweg
79244 Münstertal.
☎ 07636-881
Open: Wednesday, Saturday and
Sunday 2-5pm.

Waldmuseum
Wasen 47
79244 Untermünstertal
☎ 07636-70730 or 70740
Open: June-October, Wednesday
and Saturday 2-5pm.
Forestry.

Neustadt
Heimatstuben
Scheurlenstrasse 31, 79822 Neustadt
☎ 07651-20632
Open: mid-May to September,
Monday to Friday 2-5pm, Saturday
10am-12 noon; October to mid-
May, Thursday 2-5pm, Sunday
10am-12noon.
Exhibits include clockmaker's
workshop.

Oberkirch
Heimat- & Grimmelshausen-Museum
Hauptstrasse 32
77704 Oberkirch
☎ 07802-82178 or 82140
Open: Tuesday & Thursday 3-7pm,
Sunday 10.30am-12.30pm, 2-5pm.
Folk museum and Grimmels-
hausen memorabilia. Children free.

Oberried
Bauernhausmuseum Schniederlihof
Hofsgrund, Schauinsland,
79254 Oberried
☎ 07602-448
Open: July and August, daily
10am-6pm, May, June, September
and October, Saturday 2-6pm and
Sunday 10am-6pm.

Pforzheim
Schmuckmuseum (Reuchlinmuseum)
Jahnstrasse 42
75173 Pforzheim
☎ 07231-392126
Open: Tuesday to Sunday, 10am-
5pm. Admission free.
Museum prospectus in English.
Jewellery etc.

*Technische Museum der Schmuck und
    Uhrenindustie*
Bleichstrasse 81
75173 Pforzheim
☎ 07231-392869

Open: Wednesday 9am-12noon, 3-
6pm; 2nd & 4th Sunday in month
10am-12noon, 2-5pm. Admission
free.

Edelsteinaustellung Schütt
Goldschmiedeschulstrasse 6
75173 Pforzheim
☎ 07231-22001
Open: Monday-Friday 9am-
12noon, 1.30-5pm, Saturday 9am-
12noon. Admission free. Precious
stones and jewels.

Rastatt
Freiheitsmuseum
Herrenstrasse, 76437 Rastatt
(in Schloss)
☎ 07222-39475
Open: daily except Monday 10am-
12noon and 2-5pm. Admission free.

Wehrgeschichtliches Museum
Herrenstrasse, 76437 Rastatt
(in Schloss)
☎ 07222-34244
Open: daily except Monday 10am-
12noon and 2-5pm. Admission free.

Heimatmuseum
Herrenstrasse 11
76437 Rastatt
(opposite Schloss)
☎ 07222-972127
Open: Wednesday, Friday and
Sunday 10am-12noon and 3-5pm.
Admission free.

Schloss Favorite
Rastatt-Förch, 76437 Rastatt
☎ 07222-41207
5km (3 miles) south-east of Rastatt.
Open: March to November, Tues-
day-Thursday 9-11am and 2-5pm
(4pm in October and November).
Conducted tours. Additional
admission charge for porcelain
exhibition.

Rothaus
Heimatmuseum 'Hüsli'
79865 Rothaus
☎ 07748-212
Open: Tuesday to Saturday
9.30am-12noon and 1.30-5.30pm,
Sunday and holidays 1.30-5.30pm.
Closed November and December.

Rottweil
Städtisches Museum
Hauptstrasse 20, 78628 Rottweil
☎ 0741-494256
Open: Monday-Thursday, Satur-
day 9am-12noon and 2-5pm, Friday
9am-12noon, Sunday 10am-12noon.
Admission and prospectus free.
Folk museum, Roman collection
and *Fastnet* room, etc.

Kunstsammlung Lorenzkapelle
Lorenzgasse, 78628 Rottweil
☎ 0741-494298
Open: weekdays except Monday
10am-12noon and 2-5pm, Sunday
2-5pm.
Admission free 1st Sunday in
month. Art collection.

Römerbad
beim Stadtfriedhof
Königsstrasse, 78628 Rottweil
Always open. Admission free.
Outdoor remains of Roman baths.

Dominikanermuseum
Kriegsdamm, 78628 Rottweil
☎ 0741-7862
Open: daily except Monday 10am-
12noon, 2-5pm.
Branch of the Württemberg State
Museum.

St Georgen
Heimat und Phonomuseum
Im Rathaus
78112 St Georgen
☎ 07724-8794

Open: Monday to Friday 9am-12.30
pm, 1.30-4.30pm (6pm Thursday)
also May to September Saturday
10am-12noon. Admission free.
History of the gramophone.

Sasbach
Turenne Museum
Schwarzwaldstrasse 3,
77880 Sasbach/Obersasbach
☎ 07841-21020
Open: Tuesday-Saturday 9am-
12noon, 2-5pm. Admission free.

Toni Merz Museum
Schulstrasse 25,
77880 Sasbach/Obersasbach
☎ 07841-26079 or 28769 (Frau Degen)
Open: Sunday and holidays 10am-
1pm, also May-October, Wednesday 4-6pm.
Art gallery. Admission free.

Schliengen
Schloss Bürgeln
Obereggenen, 79418 Schliengen
☎ 07626-237
10km (6 miles) east of Schliengen
Open: March to November,
Monday, Wednesday and Sunday.
Conducted tours (obligatory) at
11am, 2, 3, 4 and 5pm.
Fine palace dating from 1726.

Schiltach
Flösserstube
Schuttesäge, 77761 Schiltach
☎ 07836-5875
Open: Tuesday-Sunday 10am-
12noon, 2-4pm. Admission free.
Recollections of timber floatage on
Black Forest rivers.

Schramberg
Stadtmuseum
im Schloss
78713 Schramberg.
☎ 07422-29215 (Information office)

Open: Tuesday-Friday 10am-12noon (except mid-September to April) and 2-6pm; Saturday & Sunday 10am-12noon, 2-5pm. Admission free. Timepieces, stoneware, castle histories etc.

Seebach
Trachten und Volkskundemuseum
77889 Seebach. ☎ 07842-3188
Open: Tuesday, Wednesday and Sunday 2-5pm.
Folklore and costumes.

Seelbach
Geroldsecker Waffenschmiede
77960 Seelbach. ☎ 07823-1066
Open: March to October Saturday and Sunday 1-5pm.
Traditional armourer's smithy.

Staufen
Keramikmuseum
79219 Staufen
☎ 07633-80536 (*Verkehrsbüro*)
Open: Tuesday, Thursday, Saturday and Sunday 3-6pm.
Branch of the Baden State Museum in Karlsruhe. Children free.

Triberg
Schwarzwaldmuseum
Wallfahrtsstrasse 4, 78098 Triberg
☎ 07722-4434
Open: May-September daily 9am-6pm, October-April 10am-12noon, 2-5pm; closed mid-November to mid-December.

Villingen-Schwenningen
Museum Altes Rathaus
Villingen,
78050 Villingen-Schwenningen
☎ 07721-822351
Open: daily except Monday 10am-12noon, also Thursday 3-5pm; closed holidays.

Heimatmuseum und Uhrenmuseum
Kronenstrasse 16, Schwenningen, 78054 Villingen-Schwenningen
☎ 07720-822371
Open: Monday-Friday 10am-12noon, 2-5pm, also 1st and 3rd Sunday in month 2-5pm.
Prospectus available.
Folk and clock museum.

Franziskaner Museum
Rietgasse 2, Villingen,
78050 Villingen-Schwenningen
☎ 07721-822351
Open: Tuesday to Friday 3-5pm.
Museum prospectus available.

Vogtsburg
Kaiserstühler Weinbaumuseum
Achkarren,
79235 Vogtsburg/Kaiserstuhl
8km (5 miles) north-east of Breisach
☎ 07662-81243 (Tourist Information)
Open: April-November, Monday-Friday 2-5pm, Saturday and Sunday 10.30am-12noon. Viticulture.

Waldkirch
Elztäler Heimatmuseum
Kirchplatz 14, 79183 Waldkirch
☎ 07861-206104
Open: April to October, Tuesday, Wednesday, Thursday, Saturday 3-5pm, Sunday 10am-1pm.
Folk museum of the Elz valley.

Wolfach
Glasmuseum Dorotheenhütte
Glashüttenweg 4, 77709 Wolfach
☎ 07834-751
Open: daily 9am-3.30pm.
Year-round Christmas shop.
Children under 6 free.

Heimatmuseum
Grosser Schlosshof
77709 Wolfach
☎ 07834-4284

Open May to September, Tuesday, Thursday and Saturday 2-5pm, Sunday 10am-12noon, 2-5pm. Rest of year Thursday 2-5pm and first Sunday of each month 10am-12noon, 2-5pm.

NATURE CONSERVATION AREAS

Feldberg
Includes the whole Feldberg area; 8km (5 miles) north-south and 10km (6¼ miles) east-west.

Freudenstadt
Parkwald on fringes of town. The biggest reserve in Germany.

Hinterzarten
Hochmoor. Adjacent to village. Bistenwald. 2-3km (1-2 miles) west of village.
Kesslermoos. 1½km (¾ mile) south of village.

Kaltenbronn
15km (9½ miles) south-east of Wildbad.

Lenzkirch
Ursee. 3km (1½ miles) west of town.

Menzenschwand
Scheibenlechtenmoos. 2km (1 mile) west of village.

Neuenbürg
Schlossberg above the town.

Pfalzgrafenweiler (Kälterbronn)
Conservation area 'Hohe Tannen'.

Rottweil
Eschachtal and Neckarburg. 6-8km (4-5 miles) north of town.

Schlüchtsee
In the Schlüchttal near Grafenhausen.

Schwarzwaldhochstrasse
Area bordering the Black Forest High Road B500.

Wutachtal and Wutachschlucht
6-20km (4-12 miles) south-east of Neustadt.

Zweribach
8km (5 miles) by road from St Peter or on foot from St Märgen.

NATURE TRAILS AND 'KEEP FIT' PATHS

The signs are *Naturlehrpfad, Waldlehrpfad* or even *Weinlehrpfad* for nature trails, and *Trimm Dich* or *Sportpfad* for those with exercise instructions and equipment.

Biberach (*Waldlehrpad*)
Starts from *W-Parkplatz* 1km (½ mile) east of station.
To Zell am Harmersbach and back, 6km (4 miles).

Ehrenkirchen (*Wald- & Weinlehrpfad*)
On the *Badische Weinstrasse* 15km (9½ miles) south of Freiburg. Starts 1km (½ mile) away in Kirchhofen.

Enzklösterle (*Waldlehrpfad*)
At edge of village; red-deer park.

Kirchzarten (*Trimm Dich* and two *Naturlehrpfade*)
On the Giersberg close to the town.

Lossburg (*Waldlehrpfad*)
Starts 0.8km (½ mile) from village on Schömberg road. 2km (1 mile) to Rodt. (*Waldsportpfad*) Starts 1km (½ mile) from village near Schömberg road. 18 exercise stations.

Nagold (*Waldlehrpfad*)
Starts from *W-Parkplatz* at the
Schlossberg. 3 ½km (2½ miles).

Pforzheim (*Naturpfad*)
Starts on the southern edge of the
town at Kupferhammer.
Restaurant and car park.

Rottweil (*Naturlehrpfad*)
In suburb Göllsdorf east of railway
about 3km (1½ miles) from town
centre.

St Blasien (*Trimm Dich*)
Close to and north-east of village.
Car park nearby.

Schlüchtsee (*Naturlehrpfad*)
From Grafenhausen round the little
lake to Rothaus, about 3km (2 miles).

PLEASURE PARKS

Wild und Freizeit Park
79843 Löffingen
☎ 07654-606
10km (6¼ miles) east of Neustadt
north of road B31.
Open: Easter-November daily 9am-
6pm. Modest admission charge,
some rides extra. Free car park.

Freizeit und Familienpark
Europapark Rust, 77977 Rust
☎ 07822-770
12km (7½ miles) south-west of Lahr.
Open: daily April to mid-October,
9am-6pm (later in summer).
Large variety of rides, shows and
entertainments; restaurants and
cafés.

SPORTS AND LEISURE ACTIVITIES

Boating and Sailing
Rowing boats and pedalos are
available at Titisee, Schluchsee and
many of the smaller lakes.

Bowling
Indoor bowling alleys are popular,
usually in a *Gasthaus* with the signs
Kegeln or *Kegelbahn* outside.

Cycling and Cycle Hire
From April to October, cycles can
be hired from most railway stations
which can provide details of
recommended tours. Cyclists
arriving by train pay only half the
hire charge.

Fishing
Most local information offices have
details of locations and facilities. A
seven-day package holiday is
available in Bad Herrenalb from
April to September. Details are in
the brochure 'Hobby Holidays'
from the GNTOs.

Riding and Pony-Trekking
Numerous stables and riding
schools offer facilities for the
visitor, many of them being listed
in *Urlaub auf dem Bauernhof*, the
handbook for farm holidays
available from the GNTOs.

Tennis
Seven-day tennis package holidays
are available at Hinterzarten and
Schluchsee, where coaching can be
in English. Details in the brochure
Hobby Holidays from the GNTOs.

STEAM AND OTHER RAILWAYS

Achern-Kappelrodeck-Ottenhöfen (Achertalbahn)
Achtäler Eisenbahnverein eV
c/o Willi Reichert, Schäffersheimer Strasse 12, 77656 Offenburg 21
☎ 0781-58789
Local address: Betriebsleitung Ottenhöfen der Südwestdeutschen Eisenbahnen AG,
Bahnhof, 77883 Ottenhöfen.
☎ 07842-2231.
Operates steam passenger trains on alternate Sundays, May to October. Three trains in each direction between 9am and 6pm. Times in *DB-Kursbuch*, table 715.

Blumberg-Weizen (Museumsbahn Wutachtal)
Stadt Blumberg Verkehrsamt, 78176Blumberg 1
☎ 07702-5127 (8am-12noon only)
Operates May to early October. Steam passenger trains Friday, Saturday, Sunday and holiday afternoons, also Wednesday and Sunday mornings and afternoons in peak holiday period. Actual times and dates in *DB Kursbuch*, table 736 and in Swiss *Kursbuch*. Children under 4 free, 4-14 years and in school groups half-fare. Museum in Zollhaus station; open 1 hour before departure of trains. No extra charge.

Emmendingen
Museumsbahnhof
Kollmarsreuter-strasse
79312 Emmendingen
Open: Saturday 2-7pm, Tuesday and Friday 7-9pm. Enquiries to Helmut Hartmeier ☎ 07691-1503.

Small collection of historic railway vehicles.

Ettlingen-Bad Herrenalb (Albtalbahn)
Albtal-Verkehrsgesellschaft (AVG), Wilhelmstrasse 2, 76275 Ettlingen
☎ 07243-18116
Operates steam passenger trains May to October, usually one Sunday per month.
Prospectus and current timetable on request. Times and dates also in *DB Kursbuch*, table 711.

Kaiserstuhl
A leisurely journey in the *Reben-bummler* steam train through the vineyards from Riegel to Breisach. Usually operates one Sunday each month June to October with morning departure Riegel to Breisach and afternoon return. Times and dates in *DB Kursbuch*, table 723. A 2-hour Rhine cruise may be taken during the stopover at Breisach. Children under 4 free, 4-12 years half-fare. Reductions for groups of ten or more. Refreshments on all trains. Cycles carried. Information from Eisenbahnfreunde Breisgau eV, Escholzstrasse 40, 79106 Freiburg
☎ 0761-77281

Kandern-Haltingen-Basel
Eurovapor, Gartenstrasse 7, 79400 Kandern
☎ 07626-8143
Operates on most Saturdays mid-May to mid-September, on one Sunday each month June-October and on certain holidays with six trains each way 8am-8pm. Eight intermediate stops, journey time for whole route 1½-1¾ hours. Historic steam and diesel locos and

railcar from 1928. Day and family tickets. Refreshments on trains. Museum. Prospectus and timetable on request. Times and dates also in *DB Kursbuch*, table 731.

Wildbad
Funicular railway to Sommerberg 836m (2,743ft). Operates daily at frequent intervals.

USEFUL ADDRESSES

Kartographischer Verlag Busch GmbH
44137 Dortmund, Germany
(For Aral motoring maps.)

DER Travel Service
18 Conduit Street,
London W1R 9TD
(Package tours and travel.)

German National Tourist Office
Nightingale House, 65 Curzon St,
London W1Y 7PE
(General information, hotel lists.)

German National Tourist Office
444 South Flower Street, Suite 2230,
Los Angeles, CA 90017, USA

German National Tourist Office
2 Fundy, PO Box 417,
Place Bonaventure,
Montreal, H5A 1B8, Canada

German National Tourist Office
747 Third Avenue, 33rd Floor
New York,
NY 10017, USA

Landesfremdenverkehrsverband
    Baden-Württemberg
Esslinger Strasse 8,
70182 Stuttgart, Germany
(General information about whole of Baden-Württemberg.)

North Sea Ferries
King George Dock, Hedon Road,
Hull, HU9 5QA.
Hull to Rotterdam and Zeebrugge.

Olau-Line Ferries
Sheerness, Kent, ME12 1SN
Sheerness to Vlissingen (Flushing).

P & O Ferries
Russell Street, Dover,
Kent, CT16 1QB
Felixstowe to Zeebrugge and cross-channel.

Sally Line
Argyle Centre, Ramsgate,
Kent, CT11 9DS
Ramsgate to Dunkirk.

Sealink Stena Line, PO Box 29,
Victoria Station, London, SW1V 1JX.
Harwich to Hook of Holland and cross-channel.

Fremdenverkehrsverband (FVV),
Bertoldstrasse 45, 79098 Freiburg,
Germany
(Detailed information about Black Forest.)

WALKING

Walking Without Baggage
A walking tour of between 4 and 11 days can be made without having to carry one's baggage by taking part in one of the organised walks which go from hotel to hotel in stages, luggage being conveyed forward as the tour progresses. The stages provide for 4 to 6 hours walking each day, the maximum distance covered is about 24km (15 miles). Information about the five tours mentioned in this book can be obtained as follows. Firm

bookings for the tours should also be sent to these addresses.
Details of other similar tours from FVV, Freiburg.

1 'Fröhliche Weinwanderung'
(Merry wine ramble — Chapter 1)
Verkehrsamt
77652 Offenburg
☎ 0781-82253

2 'Auf Spätzlespfaden'
(On dumpling trails — Chapter 2)
Herrenalber Reiseburo,
Postfach 1150,
76332 Bad Herrenalb.
☎ 07083-4553

3 'Auf der Fährte des Rothirsches'
(On the track of the red-deer — Chapter 2)
Kurverwaltung,
Postfach 440,
72250 Freudenstadt.
☎ 07441-8640 or 86428

4 'Auf dem Weg der Uhrenträger'
(In the steps of the clock carrier — Chapter 2)
Uhrenträgergemeinschaft,
Postfach 1423
78098 Triberg im Schwarzwald
☎ 07722-860236

5 'Rund um den Feldberg'
(Round about the Feldberg — Chapter 5)
Kurverwaltung,
79822 Titisee-Neustadt
☎ 07651-20668

Long-Distance Paths

These paths are waymarked as follows:
• Markings for paths running generally north to south are on a white ground.
• Those for the east-west *Querwege* are on a yellow ground.
• Paths leading to a long-distance route are marked with a blue diamond on a white ground.
• Paths connecting two long-distance routes are marked with a blue diamond with a white vertical stripe on a white ground.

Westweg (over 275km, 171 miles)
Between Pforzheim and Basel. Red diamond on white ground.

Mittelweg (over 230km, 143 miles)
Between Pforzheim and Waldshut. Red diamond with vertical white stripe on a white ground.

Ostweg (over 237km, 147 miles)
Between Pforzheim and Schaffhausen. Black and red diamond on a white ground.

Kandelhöhenweg
(110km, 68 miles)
Between Oberkirch and Freiburg. Red diamond with white K on a white ground.

Schwarzwald-Jura-Bodensee-Weg
(109km, 67 miles)
Between St Georgen and Radolfzell. Blue and yellow diamond on a white ground.

Querweg-Schwarzwald-Kaiserstuhl Rhein (110km, 68 miles)
Between Donaueschingen and Breisach. Red diamond on a yellow ground.

Hochrhein Querweg
(49km, 30 miles)
Between Rheinfelden and Albbruck. Blue and white diamond on a yellow ground.

Hotzenwald Querweg
(45km, 28 miles)
Between Schopfheim and Waldshut.
Black and white diamond on a
yellow ground.

Querweg (92km, 57 miles)
Between Lahr and Rottweil. Blue
and red diamond on yellow ground.

Querweg (51km, 32 miles)
Between Gengenbach and
Alpirsbach. Blue diamond on a
yellow ground.

Ortenauer Weinpfad
(100km, 62 miles)
Between Baden-Baden and Offenburg. Red diamond with blue
grapes on a white ground.

Querweg Freiburg-Bodensee
(177km, 110 miles)
Between Freiburg and Konstanz.
Red and white diamond on a
yellow ground.

WINE TASTING AND SALES

All along the *Badische Weinstrasse*,
one can visit wine cellars and
tastings (*Weinproben*) and buy wine
direct from the producer. Space
does not permit a listing of all the
many places where wine may be
tasted and purchased. There are
many individual vintners, but most
now belong to a cooperative
(*Winzergenossenschaft*) which takes
care of marketing.

Vineyards along the *Weinstrasse*
are divided into five main groups:
Ortenau, Breisgau, Kaiserstuhl,
Tuniberg and Markgräflerland;
listed below are representative

addresses for each area from which
details of cellar visits, wine
festivals and other assistance may
be obtained.

The amateur wine lover should
look out for *Weinproben* and
Weinverkauf (wine for sale) signs
along the *Weinstrasse*.

Ortenau (Baden-Baden to Gegen-
bach)
Winzergenossenschaft Durbach eG
Nachtweide 2,
77770 Durbach
☎ 0781-93660

Winzergenossenschaft Vorderes
Kinzigtal eG
Börsiglachenweg 2,
77717 Gengenbach
☎ 07803-2036
Town sales at Hauptstrasse 18,
Gengenbach, Monday-Saturday
8am-12noon, 2-6pm. Closed
Wednesday and Saturday after-
noons.

Breisgau (south of Gengenbach to
Freiburg)
Winzergenossenschaft Glottertal eG
79286 Glottertal
☎ 07684-339

Kaiserstuhl
Winzergenossenschaft Achkarren eG
79236 Vogtsburg-Achkarren
☎ 07662-6092

Kaiserstühler Weinkeller
im Atrium (Feierling Passage)
79098 Freiburg
☎ 0761-22984
Historic wine cellar in the *Altstadt*
(Augustinerplatz).

Tuniberg
Badischer Winzkeller eG
79206 Breisach
☎ 07667-9000
25km (16 miles) from Freiburg via
B31.

Markgräflerland
(south of Freiburg)
Winzergenossenschaft Pfaffenweiler
79292 Pfaffenweiler
☎ 07664-7081
9km (5½miles) south of Freiburg
via B3.

Weingut Fritz Blankenhorn
79418 Schliengen
☎ 07635-1092
36km (23 miles) south of Freiburg
on B3.
Tasting room open daily until 6pm
(4pm on Saturday).

Sales hours at the addresses given
and at most other outlets on the
Weinstrasse are Monday-Friday
8am-12noon, 1.30-5pm and
Saturday 8am-12noon.

ZOOS AND WILDLIFE PARKS

The many forest enclosures
(*Gehege*) for wild boar or deer are
usually accessible at all times
without charge. The list given is by
no means exhaustive and, as exact
locations are changed from time to
time, the visitor is advised to check
with the local tourist information
office before setting out.

Baiersbronn
Deer parks 3.5km (2 miles) south-
west in Sankenbachtal, 4.5km (3

miles) north in Klosterreichenbach,
9km (5½ miles) north in Schönegrund and 24km (15 miles) north-
west in Langenbach.

Enzklösterle
Red-deer park.

Kaltenbronn
Deer park. 15km (9½ miles) south-
east of Wildbad.

Löffingen
Wild und Freizeit Park.
10km (6 miles) east of Neustadt on
road B31.
For details see under Pleasure
Parks.

Oberried
Berg-Wild-Park Steinwasen,
79254 Oberried.
☎ 07671-451
5km (3 miles) south of village.
Open daily. Admission charge.
Free car park. Giant summer bob-
bahn.

Rottweil
Red-deer park at Eckhof in
Aschachtal about 6km (4 miles)
from town centre.

Steinen
Vogelpark Wiesental,
79585 Steinen-Hofen.
4km (2½ miles) north of Steinen.
☎ 07627-7420
Open 15 March to 15 November
daily, 9am-7pm. Admission charge.
Free car park.

Waldkirch
Zoo. Near town centre.
Open daily. Admission charge.

INDEX

A

Accommodation 13-
    15, 229-31
Achern 34, 38, 236
Achertalbahn (Acher
    Valley Railway)
    34-5, 38, 245
Achkarren 54, 56
Aha 200
Alb-Stausee 211
Albbruck 221, 226
Albtal 69, 91, 92, 193,
    201, 211
Albtalbahn (Alb Valley
    Railway) 91, 92,
    246
Alexander-Schanze 31
Allerheiligen 37, 91,
    92
Alpirsbach 88, 100,
    107, 232
Altensteig 97, 98, 99
Altensteigdorf 97, 99
Altes Schloss
    Hohenbaden
    (Baden-Baden) 24,
    29
Autobahnkirche
    (Baden-Baden) 25,
    26

B

Baar, the 149-160
Bad Antogast 37

Bad Bellingen 62, 65,
    66-7
Bad Boll 204, 205, 206
Bad Dürrheim 119,
    152, 153, 154, 236
Bad Herrenalb 69, 84,
    91, 92, 93, 94, 236,
    237
Bad Krozingen 62, 65,
    66, 237
Bad Liebenzell 11, 74,
    76, 230
Bad Peterstal-
    Griesbach 37, 39-
    40, 108
Bad Rippoldsau 108,
    109
Bad Rotenfels 95
Bad Säckingen 195,
    224-5, 226, 237
Bad Teinach 78, 80
Baden Wine Road
    (*Badische Wein-
    strasse*) 9, 20-68,
    129, 133, 176, 184
Baden-Baden 9, 11, 13,
    25-6, 28-9, 31, 32,
    44, 68, 232, 236
Badenweiler 62, 64-5,
    188
Baiersbronn 89, 90, 91-
    2, 237, 250
Banks and Post
    Offices 231-2

Basel 9, 10, 11, 18, 67,
    176, 185, 225, 228
Bärental 176, 177, 194,
    201
Belchen 176, 180-1,
    184, 193
Berg-Wild-Park
    Steinwasen
    (Oberried) 184,
    187, 250
Bernau 193, 212-3, 218,
    230, 237
Berneck (Nagold
    valley) 97
Besenfeld 86, 97
Biberach 120-1, 122,
    129, 244
Birkendorf 209
Birkenfeld 81
Bischoffingen 54, 55-6
Blansingen 67
Blauen 176, 187, 189,
    192
Bleibach 126, 127, 128,
    130, 133
Blindensee 123
Blumberg 208, 209,
    218
Bodensee (Lake
    Constance) 18, 41,
    56
Bollschweil 59
Bonndorf 116, 206,
    208, 237-8

Bräunlingen 154, 156-7
Breg, river 123, 124, 130, 147, 153
Breisach 52, 54, 56-7, 136, 232
Breitnau 144, 145
Brend 123-4, 130
Brigach, river 152, 153
Brigittenschloss (Sasbachwalden) 35, 38
Britzingen 66
Buchenbach 173
Buhlbach 89, 90, 91
Burg Altwindeck 34, 38
Burg Dautenstein (Seelbach) 132, 134
Burg Falkenstein (Schramberg) 106
Burg Hohenger-oldseck (Seelbach) 132, 134
Burg Hohenrode (Sasbachwalden) 35, 38
Burg Hohenschram-berg (Schramberg) 104
Burg Roggenbach 209
Burg Rötteln (Lörrach) 62, 67
Burg Staufenburg 41
Burg Steinegg (Tiefenbronn) 71, 73, 84
Burg Steinegg 209
Burg Zavelstein 80
Burkheim 52, 54, 56
Busenbach 69
Bühl 32, 34, 38
Bühlertal 33, 34

C
Calmbach 81
Calw 74, 77-8, 82, 238
Churches 232-3
Clock-making 100, 104, 105, 114, 123, 147, 150, 151, 198

D
Danube (Donau), river 9, 116, 124, 153
Denzlingen 129, 133
Diersburg 44, 48
Dietlingen 69
Donaueschingen 41, 112, 136, 153, 154, 156, 159, 232, 238
Donauquelle (Donaue-schingen) 153, 154
Dornstetten 99
Döggingen 157, 205
Dreiseenbahn (Three Lakes Railway) 201
Durbach 41

E
Ebersteinburg (Rastatt) 24, 29
Egenhausen 98
Eggenertal 192
Ehrenkirchen 59, 244
Eichstetten 57
Ellmendingen 69
Elz valley (Elztal) 127, 129, 130, 133
Elz, river 69, 70, 81, 82, 84, 85, 86, 94
Elzach 112, 124, 127, 130, 133, 238
Emmendingen 54, 58-9, 133, 246
Endingen 52, 54
Entenburg (Donaue-schingen) 154, 156
Enzklösterle 82, 86, 230, 244, 250
Erdmannshöhle (Schopfheim) 187, 193, 234
Erzgrube 97
Ettenheim 49, 51
Ettenheimmünster 49-50, 134
Ettlingen 20, 22-3, 26, 69, 92, 232, 238
Europapark Rust (Lahr) 49, 51

F
Falkenstein (Höllen-tal) 169
Farrenkopf 112
Feldberg (resort) 194
Feldberg 9, 10, 11, 176, 177, 180, 183, 187, 193, 194, 204, 243
Feldsee 10, 177, 194, 204
Felsenkranz (Belchen) 180
Fessenbach 44
Festivals 233-4
Forbach 96, 99
Förch 24
Frauenalb 91, 92-3
Freiamt 133, 135
Freiburg im Breisgau 10, 13, 18, 51, 59, 119, 160-74, 232, 238
Freiheitsmuseum (Rastatt) 24, 26
Freudenstadt 13, 23, 31, 32, 76, 86, 88-9, 91, 97, 98, 99, 100, 232, 243
Freundschaftstrasse (Friendship Road) 35, 36
Friedenweiler 159, 232
Friedrichsbad (Baden-Baden) 25
Furtwangen 105, 123-4, 126, 130, 239
Fürsatzhöhe 199, 200

G
Gaggenau 23, 24, 25, 29, 95-6
Gaisbach 40
Gasthaus 'Löwen' (Staufen) 60, 62
Gasthaus 'Schwanen' (Bad Bellingen) 62, 67
Gasthaus 'Schwarzer Adler' (Steinach) 119, 120
Gasthaus Liebeneck (Würm) 71, 74

Gasthaus Sternen
(Ravennaschlucht)
169, 172, 174
Gasthof 'Bären'
(Lossburg) 100
Gasthof 'Engel'
(Simonswald) 127
Gasthof 'Spielweg'
(Münstertal) 185,
187
Gauchachschlucht
205, 206, 218
Gengenbach 32, 38, 44,
45, 48, 122, 239
Gernsbach 29, 82, 94,
96, 99
Geroldsecker
Waffenschmiede
(Seelbach) 132, 134
Geschwend 192
Giersberg 166
Glaswaldsee 109
Glottertal 134, 135,
136-7
Grafenhausen 204,
209, 218, 230, 232
Grafenmatt 194
Grossjockenmühle
(Ravennaschlucht)
169, 174
Grunern 60-1, 62
Grüne Strasse (green
road) 56, 153, 157,
165
Gschwinghof 142
Gutach 111-2, 119,
127, 239
Gutach valley
(Gutachtal) 41, 109,
112-4, 118, 119, 127
Gütenbach 124-6

H
Haiterbach 98
Haltingen 189
Harmersbach Valley
(Harmersbachtal)
120, 121
Hasel 216
Hasenhorn 180
Haslach 117, 119-20,
127, 239

Hausach 117
Hausen 187, 193
Häusern 201
Heilbronn 9
Heiligenbronn 99
Heitersheim 62, 65-6
Herbolzheim 133
Herzogenhorn 212
Hexenlochmühle
(Furtwangen) 124,
130, 144
Himmelreich 173
Himmelsberg 133
Hinterzarten 145, 169,
172-3, 198, 243
Hirchsprung (Höllen-
tal) 169, 174
Hirsau 32, 74, 76-7, 82,
88, 232
Hochburg (Emmend-
ingen) 59
Hochfahrn 181
Hochfirst 197, 198
Hochgescheid 176
Hochkopf 176, 213,
216
Hofen 187, 188
Hohlosee 82, 85, 86
Holzen 187, 189
Horb 74, 80-1, 82, 106
Horben 164
Hornberg 105, 112,
113, 127
Hornisgrinde 32
Höchenschwand 202
Höhingen castle 56
Höllental (Hell valley)
145, 168-74
Höllentalbahn (Hell
Valley Railway)
168-9
Höllsteig 169
Hölzebruck 200
Hubacker 125
Hübschental 125
Hüfingen 154, 156
Hügelheim 66
Hünersedel 133

I
Ihringen 57
Inzlingen 62, 68, 228

J
Jestetten 217, 219, 226
Jostal 198-200

K
Kaiserstuhl 52, 53-9,
68
Kaltenbronn 82, 85-6,
96, 243, 250
Kandel 128, 129, 130,
136, 142-4
Kandelhöhenweg 35,
129, 143-4, 248
Kandern 187, 188-9,
192
Kandertalbahn 189, 192
Kappelrodeck 34, 35,
38, 44, 230
Karlsruhe 9, 20, 69,
239
Kastelburg
(Waldkirch) 128-9,
130
Katherinenkapelle 52,
53
Kentheim 78, 82, 233
Kenzingen 50, 51, 133,
135, 239
Kesselberg 152
Kinzig valley
(Kinzigtal) 38, 41,
45, 95, 100, 101,
104, 107, 108, 109,
117, 119, 121, 122,
127, 129, 132, 133,
246
Kirchzarten 165-7,
174, 244
Klettgau 219
Kloster Lichtental
(Baden-Baden) 26,
28
Klosterreichenbach 91,
92, 97, 99
Klösterle 109
Kniebis 31, 32, 109
Königsfeld 148-9
Kuhbach 49, 129
Kupferhammer
(Pforzheim) 71, 74
Kuppenheim 24, 95
Küssaberg 219, 226

Küssaburg 219, 226

L
Lahr 48-9, 51, 129
Langenbach 91, 92
Langenordnachtal 200
Langensteinbach 69
Laufenburg 221-2, 226
Lautenbach 36, 38
Lenzkirch 198, 230, 240, 243
Leopoldskanal 51
Lindenberg (St Peter) 134, 141
Loffenau 91, 94
Lossburg 100, 107, 230, 244
Löffingen 149, 154, 157, 159, 205, 232, 250
Lörrach 62, 67-8, 185, 228, 240

M
Mailänder Tor (Löffingen) 149, 154
Maisach 37
Maisachtal 37
Malsburg-Marzell 187, 192
Malterdingen 51
Mambach 192
Mantelberg castle (Haiterbach) 98
Markgrafenbad (Badenweiler) 64
Marxzell 91, 92, 240
Marzell (see Malsburg-Marzell)
Märchenwald (Simonswald) 127, 130
Menzenschwand 212, 213, 216, 243
Mines and Caves 234
Mittelweg 18, 248
Mohlin, river 59
Monakam 76
Monbachschlucht 76
Moosbronn 93-4
Motoring 235-6
Mummelsee 26, 31, 32, 91

Murg valley 10, 23, 85, 89, 90, 91, 94, 95, 96
Murg/Baden 222, 224
Museums and Art Galleries 236-43
Museumsbahn Wutachtal (Blumberg-Weizen) 208-9, 218, 245-6
Mühlentor (Bräunlingen) 154, 156-7
Mühlsbach 133
Müllheim 62, 64, 66, 240
Münstertal (resort) 185, 187, 233, 240
Münstertal (valley) 184-5

N
Nagold 74, 80, 82, 98, 233, 244
Nagold valley 69, 74, 76, 77, 82, 97
Nagoldtalsperre 97, 99
Nature Conservation Areas 243-4
Neckar valley 9, 69, 76, 81, 82, 84, 106, 152
Nessellachen 173
Neuenbürg 81, 82, 243
Neukirch 124, 130
Neunenweg 180
Neustadt 176, 198-201, 205, 218, 240-1
Niederrotweil 54, 56, 233
Nordrachtal 121

O
Oberbergen 52
Oberbühlertal 33
Obereck 124
Oberharmersbach 121, 122
Oberkirch 35-6, 38, 39, 40, 41, 44, 129
Oberkirnach 152
Oberrglottertal 136

Oberried 165, 181, 184, 187, 241, 250
Oberschaffhausen 54, 57
Obertal 89, 90
Oberwolfach 108
Offenburg 11, 36, 38, 40, 41-5, 48, 68, 112, 122, 161
Ohlsbach 45
Oppenau 36-7
Ortenauer Weinpfad (Ortenau Wine Path) 44
Ortenberg 38, 45, 48
Ottenhöfen 32, 34, 38
Ottoschwanden 133, 134, 135

P
Panoramabad (Freudenstadt) 88, 91
Paracelsusbad (Bad Liebenzell) 76
Pfaffeneck 173
Pfaffenweiler 59
Pfalzgrafenweiler 98, 243
Pforen 154, 156
Pforzheim 10, 18, 69-71, 73, 74, 76, 81, 84, 241, 244
Poppeltal 82, 86
Präg 213
Prechtal 127

R
Rankmühle (St Märgen) 134, 141
Rastatt 23-5, 26, 41, 95, 241
Raumünzach 95, 96
Ravennaschlucht 145, 169, 173, 174
Rebenbummler (steam train) 52, 54
Rench valley 35, 36, 37, 39, 41, 121
Renchen 38, 40
Rheinfelden 225, 226
Rheinheim 219, 226

Rhine (Rhein), river 8, 9, 10, 11, 12, 20, 23, 32, 41, 48, 53, 54, 55, 57, 64, 66, 69, 112, 116, 195, 201, 202, 217, 219-28
Rhine Falls (Rheinfälle) 217, 226
Rhine valley 11, 12, 31, 34, 36
Riegel 52, 54
Rohrhardtsberg 124
Rossberg 144
Rosseck 124
Rosskopf 163, 174
Rothaus 202, 204, 230, 241
Rottweil 106-8, 119, 161, 233, 241-2, 243, 244, 250
Rötenbach 159, 205
Ruhestein 31, 90
Ruine Yburg (Baden-Baden) 26, 29
Rümmelesteg 205, 206

S
Sankenbachtal 91, 92
Sasbach 53, 54, 242
Sasbachwalden 35, 44, 230
Sausenburg castle (Kandern) 187, 188, 189
Sägendobel (St Peter) 134, 143-4
Schaffhausen 217
Schapbach 101, 108
Schauenburg (Oberkirch) 36, 38
Schauinsland 163-5, 174, 176, 181
Schenkenburg 101, 107
Schenkenzell 100-1, 107, 233
Schillingerberg 129
Schiltach 104, 107, 242
Schliengen 66, 242
Schliffkopf 31, 89, 90, 91

Schloss Beuggen (Rheinfelden) 225, 226
Schloss Bürgeln 187, 192
Schloss Eberstein (Gernsbach) 96, 99
Schloss Favorite (Förch) 24, 26, 95
Schloss Ortenberg 38, 45, 48
Schloss Schönau (Trompeter-schloss), Bad Säckingen 224-5, 226
Schloss Weitenburg (Horb) 81, 82
Schloss, Rastatt 23-4, 26
Schlossberg (mountain) 56, 163, 174
Schlossberg (Neuenbürg) 80, 81, 82
Schluchsee (lake) 9, 176, 200, 201
Schluchsee (resort) 200, 201, 231
Schlüchttal 202, 204
Schlüchtsee 202, 204, 218, 244
Schniederlihof (Hofsgrund) 165, 184, 187, 194
Schonach 124, 127-8
Schopfheim 48, 187, 192-3
Schöllbronn 23
Schömberg 84-5, 101
Schönau 181, 187
Schönberg pass 129
Schönegrund 91, 92
Schönmünzach 97
Schönwald 123, 128
Schramberg 104-6, 107, 231, 242
Schutterlindenberg 48
Schuttertal (valley) 129, 132, 133
Schuttertal (resort) 49, 132-3

Schwann 81
Schwarza, river 201
Schwarzabruck 201
Schwarzach 32-3, 233
Schwarzenbach-Talsperre (Forbach) 96
Schwarzenbachtal 123
Schwarzwaldbahn (Black Forest Railway) 41, 112-3, 114, 119, 120, 168
Schwarzwaldhochstrasse (Black Forest High Road) 29, 31, 32, 33, 37, 89, 91, 94, 108, 244
Schwarzwaldtälerstrasse (Black Forest Valley Road) 89, 95, 100, 108
Schweighausen 129, 133, 134
Schwendi-Schloss (Burkheim) 54, 56
Schwenningen 149, 151-3, 154, 242-3
Schwenninger Moos (nature conserva-tion area) 152, 154
Schwörstadt 225, 226
Seebach 32
Seebrugg 200, 201
Seebuck 176, 187, 194,
Seelbach 129, 132, 134, 242
Simonswald 124, 126-7, 130
Simonswäldertal 124-7, 128, 129, 130
Sindelfingen 73-4
Sitzenkirch 192
Sommerau 113
Sommerberg 82, 83
South-Eastern Hinterland 195-217, 218
Spitzenberg 213
St Blasien 211-2, 218, 233, 244
St Georgen 112, 116-7, 152, 242

St Märgen 116, 124, 126, 134, 140-1, 142, 144
St Peter 126, 134, 137-8, 140, 141, 142, 233
St Trudpert 185, 187
St Ulrich 59-60, 62, 233
Staufen 60, 62, 65, 119, 184
Staufenburg 60
Steinach 119, 120, 133
Steinen 187,188, 192, 250
Steinwasen 184
Stöckenkopf 89, 91
Stöcklewald 123
Strasbourg 9, 41, 48, 90
Stuttgart 9, 76
Stübenwasen 176, 194
Stühlingen 208, 218, 233
Sulzbachtal 112
Sulzburg 61-2, 233

T
Teinach 78, 80
Tennenbach 134, 135
Tennenbronn 106
Teufelsmühle (mountain) 91, 94
Thurner 146
Tiefenbronn 73, 74
Tiengen 219-21, 233
Titisee (lake) 9, 116, 159, 194, 195, 197, 201, 204
Titisee (village) 195, 197, 201
Titisee-Neustadt 197-201
Todtmoos 213, 216-7, 218
Todtnau 179-80, 181, 187, 193, 194, 230
Todtnauberg 179-80
Tote Mann 181, 183

Totenkopf 53
Triberg 10, 105, 113-4, 116, 119, 123, 124, 127, 242
Tschamberhöhle (Rheinfelden) 225, 226, 234

U
Unterbühlertal 44
Unterglottertal 136
Unteribental 168, 233
Unterkirnach 148, 152
Untermünstertal 185
Urach 130, 146-7, 233
Urachtal 146-7

V
Villingen 148, 149-51, 152, 153, 154, 156, 161, 242-3
Vogelpark Wiesental (Steinen-Hofen) 187, 188, 250
Vogelskopf 31
Vorseebach 109
Vosges (Vogesen) 10, 35, 53, 90
Vöhrenbach 130, 147-8
Völkersbach 23

W
Waldachtal-Lützen-hardt 98-9
Waldbronn 69
Waldkirch 128-9, 130, 135, 233, 243, 250
Waldshut 18, 195, 201, 202, 211, 219-21
Wasserschloss Entenstein (Schliengen) 66
Wasserschloss Reichenstein (Inzlingen) 62, 67-8
Wehr 216, 218
Weil am Rhein 67

Weil der Stadt 73, 74
Weisenbach 96
Weizen 208, 218
Welschensteinach 133
Westweg 28, 188, 200, 213, 248
Wiesental 67, 176, 181-94
Wildbad 11, 81, 82, 83-4, 246
Wildpark (Löffingen) 154, 157
Wildsee 82, 85
Wilhelmshöhe (Schonach) 128
Windgfällweiher 201
Wittichen 101, 104
Witznau 209
Wolfach 107, 108, 109, 243
Wolfach valley (Wolfachtal) 91, 101, 108
Wolfsschlucht 189
Wutach, river 202, 204, 206
Wutachmühle 205, 206, 208, 218
Wutachschlucht 157, 159, 204-6, 218, 244
Würm 71, 74

Z
Zastler 177, 181
Zavelstein 78, 80
Zell (Wiesental) 193
Zell am Harmersbach 119, 120, 121, 122
Zollhaus 209
Zoos and Wildlife Parks 250
Zum Silbernen Stern (Oberkirch) 38, 40
Zunsweier 48
Zweribach waterfalls and conservation area (St Peter) 134, 141-2, 244